A Brief History
of Mexico

A Brief History of Mexico

Lynn V. Foster

Facts On File, Inc.

A BRIEF HISTORY OF MEXICO

Facts On File, Inc.
11 Penn Plaza
New York NY 10001

Library of Congress Cataloging-in-Publication Data

Foster, Lynn V.
A brief history of Mexico / Lynn V. Foster.
p. cm.
Includes bibliographical references (p.) and index.
ISBN 0-8160-3165-7 (alk. paper)
1. Mexico—History. I. Title.
F1226.F67 1997
972—dc21   97-1441

Facts On File books are available at special discounts when purchased in bulk quantities for businesses, associations, institutions or sales promotions. Please call our Special Sales Department in New York at 212/967-8800 or 800/322-8755.

You can reach Facts On File on the World Wide Web at http://www.factsonfile.com

Text design by Robert Yaffe
Cover design by Dorothy Wachtenheim
Illustrations by Dale Williams

Printed in the United States of America

MP FOF 10 9 8 7 6 5 4 3 2 1

This book is printed on acid-free paper.

CONTENTS

To My Husband, Lawrence Foster

ACKNOWLEDGMENTS

The illustrations in this book result from the generous assistance of many individuals and organizations, acknowledged next to their corresponding photographs. The majority of photographs, however, are the works of personal friends who requested no such recognition, foremost among them Donnelly Marks, whose contributions to the book are immeasurable.

Two editors deserve special thanks: Randy Ladenheim Gil, who encouraged me to write the book, and Hilary Poole, who guided the manuscript into print.

INTRODUCTION

"Whatever else Mexico may be, she is never dull."
■
—*Lesley Byrd Simpson (1962)*

Mexico and the United States share a common border, but their distinctive cultures make them seem continents apart. Where the history of the United States and its neighbor to the south overlaps, the result has too often created xenophobia rather than mutual comprehension.

Modern Mexico is foremost a *mestizo* society, a mixed race and mixed culture of Indians and Spaniards. Neither part of the mixture coincides exactly with the experience of native culture and European conquest in the United States and, except for a few regions such as the American Southwest, neither does the blending of the races. From the dawn of time Mexico has been different: over three millennia ago it spawned a sophisticated indigenous civilization and gave birth to some of the most populous cities in the world. When the Spaniards arrived, there were as many as 25 million Indians in central Mexico alone.

The European settlement and conquest of the United States and Mexico only deepened the contrasts between the two countries. The differences were not just in language and religion, but also in the economic foundations of the two nations: Britain was an industrial state while Spain remained a feudal society. Further, the course of Mexican history during the three centuries of the Spanish colony required the interaction of the pre-Hispanic and Spanish peoples. The nature of those relationships laid the foundation, sometimes for the better and other times for the worse, for modern Mexico.

The contrasts in heritage make a knowledge of Mexican history imperative for neighborly understanding and cooperation. Fortunately for the reader of Mexican history, it is as riveting as it is often tragic. Beginning with the rise of the first civilizations of North America and the cataclysm of the Spanish conquest and continuing through the Mexican-American War (in which Mexico lost half its territory) and on to the outburst of the Revolution of Emiliano Zapata and Pancho Villa in 1910, the main events of Mexican history have been dramatic enough to inspire romantic novellas and Hollywood movies. Understanding the deeper significance of these events holds the key to the national consciousness.

This history begins with the peopling of the Americas and gives broad coverage to Mexico's pre-Columbian civilizations that thrived from at least 1200 B.C. until the Spanish conquest in A.D. 1519. Even though much of this past is not recorded in writing and so is not technically "history," it is integral to understanding contemporary indigenous culture as well as Mexico's pride in its unique past. It even clarifies popular political gestures and expenditures—such as President Carlos Salinas de Gortari's 1991 gift of one-year million-dollar grants for renewed excavations at Mexico's most famous ruins. So much progress has been made in the last decades towards understanding the values and beliefs of these ancient societies that a close examination is well rewarded.

This history also lingers over the early exchanges between the Spaniards and Indians. Not only is it fascinating to examine the unexpected encounter of two civilizations, but the period is critical for the future course of events in Mexico. The Spanish empire left its mark in language and art, in religion, politics, and the economy. When Mexico gained its independence, it found itself without a political center and with an economy and social system that would hold it back for decades longer.

Mexico's struggle for political stability and independence has been achieved only in this century. It was a hard-fought effort that had to overcome centuries of colonial occupation by Spain followed by nearly a century of internal strife and regional factionalism. In the end, it took the upheaval and devastation of a revolution to set it on its modern course. These historic events define modern Mexico and, since the Revolution of 1910, they have been reformulated into national icons and have found their way into school primers as well as art and literature.

Accounts of political and cultural events too often give a monolithic and dehumanized impression of society. But many individuals do not walk in step with the main course of political events, especially not in a country of such regional and ethnic diversity. And many political events have an unexpected impact on the fabric of society and the ecology of the land. To provide more contrasts and a deeper understanding of the variety of human responses to events, this history attempts to elaborate various epochs with contemporary quotations and illustrations of period art. It also provides asides in photo captions or boxed "close-ups" about everything from religious icons to the destruction of the rain forest, from the decipherment of ancient hieroglyphs to life in the capital during a military coup.

The close-ups also are intended to amplify the unusual backgrounds of some important individuals in politics. Just as often they give voice to those who are not usually represented in the official histories: a Spaniard preferring life in a Maya village to rejoining his fellow conquistadors; a poet choosing the nunnery over the viceregal court; a successful mulatto painter in a racist society. This history also uses the close-ups to overcome a tendency in Mexican histories to abandon the fate of the indigenous people a century after the Spanish conquest. The Indians become numbing statistics about impoverished peasants. Yet many native peoples (estimated to constitute 10 to 30 percent of the populace) have struggled to preserve to this day their separate cultural identity and ancient traditions. Their growing resurgence forced an amendment to the Mexican constitution in 1991 and captured world attention in the Zapatista uprising of 1994. A number of the close-ups spotlight their diverse methods of survival. Others follow the fortunes of some Mixtec Indians in Oaxaca through the centuries after the conquest to the present day.

This history, and Mexicans' perceptions of its lessons and promises, ends with Mexico once again at a crossroads. It is hoped that this book, however brief, will shed light on Mexico's efforts to resolve its most profound political and economic challenges since the Revolution of 1910.

A Brief History of Mexico

1

THE FIRST PEOPLES: PRE-COLUMBIAN MEXICO

They had always known within themselves
the lengths of their days.
The moon, the year, the day, and the night,
The breath of life were fulfilled
and they passed.

■

—Maya Book of the Chilam Balam of Chumayel
(translated by Ralph Roys)

Mexico contains the ruins of an estimated 10,000 ancient cities dating from before the Spanish conquest. Some dominate the countryside in sublime isolation; others are mostly obscured by urban sprawl except for their too-grand-to-hide pyramids supporting monumental 16th-century Spanish churches. Others have yet to be discovered: new ones, some surprisingly large but in remote regions, are found practically every year.

These ruins represent the great pre-Columbian civilizations that flourished for 3,000 years. The earliest civilization, the Olmec, dates to 1200 B.C.—around the time in which Egypt was ruled by the dynasty of Ramses the Great but western Europe had yet to achieve a civilization, much less produce a great ruler. Pre-Columbian cities ranked among the largest in the world: Teotihuacán, known for its pyramids of the Sun and Moon that still stand outside modern Mexico City (see page 29), had a population of more than 200,000 in A.D. 600, a time in which the most populous city in the world, Constantinople, had only 500,000 inhabitants. In the early 16th century, the Aztec capital of Tenochtitlán was five times larger than London. Although massive, Mexico's great metropo-

I

lises were constructed without pack animals and with only stone-age technology: obsidian (volcanic glass) and stone tools, not metal ones; wheels were used, but for toys, not pulleys and carts.

The descendants of the people who built these pre-Columbian cities live on in Mexico today, a country named after the ancient Mexica, the Aztecs' name for themselves. Mexico's population is primarily *mestizo*, or mixed Indian and European extraction, but at least 10 million Mexicans are Indian—perhaps three times that number according to more generous estimates. Mexico's most traditional citizens preserve the mythologies of their ancestors, farm the land for the maize and beans that have sustained American Indians for thousands of years, and speak the Nahuatl, Yucatec Maya, and other languages of this pre-Hispanic land. Their legends and artistic heritage are an integral part of the national identity, inspiring 20th-century artists and writers and infusing every aspect of life from political rhetoric to haute cuisine, not to mention the pyramid-shaped hotels at beach resorts, such as Cancun. No understanding of Mexico can be complete without an examination of its prehistoric indigenous past.

Origins of the First Americans

The words of the song arrived
When there wasn't heaven and earth
There, then, it was born . . .

■

—Maya Book of the Chilam Balam of Chumayel
(translated by Peter Keeler)

In the 15th century when Europeans set out on their search for a sea route to Asia, they expected to sail their way to the East Indies unimpeded. Coming upon the land masses now known as the American continents, they assumed they had reached some islands off the coast of the Indies and forever perpetuated their mistake by calling the people they encountered "Indians." They had sailed into an entirely new world, one previously unknown to Europeans. Living in an age of romance novels, they wondered whether they had stumbled upon the fabled lands of Amazonian women and fountains of eternal youth.

Upon coming to Mexico, the Spaniards were awed by the sheer number of people in this unexpected land. In battle, as the Europeans soon learned, these Americans were "demonic-looking" with their tattooed faces and jaguar capes. They marched to a cacaphony of tortoise-

Mexico Before the Conquest *(1945), Diego Rivera's mural of the Aztec capital Tenochtitlán, in the National Palace, Mexico City*

shell drums, conch-shell horns, and shrill whistles. The stone cities of pre-Columbian Mexico were just as otherworldly: there was nothing so large in 15th-century Spain. Some of the soldiers had traveled to Constantinople and Rome, but even they never had seen anything like the Aztec capital of Tenochtitlán. The Aztecs were equally perplexed by the Europeans, whom they found terrifying with their clanging metal armor, snorting horses, and snarling attack dogs.

The curiosity concerned more than appearances: each wondered about the origin of the other. The Aztec emperor Moctezuma was uncertain whether the Spaniards were gods or humans. He ordered all the archives in the land to be searched for paintings of creatures such as these. Not one was found. While the foreign ships, described by the Aztecs as floating mountains, were still anchored in the Gulf of Mexico, he sent his prophets and wise men to the coast to observe the strangers. These messengers carried two kinds of food to the ships to see which would be eaten: the food of the gods, sprinkled with sacrificial blood, was repulsive to the Europeans; they opted, instead, for the tortillas, turkey, guavas, and avocados, revealing their humanity in the process.

The conquistadors were curious, too. Christopher Columbus, like Moctezuma, reflected on the nature of the people he first encountered. Without a tortilla test, however, he decided the Americans were *hombrecillos*—almost, but not quite, humans. His compatriots in Europe found such questions more compelling. The Catholic church, especially, needed to determine whether these were beings capable of salvation. Once answering "yes," a more perplexing issue remained: if all humans descended from Adam and Eve, as taught by the Bible, how did the Indians arrive in the New World? Even scientists would later be forced to ask similar questions, because no pre-*Homo sapiens* skeletal remains have ever been discovered in the New World. Who were these previously unknown people? Survivors of Alexander's shipwrecked fleet? Decendants of legendary lost Atlantis? Egyptians?

Such questions, and some fantastic answers, would preoccupy thinkers for centuries to come, often with a passion that is unimaginable today. Some idly speculated free of any cumbersome evidence; it mattered little, for example, that ancient Egypt possessed no seafaring boats capable of reaching the Americas. Others studied illustrated reports on the New World looking for clues as to the true identity of the ancient people. Lord Kingsborough of Ireland, for instance, collected and published at his own expense everything he could find about the New World. He bankrupted himself and died in debtors' prison without ever proving his belief that the Indians were descendants of the Lost Tribe of Israel. (Yet he did preserve a wealth of material for future scholars, including copies of those precious few pre-Columbian books that miraculously survived the devastation of the conquest.)

GONZALO GUERRERO

Today, the scientific view that the Americas were peopled by Ice Age big-game hunters has quieted most other speculation as to the origins of the first Americans. Many remain fascinated, however, by ideas of exotic, even extraterrestrial, cultural contacts with the Americas. Such ideas about the origin of civilization certainly are more dramatic than the reports archaeologists provide on the gradual evolution of native civilizations. Erich von Daniken's *Chariots of the Gods* is a case in point: he claimed that other planetary beings landed in the Americas, bringing civilization with them. He just never explained why the space age jets left behind only Stone Age tools.

The accidental shipwreck is often advanced as another means of bringing advanced civilization to the New World. A critical question seldom is asked by such theorists: how might strange-looking, storm-lost seafarers be received? One answer is recorded in history. In 1511, when Spain had yet to venture as far as Mexico, a hurricane destroyed one of its ships on the way from Panama to the Dominican Republic. Twenty men managed to grab on to a lifeboat. Just over half survived two weeks without food and water before a current tossed them onto the Mexican coast south of the modern resort of Cancun, a region occupied then, as now, by Maya Indians. Five of these bearers of European iron-age civilization were immediately killed in a sacrificial rite, according to one of the two survivors, Jerónimo de Aguilar. The others escaped from their pens and fled into the arms of more benign Maya, who only enslaved them. Aguilar himself, rescued eight years later by Hernán Cortés, lived as a servant within Maya society. The only Spaniard to thrive was Gonzalo Guerrero who completely integrated himself into Maya life, marrying a Maya noblewoman, tattooing his body, and piercing his nose and lips with gold plugs. Unlike Aguilar, he refused Cortés's offer of escape. Maybe Guerrero made a European mark on Maya civilization, but all that is recorded is his tactical advice on fighting the Spaniards. He died on the battlefield with his fellow Maya.

The only indisputable legacy from the Old World left by the shipwreck survivors was smallpox.

Although some contemporary writers toy with ideas about strange voyagers peopling and civilizing the Americas (see "Gonzalo Guerrero"), scientists believe that the first peoples in the Americas arrived from northern Asia over what is now the Bering Strait. Comparative studies of DNA support this view. During the Pleistocene, or late Ice Age that began around 40,000 B.C., the sea level was reduced by 300 feet, converting the strait into a 1,000-mile-wide land bridge connecting Siberia and Alaska. Many thousands of years before Alexander the Great built his fleet in the fourth century B.C., big-game hunters stalked bisons and mammoths, some 13 feet in height, across the tundra of this land bridge. Exactly when they started arriving in the Americas remains uncertain —some argue humans arrived during an earlier Ice Age, 100,000 years ago. There is some controversial evidence of stone tools dating to 22,000 B.C. found all the way down at the tip of South America; by at least 11,000 B.C., however, humans were definitely in central Mexico based on the evidence of a massive mammoth kill. The first peoples, then, filtered into the Americas from Asia in paleolithic times, possibly continuing to arrive until around 10,000 B.C., when melting glaciers submerged the land bridge and isolated the American continents from the rest of the world.

The Land

The first Americans, then, were big-game hunters. Over the millennia, the rainfalls and grasslands diminished; the hairy mammoths and giant armadillos and Ice Age horses became extinct around 5000 B.C. Some argue that overhunting from indiscriminate, mass kills contributed to their extinction. Humans survived, but out of necessity they evolved into seminomadic hunters of deer, rabbit and peccary, trappers of iguanas, turtles, shellfish and birds, and gatherers of wild plants, roots and seeds. Then, around 3000 B.C. when maize was domesticated in central Mexico, they became farmers.

By 2000 B.C. the first Mexicans—unlike their neighbors to the north —had become sedentary villagers, relying on cultivated crops. As surplus crops of corn, beans, chile peppers, and squash produced a wealthier and more complex culture, the villagers changed from subsistence survivors to citizens of the first American civilizations. The cultures that evolved were unique to the New World—even the basic foods were distinct from the wheat, barley, and rye of the Old World civilizations. And these cultures were unusual in their independence from outside influence: the nearest center of Old World civilization was 7,000 miles away in China,

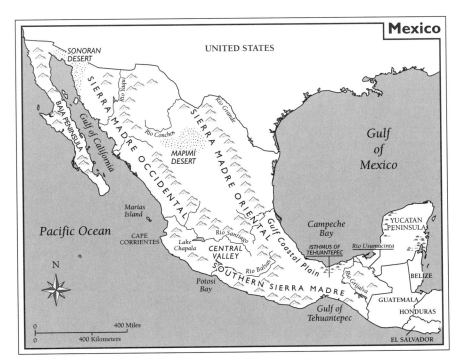

Mexico's major topographic features

a distance greater than from London to Beijing and made more formidable by the barrier of the sea.

The land provided a richly diverse setting for the evolution of these cultures. Most often pictured as the cactus desert of western movies, Mexico also is the tropical rain forest of Chiapas with howler monkeys, jaguars, and brilliantly colored macaws. It is a highland plateau dominated by snow-capped volcanic peaks, like that of Orizaba (18,700 feet), one of the three highest peaks in North America. It is the tangled green tropical lands of the coasts and riverine lowlands, as well as the cool, pine-forested regions of the Sierra Madre mountains.

The mountainous land contrasts with its largest flat area, the Yucatán peninsula, a limestone shelf barely above sea level. Other coastal lowlands are found along the Gulf of Mexico and the Pacific Ocean. Not all level areas are in the lowlands, however. Many highland plateaus, such as the central basin surrounding today's Mexico City (a city 7,349 feet in altitude) are cut off from each other by the various chains of the Sierra Madre. In this land, altitude determines the climate as much as season: really only two seasons exist, one with rains and one without. Half the year most vegetation dies from lack of rain, and the other half it is miraculously reborn by torrential downpours. There are lakes, rivers, natural springs, 3,000 miles of coast, and geysers—and deserts.

Mesoamerica

The territory occupied by the great cultures of Mexico didn't coincide with the country's present political borders. The northern deserts, rarely hospitable to the agriculture necessary to sustain the settled lifestyle of urban civilization, formed a natural buffer zone with the cultures in what is currently the U.S. Southwest. To the south, the Maya civilization spilled into what are the modern states of Belize, Guatemala, and parts of Honduras and El Salvador. This ancient cultural region, covering about 400,000 square miles, is called Mesoamerica by archaeologists.

Throughout the millennia the farthest points of Mesoamerica were in contact, primarily through trade. Although there were no wheeled vehicles or pack animals, canoes trafficked the rivers and coasts. Sea trade, in fact, was quite extensive. Christopher Columbus reported intercepting some canoes off the coast of Honduras that belonged to Maya

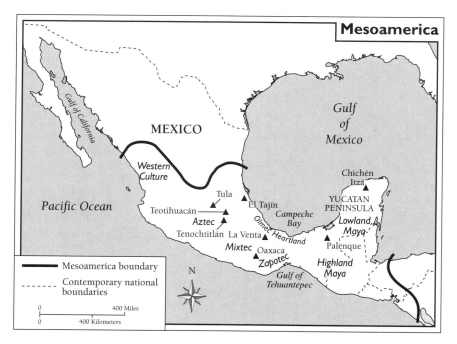

The pre-Columbian civilizations covered a somewhat different territory than modern Mexico. Less northern in its reach, Mesoamerica did extend farther south into Central America.

traders from Yucatán, a people and land unknown to him. In 1984 archaeologists discovered a port, with massive masonry docks, for the ancient inland Maya city of Chichén Itzá. The large dugout canoes must have pulled into port laden with the many objects excavated at that Yucatec city: gold leaf from as far away as Panama as well as green obsidian from north of Mexico City and turquoise from near what is now Cerillos, New Mexico—almost 3,000 miles away. And there is evidence of pre-Columbian trade along the 2,000 miles of Pacific coast between Mesoamerica and faraway Peru.

For land transport, human carriers, as onerous as their burdens must have been, more efficiently maneuvered the mountain passes and scrub jungles than carts ever could, given the technology. From the lowland rain forests they carried quetzal bird feathers and from the tropical ranges, cacao beans for making chocolate—the favorite drink of Moctezuma when spiked with vanilla, brought from the rainy slopes of Veracruz. Cacao was so valued it also was used as currency. From coastal regions like Yucatán came cotton, salt, and honey. From the highlands was traded much needed obsidian, essential for tools and weapons as well as shamans' mirrors, and textiles woven from feathers and maguey, a cactus-looking plant also used to make alcoholic *pulque*. As told by a Spanish conquistador, all these objects, and much more, could be bought in the great marketplace of the Aztec capital:

> . . . gold, silver, and precious stones, feathers, mantles, and embroidered goods. Then there were other wares consisting of Indian slaves both men and women . . . in another part there were skins of tigers and lions, of otters and jackals, deer and other animals and badgers and mountain cats, some tanned and others untanned . . . Let us go on and speak of those who sold beans and sage and other vegetables . . . fowls, cocks with wattles, rabbits, hares, deer, mallards, young dogs . . . let us also mention the fruiterers, and the women who sold cooked food . . . then every sort of pottery made in a thousand different forms from water jars to little jugs . . . But why do I waste so many words in recounting what they sell in that great market?—for I shall never finish . . .
>
> ■
> —*Bernal Díaz Del Castillo (1928:215–216)*

Fundamental Traits of Mesoamerica

Mesoamerican cultures were extremely diverse in their political and artistic attainments. Between the time of the earliest Olmec civilization in 1200 B.C. and the Spanish conquest in A.D. 1521, the classic Maya city-states flourished (A.D. 250–900) in the southern lowlands, and the great city of Teotihuacán (150 B.C.–A.D. 750) dominated the central highlands. In the tropical valleys and fertile basins of the Sierra Madre that separated these famous Mesoamerican cultures, many other groups, such as the Zapotecs, Mixtecs, and Totonacs, built their own distinctive cities. Such regional diversity continued throughout the final phase of Mesoamerican civilization, which was dominated by the Aztecs (A.D. 1345–1521). Before looking at these regional cultures individually and examining the conditions, and remaining mysteries, surrounding their rise to power and collapse, it's important to consider what unifies them and makes them distinctively Mesoamerican.

Maize

The Aztec emperor chose from among 30 dishes for his dinner each day. The ordinary citizen, however, was sustained primarily by maize and beans—a perfect protein complex. Ground on a stone mortar, called a *metate*, and mixed with water to make cornmeal, the maize was consumed as a thick gruel called *atole* or was cooked with various ingredients (such as beans and chile peppers) for *tamales* (very Mayan), or patted into flat maize cakes called *tortillas* (very central Mexican).

Maize was so essential for survival that the Mesoamerican world view parallels its recurring agricultural cycle of harvesting (death) and sprouting (rebirth). In the Maya creation myth from the surviving book of the *Popol Vuh*, the maize god is central to the birth of the sun and the dawning of the world of the Maya where the first humans were shaped out of cornmeal (see page 15).

> the making the modeling of our first mother-father, with yellow corn, white corn alone for the flesh, food alone for the human legs and arms for the first fathers, the four human works.
>
> ■
> —Popol Vuh *(translated by Dennis Tedlock:164)*

For the Aztecs, too, cultivated corn was "precious, our flesh, our bones" (Sahagún 1950–82, 11:279). Moreover, the world created in the *Popol Vuh* myth is a "cosmic corn field" (Taube 1993:54), measured and dedicated in the same manner as a *milpa* (cornfield) was prepared centuries ago and just as it is in Yucatán today.

Despite the cultural upheavals experienced by the indigenous peoples of Mexico, corn remains venerated—there are hundreds of varieties in Mexico, from blue husked to yellow, white speckled with black to reddish. The three-stone hearth for cooking cornmeal is the same as it has been for millennia, and it is held sacred. According to contemporary Maya of Chiapas, the mistreatment of maize is one of the greatest offenses against the ancestors and may cause soul loss and, sometimes, death. The *milpa* demands such respect that 19th-century rebel Maya, who had just about driven all Europeans from Yucatán, abandoned their very successful war because it was time to tend to their fields. Contemporary poet Homero Aridjis believes that a change in the quality of tortillas would seriously indicate a deterioration of Mexican life. From its Mesoamerican beginnings to the present, maize has been a symbol of life itself.

Calendars, Computations, and Celestial Events

The sciences which they taught were the computations of the years, months and days, the festivals and ceremonies, the administration of the sacraments, the fateful days and seasons, their methods of divination and their prophecies, events and cures for diseases . . .

—*Bishop Diego de Landa, 16th century*

By measuring the days and years and by studying the seasons and movement of celestial bodies, the ancient Americans hoped to understand and to influence, if not totally control, the most important events of their world. The study of the planets and stars, believed to be manifestations of the gods, led to the development of calendars for guiding people through the agricultural and ritual cycles of their lives.

Naked eye astronomy was aided by building alignments and window slats. Sometimes entire complexes were constructed for observatories, such as the Caracol at the Yucatec city of Chichén Itzá. Mesoamerican skywatchers plotted the movements of the stars in the night skies so skillfully they could predict the positions of Venus for over 500 years with only a two-hour margin of error. Entire cities could be aligned with an astronomical event, such as the heliacal set of Pleiades—known as "the rattlesnake" by the Mesoamericans—that divided the year into rainy and dry seasons. Or a sacred building, such as a great ruler's tomb, might be designed to glow in the setting sun at solstice, a symbolic moment when the sun was believed to enter the Underworld, the realm of the dead.

These astronomers excelled in their mathematics. Neither ancient Greeks or Romans had the concept of zero. The Mayas did, and they used

MAYA BOOKS

A Maya scribe paints a book, pictured on a late classic-period vase in the Museum of the American Indian, New York. With the decipherment of Maya hieroglyphics, scholars now know that scribes belonged to the nobility; some were women and some signed their works. Drawing by Cherra Wyllie (after Persis Clarkson, © Foundation for Latin American Anthropological Research)

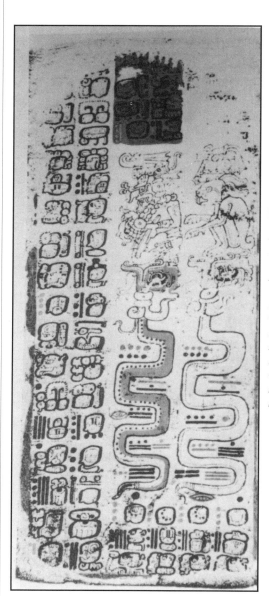

A page from the Dresden Codex, one of only four surviving Maya hieroglyphic books (Courtesy of the American Philosophical Society)

The great Mesoamerican civilizations were the only ones in the Americas that created writing and used it to compose books: books of poetry and ritual, books of astronomical cycles (and associated astrological events), books of history, and books that told the legends of world creation.

it in computations that took them thousands of years backwards into mythic time when the original ruler-gods were born and the sun first dawned. While Europe tried to calculate with unwieldy Roman numerals, the Mayas used a positional system comparable to our decimal system; theirs had a base of 20, however, not 10.

These sophisticated scientific innovations resulted from a fatalistic view of the universe. Mesoamericans viewed the world as repeating cycles, repeating prophecies. What had happened in the past, surely would happen again—in its right time. For the Yucatec Maya, for example, every period called "Katun 13 Ahau" was a period when "things fall to ruin." Perhaps they felt no surprise in seeing Spanish ships on the horizon during just such a katun period. Many centuries before, according to their books of the Chilam Balam, the great city of Chichén Itzá had been abandoned during the same cycle of time. All was determined by the "divine mandate" of the ever recurring calendrical cycles.

Knowing when to expect the worst and when to perform rituals and sacrifice to avert calamity was essential. For the learned ones, the priests, there was no distinction between astronomy and astrology. They studied the calendars and sky and predicted dangerous times, like eclipses, and times of war, like Venus stations. They read the omens and understood when there would be good crops and when not. Using books as accurate as any astronomer's chart, as indispensable as a farmer's almanac, and as prophetic as an astrologer's table, the priests advised rulers and commoners alike. All was based on the calendars and celestial cycles; all was done to please the gods who could be as menacing as they could be benificent and for whom perfect ritual performance counted. Good intentions were not enough.

> They [Yucatec Maya] had a high priest . . . the lords made him presents and all the priests of the towns brought contributions to him . . . In him was the key of their learning.
> ■
> —*Bishop Diego de Landa, 16th century*

There were many cycles and calendrical correlations. The most important were:

Solar Calendar The Mesoamericans devised a solar-year calendar as accurate as our Gregorian calendar, and more accurate than the calendar used by their contemporaries in Europe. The solar calendar was composed of 18 months of 20 days each; an additional five-day period occurred at the end of each year, a period believed to be fraught with danger.

Sacred Round Another calendar, used for divinations, was the 260-day sacred round. Archaeologists speculate this calendar may have been based on the nine-month agricultural cycle and the nine months of human gestation. Probably the oldest system of measured time in the New World, the earliest known example of a sacred round was found in highland Oaxaca and dates from about 500 B.C. The origin of the calendar, however, may very well have been in the Olmec lowlands because some of the days are named after tropical creatures such as crocodiles, jaguars, and monkeys. The nature of a king's rule was determined by the day he acceded to power, and people's destinies were determined by their birthdays in this calendar, the name of the day becoming part of their own name—the clever could manipulate their fate, however, by choosing another day for "christening." In the sacred round, numbers 1 through 13 rotate consecutively with 20 day names, then begin at 1 again with a new order of the same day names so that there is an unrepeating cycle of 260 numbered days.

Calendar Round Throughout Mesoamerica, religious festivals and dynastic events were dated by the sacred round combined with the solar calendar. In this calendar round, any given day had two names, one in each cycle—something like saying, "January 10th, the second Tuesday." It took 52 years before the dual name of any day would repeat, a period of time in the Mesoamerican system comparable in significance to our century. During the final five days, though, instead of a blow-out centennial new year's celebration, the Aztecs extinguished all fires, broke all their pottery, sacrificed, fasted, and prayed for the gods to permit the cycle to begin anew and their world to continue.

The Long Count Mesoamerican history is difficult to reconstruct using the 52-year calendar round: the dates yielded are like '92, with no distinction made between 1292 and 1992 or any other century. An additional cycle of time, most often associated with the Maya but used in the Mesoamerican lowlands from Veracruz in Mexico to Copán, Honduras, has permitted archaeologists to date Mesoamerican history with far greater accuracy. Called the "long count," the system begins with zero (August 11, 3114 B.C. in our calendar) and counts forward without repeating for over 5,000 years—enough time to cover the flourishing of Mesoamerican civilization 1,500 years before the arrival of the first Europeans. While many archaeological techniques, such as radiocarbon dating, are accurate within only a few hundred years, the long count dates that were carved into stone monuments from 32 B.C. to A.D. 909 have enabled archaeologists to reconstruct the chronology of ancient Mesoamerica in unusual detail.

Creation Myths and World View

And here is the beginning . . . Whatever might be is simply
not there: only murmurs, ripples, in the dark, in the night.
▣
—Popol Vuh *(translated by Dennis Tedlock)*

There was never a Garden of Eden in the Mesoamerican world view. The
first people, molded out of ground maize dough, never sinned, they never
fell from grace. They were, instead, the most recent efforts by the gods
to create creatures to speak and pray to them and honor them through
sacrificial offerings. In return, the people of maize would be fed and, as
the Aztecs thought, given the gift of laughter and sleep "so that [they]
would not die of sadness" (Sahagún 1950–82, 6:93).

The gods previously had tried to create appropriate earthly compan-
ions. They had always been disappointed, however, by the inability of
these earlier races to nourish them through prayers and offerings and, at
times, by their overweening arrogance. So the gods had destroyed their
own creations. According to the Aztecs, the very first creatures were
giants that the gods had devoured by fierce jaguars; the most recent were
transformed into fish when floods destroyed the mountains and the sky
crashed to the earth.

According to the Maya *Popol Vuh*, the gods continually tried to create
a more perfect world, looking for a race that could speak in order to pray,
that could remember the gods in order to be thankful. After their previous
attempts (four for the Aztecs; three for the Maya), the gods finally created
this one, the world of the true sun and moon, of maize and humans.

Lifting the sky from the sea, where it had crashed in the floods, and
naming the mountains and caves and places of the land, they created the
middle world of earthlings. The world of the maize people was ordered
into four directions and centered by the world tree that reached into the
earthly underworld with its roots and raised up to the heavens with its
branches. For all Mesoamericans this world was created through the
ultimate self-sacrifice of the gods. To create the sun and moon, two Aztec
gods had thrown themselves onto a raging fire; and Maya ancestral deities
had entered the Underworld where they were defeated and decapitated
in a game of hipball (see "The First Ballgame") by the gods of death and
disease. Eternal night was banished, and the world was ordered and
perfected for humans only through the blood sacrifices of the central
Mexican god Quetzalcoatl ("feathered serpent") and the Maya hero
twins, all of whom traveled to the Underworld to find the skulls and

15

THE FIRST BALLGAME

Mesoamerica produced the first rubber ball; the rubber came from the milky sap found in the *guayule* trees of the tropical zone, which was occupied by the earliest civilization, that of the Olmecs. The Aztecs later imported 16,000 rubber balls a year from this Gulf coast region. The ball was used in any number of games, from a hockey-like stick ball (seen in the murals of the city of Teotihuacán, near Mexico City) and a baseball version (seen in ceramic figurines from Western Mexico) to the more prevalent hipball game in which the ball—solid and packing a wallop—was bounced off hip protectors, not the hands or feet. Aztec hipball matches, according to Spanish witnesses, were accompanied by considerable betting. A team could lose by allowing the

A Maya vase (A.D. 700–850) depicts a nobleman playing a ritual game of hipball. The size of the rubber ball is exaggerated. (Dallas Museum of Art, gift of Patsy R. and Raymond D. Nasher)

ball to hit the ground or go out of bounds. Scoring in one version of hipball required the ball to pass through narrow stone rings; this was so rarely achieved that when it happened spectators showered the scoring ballplayer with their jewelry. Fascinated by the game, the conquistador Hernán Cortés took two teams back to Spain on his first trip to report to Emperor Charles V, thereby introducing ballgames to the Old World. Others simply tried to describe to the uninitiated exactly what was so remarkable about a rubber ball:

> Jumping and bouncing are its qualities, upward and downward, to and from. It can exhaust the pursuer running after it before he can catch up.
> ■
> —*Friar Diego Durán, 1579*

The competitive games played today, however, have none of the cosmic significance the ancient Americans attached to ballgames. Most of the great pre-Columbian cities had stone ballcourts in their very center next to the most sacrosanct buildings. In the Aztec origin myth, the patron god Huitzilopochtli (weet-zee-loh-POACH-tlee) slays the forces of night in a ballcourt. The Maya story of creation as told in the *Popol Vuh* involved ballplaying hero twins who, through self-sacrifice and cleverness, defeated the gods of evil and prepared the world for the birth of the sun, the dawning of the ancients' universe. When rulers took the throne in the seventh century A.D. at the beautiful Maya city of Palenque, they assumed the title of "ballplayer," just like the hero twin gods they were believed to embody. And when the game was played, creation was reenacted: decapitation of the losers paralleled the sacrifice of the creator gods in the Underworld ballgame; the arching ball signified the movement of the sun. The game had agricultural significance, too: central Mexican kings were said to play the rain god for bountiful crops. Momentous matters of state—alliances, border disputes, and ruler legitimization rituals—were decided on the sacred ballcourt.

The Great Ballcourt at the Maya city of Chichén Itzá. The scoring ring is visible on the right wall.

Xochipilli, an Aztec god of spring, is associated with flowers, song, and male fertility. (National Museum of Anthropology, Mexico City)

bones of their ancestors in order that they could be magically reborn in the sky. It was from these sacrifices that maize sprouted and the primordial ancestors ground the kernels to shape the first humans out of cornmeal.

The creation myths provided a metaphor for proper human behavior. The gods had sacrificed themselves in order to be reborn as the sun and moon; so the sun required human sacrifice before it would dawn again after a night in the Underworld. The gods went into the Underworld to defeat the lords of death and to honor their ancestors; so all Mesoamericans must sacrifice in order to honor their gods and ancestors. To keep the people of maize from becoming too arrogant and believing themselves godlike, the gods invented alcoholic *pulque* to blur their vision like "breath on a mirror": modesty and a sense of one's place in the cosmos were imperative.

The myths also infused the world with spiritual meaning. Nature itself was animate and willful, the winds and rains and storms and drought were godly expressions. The stars represented an aspect of the gods, caves were portals to the frightening Underworld, mountains were home to ancestral deities.

The myths justified the political order. Rulers embodied the creator gods, their deified ancestors. They wore god emblems on their costumes and communicated with the ancestors during shamanistic trances brought on by autosacrifice and hallucinogens. Their cities often were constructed as cosmograms, or replicas of places of creation—pyramids represented the sacred ancestral mountains and the place where corn was born; the small temple interiors represented caves or entrances to the Underworld, places where rulers communicated with the gods.

Like the Bible, the creation myths of Mesoamerica explained the genesis of the world and prescribed correct social and political behavior.

Irreverence would result, not in hell, but in the destruction of the maize world, by earthquake according to the Aztecs. Although a few late versions of these myths have been preserved through the Spaniards' contact with the last Mesoamerican civilizations, older ones have recently been deciphered in the hieroglyphic texts of the ancient Maya. Even earlier, these myths can be identified in the art of the Olmec, dating from three millennia ago. And the myths continue to infuse the world view of many indigenous peoples today: from Maya communities in highland Guatemala to Nahuatl ones near Mexico City, ancestral mountains are still worshipped and the skies are watched for the activities of the old gods.

Human Sacrifice

. . . when they sacrifice a wretched Indian they open the chest with stone knives and hasten to tear out the palpitating heart and blood, and offer it to their Idols, in whose name the sacrifice is made.
■
—*Bernal Díaz del Castillo (1928:213)*

Grisly tales of human sacrifice permeated the conquistadors' reports to Europe. Atop the towering pyramidal platforms, in front of the most sacred temples, priests stretched their still-living victims over sacrificial stones and cut out their hearts. Sometimes they cut out the entrails, too, and flayed the skin in order to make "cloaks" worn by priests in honor of Xipe Totec, a god of spring. The remaining corpse would be rolled down the steps of the Aztec Great Temple where the captors of the prisoner had the right to take home various parts for a cannibalistic corn stew.

The Spaniards reported that thousands of victims at a time were dispensed in this manner. Twenty thousand war captives were sacrificed just to dedicate the temple to the Aztec patron deity, Huitzilopochtli. Over 100,000 skulls of victims were displayed in the sacred center. Or so it was said.

Other early civilizations are known to have practiced human sacrifice—even in the Bible, Abraham vows to sacrifice Isaac, and the ancient Romans subjected gladiators and slaves to torturous deaths simply for sport. Likewise, cannibalism has been identified as ritual behavior in various tribes. The massive scale of ritual sacrifice reported for the Aztecs, however, has often been considered unique in world history.

Time-motion computer simulations have cast doubt on the actual number of sacrificial victims reported by the conquistadors. Scholars now emphasize that at the time of their reports, the Spaniards were mistreating the Aztecs and had much to gain by portraying them as despicable. Careful studies of the reports made by the first missionaries on the native religion indicate there were really not a great number of human sacrifices performed for the annual rituals and that cannibalism was extremely rare, more a kind of religious sacrament. How many sacrifices were performed remains a matter of controversy. But they were performed, and with considerable variety, depending on the feast day.

Until recent decades, archaeologists believed the Aztecs had a barbaric streak that made them more bloodthirsty than their predecessors in ancient Mexico. Now human sacrifice is recognized as a religious practice in all Mesoamerican cultures. Exactly why their world view evolved to demand such behavior remains obscure, but the land itself, with its stark seasonal contrasts of drought and rain, desiccation and verdure, deprivation and abundance surely reinforced any tendency to believe that from hardship and sacrifice and death came the rebirth of maize and life itself. Although the details of Mesoamerican resurrection cosmology are unique, human sacrifice is far from unusual in early civilizations—large numbers of sacrificed individuals have been found in ancient tombs in both Mesopotamia and China.

Carved stone skull rack excavated from the Aztecs' Great Temple in Mexico City

The Mesoamerican world was created by sacrifice of the gods, according to native myths. For that world to continue, humans had to reenact the original sacrifice. Nobles sacrificed their own blood, spattered and burnt it on paper and sent the smoke as food for the gods. Men perforated their genitals with stingray spines or obsidian in order to let blood. Both men and women pulled ropes of thorns through their lips; priests pricked their tongues and lips so often they barely could speak. Commoners marched into holy wars to capture sacrificial victims, or to become victims themselves. These sacrifices of Mesoamericans provide compelling evidence of their faith. However, few willingly gave their lives or those of their loved ones to the temple priests: most sacrificial victims were, at the time of the Spanish conquest at least, prisoners of war, orphans, or slaves.

Sacrifice was necessary to keep the sun on its course, to bring on the rains, to assure order by maintaining the cycles of human existence. The world was particularly at risk during the completion of a cycle of time or a transition between seasons or rulerships. At such times, human sacrifice was especially demanded: hearts were needed to feed the sun and guarantee its cyclical renewal; small children were offered to bring on the rains—the worse their cries, it was said, the more Tlaloc, the rain god, was pleased.

For the Mesoamericans, their world could continue only by sacrifice. Such was the unremitting fate of the New World inhabitants, a tragic fate that infused every aspect of their lives.

2

DIVERSITY OF MESOAMERICAN CIVILIZATION

Mesoamerican civilization survived 2,500 years. Mesoamerican trade goods and trade patterns changed over these many centuries, as did the environmental and political setting. And with those changes, cities achieved moments of greatness, then expired. Vast regions sometimes were bypassed by new political and economic arrangements, until they, too, passed away. As a result, the variety in Mesoamerican art and architecture is extremely rich.

Archaeologists have identified these different cultural and temporal horizons. The preclassic period was dominated by the earliest Olmec culture from 1200 B.C. to 400 B.C.; and during the protoclassic period from 400 B.C. to A.D. 250 many cities first made their appearance throughout Mesoamerica, from the great city of Teotihuacán near modern Mexico City to the many southern cities, such as Izapa near the Guatemalan border, Monte Albán in Oaxaca, and the earliest Maya sites. During the classic period from A.D. 250 to A.D. 900 many of the protoclassic cities achieved their greatest heights, from Teotihuacán and Monte Albán to Maya cities like Palenque in Chiapas and Uxmal in Yucatán. Then, during the early post-classic period from A.D. 900 to A.D. 1200 many of the classic cities were forever abandoned while others, such as Tula in central Mexico and Chichén Itzá in Yucatán, flourished. Finally, during the late post-classic period much of Mesoamerica was dominated by the Aztecs. This last Mesoamerican horizon came to a calamitous end with the Spanish conquest (see chart on page 23).

The contrasts in geography, not just in time, also influenced the different regional cultures. The art of Mesoamericans of highland central Mexico tends towards geometric and abstracted figures, hard-cut and deeply shadowed sculpture (see pages 18 and 39). The art is powerful and awesomely expressive, if often impersonal. By contrast, the lowland areas of the Gulf coast and the Maya region concentrate far more on portraiture (see page 26; pages 16 and 35) and Maya art often has the soft, curved forms and lush foliate designs of the tropical environment that surrounded those people.

The Preclassic and the Olmec (1200 B.C.–400 B.C.)

Not until the 1950s, when radiocarbon tests were developed to date excavated materials, did archaeologists realize how old Mesoamerican civilization was. Equally surprising, at least to some archaeologists, was that the earlier dates belonged to the Olmec culture (1200 B.C.–400 B.C.), not to the more famous peoples of the central highlands and not to the Maya of the southern lowlands. Some had thought the Olmec culture might be a provincial branch of Maya civilization. Instead it was proven older, much older.

The Olmec culture had been discovered only in the late 19th century, when a farmer clearing his field had found a colossal basalt head (see page 26)—the first of 17 that would be uncovered in southeastern

CHRONOLOGY OF ANCIENT MEXICO

		Central Mexico	Oaxaca	Gulf Coast	Chiapas	Yucatán Maya	Michoacán/ Mexico West
Post-classic Period	A.D. 1520– 1200–	Aztec	Mixtec	Zempoala	C H I A P A	Tulum Mayapán	Tarascan
Classic Period	900– 600–	Toltec Xochicalco	Monte Albán IV Monte Albán III	El Tajín	Palenque	Chichén Itzá Uxmal Edzná Cobá Kohunlich	Shaft Tombs
Protoclassic Period	250–	Teotihuacán	Monte Albán II	Tres Zapotes	Izapa		
Preclassic Period	B.C. 100– 500– 900– B.C. 1200–	Cuicuilco Tlatilco	Monte Albán I San José Magote	La Venta San Lorenzo	O L M E C		Chupícuaro Guerrero Olmec

23

The Great Goddess, one of the three patron deities of Teotihuacán, is frequently depicted in murals, such as this one, painted on palace walls.

Veracruz, the most recent one just in 1994. These bodyless basalt heads, found at many Olmec sites and now thought to be portraits of Olmec rulers, are 5 to 11 feet high and weigh up to 20 tons.

By the time of their rediscovery, the largest Olmec cities of La Venta and San Lorenzo Tenochtitlán had been abandoned for 2,500 years. No subsequent cities had been built over them to link them with later times and later peoples. The Aztecs, Mayas and Zapotecs had been encountered by Spanish conquistadors and written about by evangelizing friars, but it was unclear if the Mixe-Zoque residents of the region were the Olmec themselves or later settlers. Too much time had lapsed. The region, no longer densely populated, seemed rather abandoned—and mysterious.

The first civilization arose in one of the wettest and most bountiful regions of Mesoamerica. Many rivers, including the Coatzalcoalcos and Papoloapan, cut through tropical rain forests and mangrove swamps on their way to the sea. Jaguars, monkeys, crocodiles, wild turkeys, boar, and deer thrived. Shellfish, turtles, and fish abounded in the estuaries. Heavy rains and mists made the dry season practically unknown and allowed crops to grow year-round. Even without cultivated crops, the region was rich and had evolved into sedentary villages well before 1200 B.C. With the introduction of maize from the highlands, it became a land

24

of plenty, and the villages grew into important political and religious centers.

With extra crops and goods, the Olmec set about spending their surpluses. They traded their crops and rubber balls for central highland obsidian to make tools and southeastern lowland green-blue jade to create magnificently polished objects. They exchanged their magnificently carved ornaments and worked shells for Oaxacan iron-ores in order to make polished mirrors—mirrors known to be used later in Mesoamerica by shamans and rulers for communicating with the gods and ancestors.

At home, the Olmecs constructed the first monumental buildings. The buildings were earthen, not stone like later cities, but while other areas of Mesoamerica were mere villages of wattle and daub (interwoven poles plastered with clay), the Olmecs of San Lorenzo (1200 B.C.–900 B.C.) constructed an immense artificial plateau, 3,000 feet long and almost 2,000 feet wide. On top were 200 earthen mounds for residences and ceremonial buildings and an elaborate drainage system connecting artificial ponds. At La Venta (900 B.C.–400 B.C.), the local population, numbering 18,000, constructed the first great pyramid, 100 feet high and shaped like a fluted, conical effigy of a nearby volcano. Here they buried, perhaps as offerings to the Underworld gods, immense deity masks (16.5 × 20 feet), stone mosaics, and colored clays, 3,022 pieces of precious polished jade and, in one burial alone, 1,000 tons of serpentine stone imported from the Pacific coast!

The Olmec built their great centers and carved their delicate bas reliefs with the stone age kit that would persist until the Spanish conquest. What they undertook with such limited technology is often astonishing. The nearest basalt to San Lorenzo was 30 miles away and from La Venta, 80 miles. Yet vast quantities of this stone were imported for carving colossal heads of rulers and 50-ton thrones showing their divine descent. The stone had to be cut without metal (probably rope-and-water abrasion assisted by drilling) and transported without wheeled cart or pack animal. Most likely the basalt was dragged to a river then floated on rafts to the centers. Some estimate these monumental stones required crews of 1,000 people to move them.

It remains unknown why the Olmec civilization ended. Their hallmark art style—jade bas reliefs of snarling jaguar-human figures (probably part of a shamanistic cult) and more portrait-like freestanding sculptures of rulers with slanting eyes, flaring noses, and thick lips—gradually disappeared. The monolithic sculptures were ritually muti-

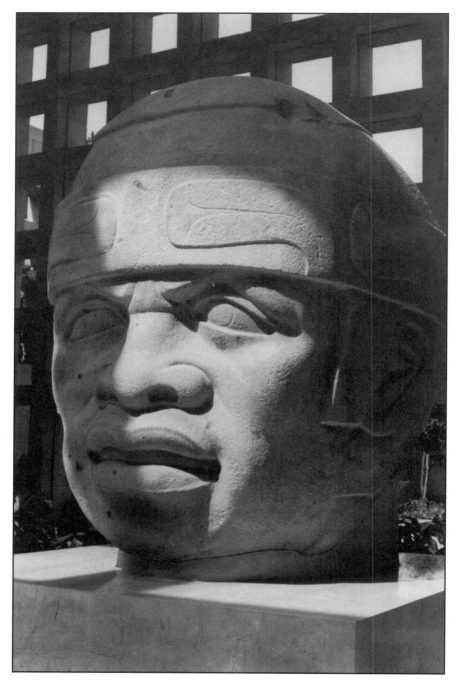

Over 7 feet high, this portrait head of an Olmec ruler dates between 1200 and 900 B.C.
(Photo: Michael Edwards)

lated, then carefully buried. Olmec political centers were abandoned one by one. The power centers of Mesoamerica shifted elsewhere.

But the Olmecs left a legacy. Their trade into Honduras and across Mexico to the Pacific coast, and the spread of their art and ideas, geographically defined Mesoamerica. Olmec trade stimulated the development of other emerging cultures into more complex societies. Their religious and artistic symbols were borrowed by new elites as badges of social prestige and authority—burial sites as far away as Honduras have been found to contain Olmec jades and pottery. And the inherited shamanistic power of the rulers created a rigid class structure that was maintained even after the Spanish conquest.

As archaeologists dig deeper into the long-held secrets of the earth, they may find other civilizations as important or more ancient than the Olmec. Current evidence suggests, however, that it was the mother culture of Mesoamerica. Most of the traits that characterize later pre-Columbian societies can be identified in this earliest period of civilization, from shamanism and rulership to Underworld offerings and pyramid construction, from the rubber ballgame and human sacrifice to the feathered serpent deities and, of course, the gods of maize, rain, earth, and fire.

Before the end of the Olmec culture, other cultures flourished throughout Mesoamerica—calendrical dates were recorded in the Zapotec highlands of Oaxaca, and the pyramids were built by the Mayas and central Mexicans. During the protoclassic period (400 B.C.–A.D. 250) writing was carved into stone monuments; some of the earliest examples come from the Olmec heartland. The region shifted into second-class status, however, with newer, more urban centers taking control elsewhere.

The Classic Period: Teotihuacán, Monte Albán, and Maya Cities

The classic period was first named for those centuries when cultures flourished throughout Mesoamerica, from the Maya and Zapotec to the highland Mexican and Gulf coast cities. This was a period of urbanization. And it was a period of widespread literacy; a period when the Maya used the exact long count system of dating. There was also a great diversity of city-states—hundreds in the Maya area alone, quite a number with populations of 50,000 to 100,000. The richness and variety in art was never greater.

Until recently it was believed these classic cultures were peace-loving, theocratic states that engaged in neither war nor human sacrifice.

Such notions have been forever dispelled by the work of archaeologists as recently as the 1980s. At Teotihuacán, archaeologists discovered a ritual burial of over 200 sacrificed individuals symmetrically arranged inside the base of the Pyramid of the Feathered Serpent; most of them, including the women, were outfitted as warriors. In the Maya area, archaeologists have uncovered signs of devastating warfare, and epigraphers have translated hieroglyphs about battles between cities.

The classic period then, was not an especially stable time. By its end, entire cities were abandoned, and power and trade alliances had shifted to new sites on the periphery of the classic regions—such as Chichén Itzá in northern Yucatán, El Tajín in Veracruz, and Cacaxtla and Xochicalco on the edges of the basin of Mexico. Some Maya regions were depopulated, not to recover until the 20th century. The possible causes of these various collapses have been the subject of considerable archaeological study.

Near the Gulf coast, cities, which may have been very large, have been rediscovered in the 1990s. At the same time, the Pacific coast is being more closely examined for sites and cultural affiliation. Excavations in these areas will surely change archaeologists' understanding of Mesoamerica. For now, it is only the better excavated and better understood cities that can be described. As a sample of the diverse settings and cultures of Mesoamerica, it is worth examining some of the most important: Teotihuacán, the Maya, and Monte Albán.

Teotihuacán (150 B.C.–A.D. 750)

Once the sixth largest city in the world, the ancient city of Teotihuacán was one of the greatest powers in the 2,500-year span of Mesoamerica. Located near Lake Texcoco, about 30 miles from modern Mexico City, Teotihuacán still proclaims its mighty presence with its monumental Pyramid of the Sun and Pyramid of the Moon. It once controlled a region about the size of Belgium. Its influence was felt in cities as far away as in Honduras; its trade reached to northern Mexico and the Pacific coast. Its emissaries—warrior merchants, most likely—can still be seen depicted in the art of foreign cities, such as the Maya site of Tikal in Guatemala and the Zapotec city of Monte Albán.

So much prestige was invested in Teotihuacán, "the place where the gods were made," according to one myth, that the Aztecs venerated it at the time of the conquest when Emperor Moctezuma made regular pilgrimages there—900 years after Teotihuacán's fall. The Aztecs believed they lived in the age of the Fifth Sun, which was created when the

New World Pyramids

yramids in the New World, such as the Pyramid of the Moon at Teotihuacán shown below, are unlike those in Egypt in that, rather than coming to a peak, they are level atop, forming platforms for temples. American pyramids often achieved their monumental proportions because their builders, rather than starting from scratch, would envelope old structures as fill. The Cholula pyramid, with a volume of 3 million meters, a base covering 46 acres, and a height of 198 feet, has been said to be the largest preindustrial building ever erected on earth. Yet its final bulk was achieved by various building projects over the centuries that incorporated earlier pyramids—larger than the Pyramid of the Moon. Like their Egyptian counterparts, however, the pyramids sometimes contain royal tombs painted with murals and accompanied with precious jades and, in the post-classic period, gold ornaments. Although many have speculated about burials inside Teotihuacán's Sun and Moon pyramids, no tombs have been discovered to date.

Pyramid of the Moon, Teotihuacán

sun and moon were born at Teotihuacán. Teotihuacán's rise to power may have been related to just such a religious belief about its cosmic importance. Archaeologists have discovered a sacred cave, a place of emergence for Mesoamericans, beneath the Pyramid of the Sun; astronomers now argue that the alignment not only of the pyramid but of the entire city may correlate with ancient beliefs about the creation of the Mesoamerican world.

More than religion propelled Teotihuacán into power. Located near the highland lake where the Aztecs would eventually build their island capital, Teotihuacán had access to fish and fowl as well as to the agricultural potential of the central basin. Teotihuacanos also controlled vast quantities of precious obsidian, the glass "iron" from which Mesoamerican tools were made and their major item of trade. Teotihuacanos' wealth paid for the Pyramid of the Sun, completed by A.D. 150, and covering about the same area as the Great Pyramid in Egypt, but with only half its height. That great effort of human construction was followed by others, including the Pyramid of the Moon and a 48-acre administrative and market complex, larger than the Pentagon in Arlington, Virginia (34 acres).

Yet for all of Teotihuacán's recognized greatness, its rulers remain anonymous: nowhere in the art of the city are their portraits discovered, and nowhere on the monuments and great buildings were any writings inscribed about their achievements. Yet their presence is felt in every element of the city's design. A rigid grid plan prevails for over eight square miles. No natural feature was permitted to interfere with the layout: the San Juan river was canalized to conform to the grid as it passed through the city. Symmetry was the aesthetic mandate, from the composition of paintings in palaces to the urban plan for the city.

The urban plan invaded even private homes. The population—who, based on depopulation studies of the surrounding countryside, were probably coerced into living in the city—resided in 2,000 apartment complexes for 60 to 100 individuals each. These complexes could vie with modern housing projects in the uniformity of their plan: one-story, windowless buildings with rooms constructed around interlocking, open courtyards. These complexes included a semipublic space for worship, especially of the city's patron, the Great Goddess, from whose yellow hands flowed streams of jades and shells and other symbols of fertility and wealth (see page 24). Of course, the elite classes lived in grander complexes decorated with bas relief sculptures and murals. There were warrior enclaves as well as neighborhoods of potters and obsidian workers. Archaeologists have identified foreign neighborhoods, too: residences with cultural traces from the Zapotec, Gulf coast, and Maya regions that may have housed traders and artisans.

Many aspects of life in Teotihuacán remain mysterious. Some Mesoamericanists wonder whether the objects in the precious stream flowing from the Great Goddess's fingers are in fact signs that constitute a form of writing. If not, then there is no writing known from this great city despite the fact that the Teotihuacanos were exposed to the hiero-glyphs of other Mesoamerican cultures, such as the Maya. Could they have consciously rejected literacy? Many believe records were kept, but on perishable bark paper rather than stone. Because there is no written record from this period, the language, and ethnic identity, of the Teoti-huacanos is unknown.

Sometime between A.D. 650 and A.D. 750 Teotihuacán's elite lost control. The sacred center of the city was burned and sacked and never again occupied. The city never recovered its farflung trade or prestige. Archaeologists remain uncertain as to whether the populace rose up in rebellion against oppressive ruling powers or whether other city-states, competing for the lucrative trade of Teotihuacán, invaded the city. What is certain is that after 800 years, Teotihuacán ended cataclysmically.

Southern Lowland Maya (600 B.C.–A.D. 900)

In contrast to highland Teotihuacán, the Maya flourished in the southern lowland rain forests of Mexico, Guatemala, and Belize (see map 2) where colorful bird feathers and jaguar pelts were valued trade items. They also thrived in the northern scrub jungles of Yucatán where cotton and salt were items of exchange as well as in the highlands of Guatemala where obsidian was a resource. Although the Maya built large cities, quite a number with populations from 50,000 to 100,000, they built too many of them, perhaps, for any one to achieve the kind of centralized control that occurred at Teotihuacán.

The aesthetic sensibilities of the southern lowlands and central Mexican highlands could not be more different. The Maya cities were never built to a grid plan; more often they conformed to the irregularities of the natural landscape. Their buildings were constructed with a corbel arch (the closest Mesoamerica ever came to using the true arch), permit-ting greater height. Splendid tombs of rulers and other nobility have been found incorporated into the pyramidal platforms of temples; some are connected to the temples by ceramic tubes, or what have been called psychoducts—the Maya may have used them to communicate with venerated ancestors. Maya art is never anonymous, but full of portraiture, whether a ruler or ballplayer or tormented captive is the subject (see pages 16 and 35). Even Maya gods have faces, and many of them are deified ancestors and former rulers.

Another major contrast with Teotihuacán is the use of writing on stone monuments that have preserved their texts till this day. Although archaeologists have uncovered sizable Maya cities dating back to middle Olmec times (600 B.C.), the earliest known Maya hieroglyphic text with an exact long count date (see "Calendars" in chapter 1) occurs in A.D. 292, and the last long count date known to archaeologists is A.D. 909: these dates have been used to define the temporal limits of the classic period. Most of the dated Maya monuments are found in the southern lowlands, called the Maya heartland. Here are the most famous ancient cities of classic Maya civilization, such as Palenque in Mexico, Tikal in Guatemala, and Copán in Honduras.

Other Mesoamerican cultures, such as the Zapotecs in Oaxaca and the Aztecs, recorded brief hieroglyphic statements in stone; many also had bark paper books, but few of these survived. Pottery shards and artifacts are all that can be pieced together to tell us about the Olmec and Teotihuacán civilizations. The Maya, however, developed a partially phonetic writing system and left long enough texts for the hieroglyphic statements to be deciphered by 20th-century scholars. In recent decades, epigraphers have made enormous strides in translating these hieroglyphs. They have revealed the first written history of the Americas—a very biased history, one based on rulers' proclamations and boasts, but a brief history nonetheless of the classic period Maya world. Archaeologists now can enhance their understanding of the Maya with these deciphered writings. Rulers, a few of them women, now have names. In addition to the names, a system of governance has been revealed through the deciphered texts. The rulers' inherited right to rule is asserted through dynastic lists; their divine right to rule is proclaimed by associating the gods with royal ancestors. Political and marriage alliances are recorded, wars and noble captives boasted about, and religious ceremonies with royal bloodletting described.

Despite the remarkable contrasts between the lowland Maya and Teotihuacán, there was considerable contact between them. The Maya presence is clear at Teotihuacán in one of the apartment complexes and in trade items, such as carved jades. Teotihuacán-style buildings, ceramics, and obsidian are found at numerous Maya sites, and Teotihuacán symbols were adapted by Maya rulers as part of their war costume. Although some archaeologists have argued that Teotihuacán conquered some Maya cities or even founded them, most now believe the evidence equally supports mere trade relationships. Whatever influence Teotihuacán had, there is major growth in the number and size of Maya cities after the fall of that central Mexican state.

The collapse of classic-period Maya civilization has been one of the great Mesoamerican mysteries. Drought, disease, and incessant warfare have all been suggested as causes. The collapse was most likely caused by a combination of such factors. But one additional element of the collapse cannot be overlooked, that of the environment.

The classic-period Maya radically altered their rain forest environment. Two hundred cities replaced the forest. Palaces and temples and ballcourts covered the most fertile land. More forest had to be cut for farming, and trees were needed to burn limestone for the stucco the Maya used to plaster their buildings both inside and out—20 trees with all their branches, it is estimated, produce only a small 3-foot-high pile of stucco. Still more trees had to be felled for wood-fired pottery kilns. The result, based on pollen studies, was massive deforestation that caused soil erosion and environmental degradation.

It is not difficult to imagine that the lowland Maya may have outstripped the carrying capacity of the lowlands. Some archaeologists have argued that overpopulation and deforestation caused the collapse of their civilization. Examination of skeletal remains suggests severe malnutrition among the poorer classes and, in some instances, among the elite as well. The fact that the southern lowlands were abandoned by the end of the classic period certainly suggests problems with the environment. The degradation of the ecosystem, even if not the sole cause of the collapse of the lowland Maya, could have rendered them vulnerable to other pressures, including prolonged warfare and drought.

From A.D. 800 to A.D. 900, cities gradually stopped erecting monuments and an increasing number were abandoned. Some were surrounded by defensive walls. After A.D. 909, not a single ruler is proclaimed anywhere in the long count calendar. The Maya continued to thrive in northern Yucatán, parts of Belize and highland Guatemala—all regions where they live today—but not in the southern lowlands. By the time of the Spanish conquest, the southern lowlands had reverted to tropical rain forest and the classic-period cities of stone, once so numerous, were hidden under the jungle growth. Hernán Cortés, marching through the region in 1526, considered it a wilderness.

Monte Albán (500 B.C.–A.D. 700)

The Zapotec city of Monte Albán never was large compared to Teotihuacán—its entire ceremonial center would fit under the Pyramid of the

Eighth-century A.D. *palace at the Maya ruins of Palenque*

K'AN XUL II, MAYA KING

The unusual tower of the palace at the ruined Maya city of Palenque in Chiapas, Mexico, is believed to have been built by Lord K'an Xul who ruled the city from A.D. June 3, 702 to August 30, 711. Considerable historical knowledge, such as K'an Xul's name (now known to be more accurately spelled phonetically as K'an Hok' Chitam) and his royal lineage, has resulted from rapid advances in interpreting Maya hieroglyphs. Scholars have known for the past century how to translate the Maya long count into our Gregorian calendar, but the rulers' names, their births, accession, and other events in their lives have been translated through phonetic decipherments only in the past few decades.

In the Palace Tablet K'an Xul, sitting between his parents who legitimize his right to rule from the realm of the dead, accedes to the throne of Palenque. This scene is part of a beautiful hieroglyphic panel that begins on the left with a long count date after which it states the royal ancestry of K'an Xul and tells of his accession to the throne of Palenque. The glyphs in the top scene name the actors and events.

Even after many of the texts at Palenque had been deciphered, scholars were not able to determine when K'an Xul died. He simply fell out of the written history of Palenque. The discovery of the carving at the nearby

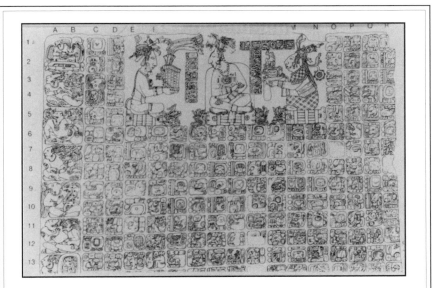

Palace Tablet, Palenque   (Drawing by Merle Greene Robertson; used with permission)

site of Tonina revealed the historical truth that Palenque scribes had avoided telling. The scene depicts a lord, his arms bound, who has been captured by Tonina. Identified by the hieroglyphs on his thigh, this victim is none other than K'an Xul of Palenque. The hieroglyphs to the right state that a war occurred on a certain date.

Tonina Monument 122   (Drawing by Ian Graham, courtesy Peabody Museum, Harvard University)

Sun. It was not large compared to the great cities of the Maya either. But Monte Albán, set atop a mountain, required a herculean effort to construct. First the mountain was flattened and the city laid out symmetrically, but not in a Teotihuacán-style grid. Then building materials were carried up the mountainside—without pack animals or wheeled vehicles. Stone for columns, the first known in Mesoamerican architecture, were hauled up for the construction of a colonnaded hall. And, finally, the city of 26,000 people was continually supplied with food and water.

Located in the middle of a series of narrow valleys created by two converging chains of the Sierra Madre, Monte Albán may have been chosen for its central, and easily defensible, position. Archaeologists have argued that a confederacy of the nobles from the valleys jointly chose the site as their capital for ruling highland Oaxaca. Although people continued to populate the valleys (unlike the basin surrounding Teotihuacán), there is evidence that the elite no longer did. The only city-state in Oaxaca with any concentration of power (unlike the Maya region), Monte Albán dominated a vast region, at least according to the hieroglyphic proclamations of conquest carved into its buildings.

In its earliest history, the Oaxaca valley had close cultural contacts with the Olmecs with whom they traded magnetite for mirrors, and, later, with the Maya to the south. Throughout the classic period, the Zapotecs followed the Maya practices of erecting sculptures carved with hieroglyphic texts extolling the military exploits of their rulers, and building stone ballcourts in their most sacred centers. Great tombs were built for their rulers and the nobility, and there is evidence of ancestor worship, just as there is in the Maya region.

But Monte Albán's most important contact during the classic period was with Teotihuacán. Whether that contact was always peaceful is unclear, given the defensive position of Monte Albán. Yet there was an enclave of Oaxaqueños at Teotihuacán, and archaeologists have found remnants of a Teotihuacano-style palace at Monte Albán from the early classic period. The two cities certainly traded, but whether this trade was in the form of tribute or exchange remains uncertain. Although Monte Albán differed from the central Mexican city in its artistic preference for portraiture and its use of writing on public monuments, the warrior dress of its rulers and the mural art of its elaborate stone tombs shows borrowing from that great city.

Monte Albán's power eroded with the collapse of Teotihuacán. The grand carvings dedicated to its leaders' war victories were replaced with less grandiose ones about marriage alliances and lineages. Numerous, competing cities appeared in the Oaxaca valleys. Monte Albán was abandoned until a new group made its appearance: the Mixtecs.

Post-classic Mixtecs and Aztecs

The deepest understanding we have of Mesoamerican culture comes from its final phase. A few of the codices painted on bark paper have survived from this time. The conquistadors left eyewitness accounts of the peoples they conquered, and after the conquest, the Catholic friars recorded many of the myths and oral histories of the peoples they converted, such as the Yucatec and highland Guatemalan Maya, the Mixtecs of Oaxaca, and the Nahuatl-speaking groups of central Mexico, especially the Aztecs. Ironically, this phase is often poorly known archaeologically because the Spaniards usually built over the cities they conquered, including the Aztec capital at Tenochtitlán which now lies beneath modern Mexico City.

Preceding the final phase of Mesoamerica, there was a decided shifting of power and movement of peoples throughout the Mexican region. From the collapse of the classic period cultures rose new cities in Veracruz (El Tajín), northern Yucatán (Chichén Itzá), the northern Basin of Mexico (Tula), as well as other areas. The inhabitants of these cities borrowed from both their Maya and Teotihuacán predecessors to create a more eclectic, more pan-Mesoamerican art style: they carved hieroglyphs on stone monuments, but only short texts; their art was naturalistic like that of the Maya, but stylistically was more sharp-edged and rectilinear like that of Teotihuacán (see page 38). Their political and religious cults placed special emphasis on the ballgame; and their ballcourt art elaborately depicted human sacrifice and was associated with skull racks. They created a trade route more expansive than that of even the classic period, and searched far and wide for turquoise and gold and cacao beans, which were used for money as well as chocolate. The Aztecs would build on the foundation laid by these earlier cultures.

By A.D. 1200, most of the early post-classic cities were either abandoned or greatly diminished in power. The Aztecs moved into the cultural void that ensued—they may even have had something to do with the collapse. According to their origin myths, they were nomadic barbarians at this time and only ended their migrations from the north a century later when they settled in the central valley of Mexico and received the veneer of civilization by marrying into more noble groups.

The Aztecs' historic myths indicate that in 1345 their nomadic ancestors witnessed an eagle devouring a serpent (a symbol borrowed for the Mexican flag); the sign, according to their patron deity, meant their wanderings had ended, their promised land had finally been reached. Archaeologists, however, believe the Aztecs settled on an isolated island in Lake Texcoco much earlier, forced there by other groups in the central valley.

It would take the Aztecs over a century before they even achieved independence as a city-state. In the meantime they expanded their island

Warrior column (15 feet in height) from post-classic city of Tula in central Mexico (National Museum of Anthropology, Mexico City)

38

Aztec stone sculpture of a jaguar   (National Museum of Anthropology, Mexico City)

by heaping mud from the lake bottom on rafts; plants anchored their roots to the mud, and the landfill became rich farmland. Through considerable engineering ingenuity, they built dikes to control flooding and aqueducts to carry fresh water. In the exact center of this five-square-mile artificial island was the Templo Mayor, the double-temple pyramid to Tlaloc, the rain god, and Huitzilopochtli, the Aztec sun god of war. Slightly askew from true north, the great temple was instead aligned with sacred mountains on the mainland and astronomically aligned with the rising sun at equinox. From this holy center four avenues divided the city into Mesoamerican divine order.

Despite their humble beginnings, the Aztecs flourished and evolved into a highly complex city-state based on rigid class distinctions—commoners were severely punished for emulating noble dress, for example —and ruled by a divine king. They created and built Tenochtitlán, the center of a 19-island lake kingdom, crisscrossed by canals and reached from the mainland by three monumental causeways. From their islands, the Aztecs forced a triple alliance with their most powerful neighbors and imposed tribute, not just trade, on conquered regions as far away as Guatemala. Their commerce was so great that some estimate nearly 100,000 canoes trafficked the lake and canals. Eventually, the kingdom of the eagle and serpent became the capital of Mesoamerica's strongest empire.

As archaeologists now know, the Aztecs were not the first militant culture in Mesoamerica. Nor did they introduce personal bloodletting and human sacrifice to the pre-Columbian world. Rather, they incorporated the religious practices of the cultures that had preceded them—perhaps embellishing them in the process—in order to appease their gods (and, probably, intimidate their enemies). Ritual wars, called flowery wars, were imposed on their Tlaxcalan neighbors so the Aztecs could capture sacrificial victims—certainly a gruesome practice and a grim world view, but one not unique to the Aztecs.

NEZAHUALCÓYOTL: POET KING

◆ut of the native histories compiled by the early Franciscan friars emerges a portrait of a king who could rival Lorenzo the Magnificent of Renaissance Florence in his learning and support for the arts. Almost 50 years before the Spanish, Nezahualcóyotl (nay-zah-whal-KOH-yohtl; meaning Hungry Coyote) ruled Texcoco, part of the Aztec Triple Alliance. He codified Aztec law, studied astronomy, engineered elaborate aqueducts, and designed his garden to include fountains and a zoo. A war captain, he battled for Aztec supremacy while also setting aside part of his palace for poets, philosophers, and historians to gather and teach. This most learned man was also a poet whose name and work has been preserved for us from the pre-Columbian world. He died in 1472, but is a culture hero in modern Mexico, with streets and even a neighborhood named after him.

> We are not here forever,
> But pause only for a moment in time.
> Though it be of jade it will shatter,
> Though it be of gold it will break,
> Though it might be of quetzal feathers it will decay.
> Nothing endures for eternity on this earth,
> But is here only fleetingly.
> ■
> —Nezahualcóyotl (after Nigel Davis 1973:117)

Aztec art was interregional, particularly so because artists were brought to Tenochtitlán from all other parts of Mesoamerica, especially from Oaxaca and Veracruz. Aztecs sculpted in a rectilinear and often fearsome style (see page 39) that also could be exceptionally realistic, whether depicting nature or human sacrifice (see page 18). They produced three-dimensional sculptures that were among the greatest artistic works of Meso-america.

The Aztec empire was so powerful it rendered other regions weaker. After the collapse of Mayapán in A.D. 1446, for example, the Yucatec Maya no longer built grand cities of stone and plaster, but rather lived in the older ones of their ancestors or built smaller shrine-like centers, such as Tulum. Although never conquered by the Aztecs, these Maya seemed diminished and peripheral to the main course of Mesoamerican events.

The Mixtecs of Oaxaca, however, flourished during the late post-classic period. The long-time occupants of the mountainous regions of Oaxaca, they had been overshadowed by both Monte Albán and Teotihuacán in the classic period. In the post-classic, however, they may very well have dominated the Zapotec area. Mixtec pictographic codices (see pages 74 and 75) boast of marriage alliances, probably achieved through military conquest, with the Zapotecs; Mixtec murals and zigzag fret

Mixtec gold pendant from a tomb in Zaachila, Oaxaca

designs are found on many Oaxacan valley buildings, such as at Mitla. The Mixtec warlords demanded, and received, tribute from the Zapotecs.

Just before the conquest, the Mixtecs were subjugated by the Aztecs and forced to pay tribute themselves. The Aztecs left the region to itself, however, and so failed to influence the local art style. Mixtec wealth is reflected in the tribute paid to the Aztecs: 40 sacks of cochineal (used to make purplish red dye), 20 bowls of gold dust, two strings of precious green stones, 800 bundles of quetzal feathers, and thousands of bundles of finely woven and decorated mantles and loincloths.

Mixtec polychrome pottery and exquisite gold jewelry were prized possessions, and often were imitated throughout Meso-america in the late post-classic period. Some of the finest examples of Mixtec jewelry were excavated from tombs at Monte Albán, which the Mixtecs reused when burying their own lords.

In 1519 Mesoamerica was a checkerboard of cultures, just as it always had been. Unprecedented, however, was the Aztecs' domination of most of the land and their onerous demands for tribute. Their enemies soon would find an opportunity to fight back.

3

THE AGE OF CONQUEST

They came in battle array, as conquerors, and the dust rose in whirlwinds
on the roads, their spears glinted in the sun, and their pennons fluttered
like bats. They made a loud clamor as they marched, for their coats
of mail and their weapons clashed and rattled . . .
they terrified everyone who saw them
■
—An Aztec account (translated by Miguel León-Portilla)

The greatest thing after the creation of the earth,
excepting the incarnation and death of he who created it,
is the discovery of the Indies.
■
—Francisco López de Gómara, 16th century

One of the most gripping events in world history is the Spanish conquest of Mexico, that collision of two totally foreign civilizations, each previously unknown to the other. For Mexico, the conquest defines the beginning of the modern mestizo nation of mixed indigenous and European peoples, a defining event commemorated with a singularly Mexican twist: not one statue in the land honors the captain of the conquistadors, Hernán Cortés, yet many recall the heroism of Cuauhtémoc, the last Aztec emperor. For Spain, the Aztec conquest would eventually lead to an empire strewn across the two New World continents and 40 times its own size.

Moctezuma's Empire
On the eve of the conquest, the Aztec emperor Moctezuma II, grandson of an Aztec king, ruled an empire the size of modern Italy—and it was still expanding. The capital of this realm, Tenochtitlán (see page 3), with a population approaching 250,000, was one of the largest cities in the world. The empire dominated central Mexico, which may have had as

43

many as 25 million inhabitants. Spain in its entirety had less than 8 million people.

Tenochtitlán, an independent state since just 1427, had achieved legitimacy through marriage alliances (Moctezuma had four wives) into the older, more noble cities of central Mexico. Its expansion from a small island city to an empire had been achieved through the Triple Alliance with neighboring city-states and through trade, but above all through military conquest. The Aztecs' major concern in expanding beyond Tenochtitlán and the central basin of Mexico was tribute, tribute that included not only prestige items and wealth for the ruling classes, but basic foodstuffs for subsistence as well.

The Aztec empire was only loosely held together. Tenochtitlán had no large standing army to maintain the empire; it often left local, conquered rulers in office. But it kept itself well informed: long-distance merchants were known to be state spies, and relay runners were positioned every few miles throughout the empire for rapid communication. And the Aztecs were intimidating. Every adult male received military training and military success was a means to social advancement for both commoners and nobles. From this pool of half a million trained citizens (the Spaniards found them sophisticated and brave in battle), the Aztecs frequently mobilized armies of 7,000 or more. When necessary, Aztec governors were installed in trouble spots, accompanied by a small Aztec garrison.

During his 16 years of rule, Moctezuma put down numerous rebellions and maneuvered his partners in the Triple Alliance into subordinate positions. In 1515, the death of one of the rulers in the alliance resulted in a struggle for the Texcoco throne. The loser never forgot Moctezuma's role in his defeat; in exile, he remained a constant threat to Tenochtitlán. The Aztecs had many enemies, and war with remaining independent states, such as Tlaxcala, intensified in the final years of the empire as the Aztecs tried to gain more control and more tribute.

Aztec Omens

The last 10 years of Moctezuma's reign were troubled by a series of disturbing events, all taken as signs of divine displeasure. A drought in 1505 created a severe shortage of maize. An unusual lightning bolt, without thunder, destroyed a temple in Tenochtitlán's sacred precinct. In 1517, the very year the Spaniards landed briefly in Yucatán, a comet flamed over the land and showered it with red hot sparks.

For Moctezuma, who was not merely a political and military leader but also the spokesman for the gods (his title, like all Aztec rulers, was *tlatoani*, or speaker), such messages from the gods required careful translation and consultation with priestly advisers and shamans.

> Tell the magicians to say what they believe: whether sickness is going to strike, or hunger, or locusts, or storms on the lake, or droughts . . . If war is threatening Mexico, or there will be sudden deaths . . .
> ■
> —Crónica mexicana *(León-Portilla 1962:14)*

One noble sage interpreted the omens as proof the empire was soon to end in violence. Refusing to believe such an apocalyptic prophecy, the emperor challenged the sage to a game of ball; the winner—chosen by the gods, the Aztecs believed—would determine the truth. Moctezuma lost.

Amid such internal stresses and ill omens, the Spaniards appeared along the Gulf coast of Moctezuma's empire. Their arrival, like that of Juan de Grijalva's expedition the previous year, brought all the evil portents to a climax.

Spain's War Machine

> Our Spaniards in sixty years of conquest have discovered, explored, and conquered so much land . . . Blessed be God who gave them such grace and power.
> ■
> —Francisco López de Gómara, 16th century

The conquistadors off the coast of Moctezuma's empire were the product of a country that had the greatest war machine in all of Europe. For several centuries Spain had fought to rid itself of the Moorish infidels. Anarchy had ruled the land until 1492, when the last Islamic outpost surrendered at Granada. In recognition of the defeat of the Muslims, the pope granted Spain's rulers the extraordinary privilege of heading the church in all their dominions. In the very year Christopher Columbus set sail, Spain was unified as a Christian nation under the Catholic despots, Ferdinand and Isabella, and soon thereafter under Holy Roman Emperor Charles V.

At the time Christopher Columbus proposed his voyage, Spain was in an unusually strong position to consider overseas expansion. Isabella was captivated by the promise of new souls for the church as much as

Ferdinand was interested in a new trade route for exotic spices and silks from the Orient. After so many centuries of war, the nation had a ruined economy and little standing among European trading nations. Fighting holy wars, however, had become a Spanish specialty. When Columbus did discover the West Indies for the Crown, it was taken as a sign that God had chosen Spain over all other nations to civilize the New World. The pope concurred.

Returning to Spain with proof of his discoveries, Columbus presented to the court six kidnapped Indians, an iguana, 40 parrots and a pile of gold. His announcement excited many Spaniards, who took the divine mandate as an excuse to enrich themselves. Centuries of crusading battles had made warriors, not merchants, out of them. Years of plundering farms and pillaging villages had done much to hurt the economy and little to promote industriousness. Quick-rich dreams associated with new lands, Indian slaves, and untapped gold mines appealed to impoverished aristocrats and unemployed soldiers of fortune alike.

Hernán Cortés

Hernán Cortés, unusual in his cunning and leadership, was otherwise typical of many Spaniards who joined the ships to the New World. A member of the bankrupt lesser aristocracy, he could make his fortune only through the military. He learned soldiering from his father, who had fought at Granada. At the age of 18 he was on his way to fight in the Italian wars, but when he heard of Columbus's discovery, he headed for Seville instead. Delayed nearly a year by an injury from an amorous escapade in which he fell from a window, he sailed for the New World in 1504—along with other penniless nobles, debtors, and criminals.

On reaching the island colonies, Cortés discovered, like so many others, how meager the prospects really were for wealth. It is said that he initially refused the offer of land, preferring gold mining to dirtying his hands like a peasant. Eventually he owned a sugar plantation as well as some gold mines in Cuba, and he held minor positions in the local government where he was well known as a convincing speaker. He remained poor, however, spending the money he gained on finery, entertainment, and gambling. For someone who had once proclaimed he wanted either to dine triumphantly to trumpets or die on the scaffold, colonial life must have been disappointing indeed.

There was too little gold to satisfy any of the colonists' grand dreams. Their own brutality, whether soldier or settler, eventually exterminated

BARTOLOMÉ DE LAS CASAS

In 1516, it was reported that the Taino Indians of Hispaniola (the island comprising the Dominican Republic and Haiti) would soon be extinct (which they became), because their numbers had been reduced to as "few as grapes after the harvest." Such statistics on the native death rate in the New World speak only too plainly about the exploitation of the Indians. Yet not all Spaniards, or even Spanish policy, condoned such brutality. No one better exemplified the struggle to protect the Indians than Father Bartolomé de Las Casas. Himself a colonist in Cuba, his father a companion of Columbus and a colonist of Hispaniola, Las Casas witnessed the suffering of the Indians. In order to protect them, he became a priest. His book, *Historia de las Indias*, and his decades of tireless lobbying in Spain, eventually led to the reform laws of 1542 governing the treatment of Indians in Mexico and all of Spain's New World dominions.

the native population—the very pagans they were supposed to save, not to mention the only available labor supply. When the Crown sent a commission to investigate Indian abuses, it found the villages tragically empty of natives to interview. Around this time in the early 16th century, explorations started once again for slaves and gold, for new lands and, perhaps, a passage to Asia, which was thought to be quite near.

Spaniards Land in Yucatán

In 1517, Hernández de Córdoba landed on the Yucatán peninsula and reported an entirely new level of civilization; one that had not been encountered in the previous 25 years of exploration. In Yucatán the natives wore finely woven textiles and gold ornaments in their noses and ears. Their cities were larger than Seville, and their homes and temples were well constructed in stone. And they were fierce. Armed with bows and arrows and obsidian-pointed spears and clubs, they successfully routed Córdoba—more than a quarter of his men were killed, the rest were wounded, and Córdoba himself suffered 30 wounds from which he eventually died.

Excited by Córdoba's report, Diego Velázquez, governor of Cuba, sent his nephew, Juan de Grijalva, to learn more while he himself applied to Spain for a license to colonize Yucatán. Grijalva sailed around the tip of Yucatán and continued up the Gulf coast to what is now Veracruz. On his travels he traded glass beads and pins and needles for 20,000 pesos in gold. At Veracruz, he heard about a great city in the interior of the land. He did not venture to look for it, however. He claimed that his men were tired of the year-long journey and had convinced him to turn back to Cuba. His chaplain thought him simply too timid to attempt a conquest. At the very least, if Grijalva had lingered a bit longer, he would have received the feathered headresses and gold bracelets Moctezuma was preparing for him. Moctezuma's messengers had kept him well-informed of the foreign presence.

The Cortés Expedition

With no prior experience commanding soldiers, much less an expedition, Cortés would nonetheless succeed where his predecessors had failed. His gambling instincts, his audacity, his intelligence, and his consuming desire for glory would enable him to defeat a nation of millions with soldiers numbering in the hundreds.

If Governor Velázquez had suspected the greatness of the land, he would not have sent so few. On the other hand, if he had realized the historic importance of the expedition, he would have appointed no one but himself to conquer "the island" of Yucatán. In fact, Cortés's first challenge was to escape Cuba with his ships fully outfitted before Velázquez could retract his commission; to do so, his men stole the entire meat supply of the town of Santiago. And because Cortés was authorized only to trade with, but not colonize, the new land, his actions throughout the conquest were of questionable legality. Cortés gambled that Spain's new king, the Holy Roman Emperor Charles V, would not be punitive when offered a conquered kingdom, especially if it turned out to be a rich one.

In the year 1519, the Aztec year of One Reed, Cortés landed on the Maya island of Cozumel. Accompanying him were 550 Europeans, 16 horses, attack dogs, and some small cannon. The conquistadors were mostly foot soldiers and sailors, a few were crossbowmen, carpenters, and artillery officers. There was also a chaplain and four other priests, a doctor, a few women housekeepers, so it is said, and hundreds of slaves (a few from Africa, the majority from Cuba). The conquistadors were predominantly poor, young, and Spanish—although others joined, a few Portuguese, African freemen, and Italians among them. All were hellbent on making their fortune in the name of God and country.

Hernán Cortés, portrait from the Hospital de Jesús, which he founded, in Mexico City

HERNÁN CORTÉS (1485–1547)

From the bounty and honors bestowed on him, Hernán Cortés became one of richest men in Spain and married into a noble family. He was later reviled in Mexico, however, as a symbol of foreign domination. During Mexico's War of Independence, his remains had to be hidden so they wouldn't be destroyed. Diego Rivera's malicious portrait of the conquistador —a notorious womanizer—as the syphilitic destroyer of native civilization captures the nationalistic spirit following the Revolution of 1910.

Hernán Cortés (left), from a detail of Diego Rivera's mural Mexico of Yesterday *(1945) in Mexico City's National Palace*

From reports of the previous expeditions, Cortés knew that shipwrecked Spaniards were rumored to live on the mainland across from Cozumel (see Gonzalo Guerrero in chapter 1). Only one, Jerónimo de Aguilar, responded to the messengers offering refuge with their countrymen. Aguilar, by then a fluent speaker of Yucatec Mayan and a nine-year observer of local manners, became a translator for Cortés. Then, after a squirmish on the Gulf coast, Cortés received a peace offering that included the slave girl, Malinalli, who was baptized "Marina" by the conquistadors. Having grown up in a Nahuatl-speaking area of central Mexico, but sold by her mother to a Maya *cacique* (chief), Marina was bilingual. With Aguilar and Marina able to speak to each other in Mayan, Cortés could communicate extensively with the native populations; he could flatter and threaten not only the Nahuatl-speaking Aztecs, but their enemies as well.

Cortés rapidly distinguished himself from the preceding expeditions by actually starting battles—and successfully finishing them. He often bullied even friendly people with cannon shots and skirmishes. This created a fearsome aura of indestructibility, especially when his small force easily won battles against forces 10 times its size.

An astute observer, Cortés noted the native reaction to European weaponry. Although he found the local cotton armor provided adequate protection against obsidian-tipped arrows and spears, Cortés realized the awesome psychological impact steel armor made on the Indians and so continued to use it. Horses "as tall as a roof" (León-Portilla 1962:30) and cannon with an odor that "penetrates even to the brain" (León-Portilla 1962:30) created understandable confusion in the ranks of Indian soldiers: mounted horses initially were thought to be strange unicorn-like creatures, and the power of the awful cannon to rip holes in mountains was "unnatural." As Cortés sailed along the Gulf coast toward the central region where Grijalva had heard so much about a great city in the mountains, Moctezuma's messengers carried the terrible news to Tenochtitlán: "the strangers brought arms which could shoot fire, and wild animals on leashes" (from an Aztec account, translated by León-Portilla).

Moctezuma and Cortés

Believing the conquistadors represented the fulfillment of the ill omens reported throughout his empire, Moctezuma faltered. Instead of moving to destroy the strangers with his armies, he sent magicians and shamans to cast spells. When these failed, he became all the more indecisive. Then

WOMEN IN
MESOAMERICAN SOCIETY

Marina was Cortés's translator, mistress, and loyal companion. Without her, he could not have negotiated with the Tlaxacalans, his allies against the Aztecs. Known as "Malinche" in Mexican histories, her very name has come to mean traitor. Marina bore Cortés a son, Martín, but she eventually married another conquistador. About the 19 other female slaves accompanying Marina, nothing is known. That Marina, along with other slaves, would be handed over to the conquistadors as gifts leaves us with a dispiriting view of the importance of women in ancient Mesoamerica. In pre-Columbian society rulers are known to have had many wives and noble mistresses and to have used such relationships to form political alliances. In just such a symbolic gesture, Moctezuma later gave Cortés his daughter Tecuichpo (baptized "Isabel"), with whom Cortés also had a child. Women were not merely chattels, however. They had essential roles in religious rituals and were integral to the economy: textiles were a valued trade item, for example, and women were the master weavers. Marina's own mother was *cacique* (chief) of a small town, and women are known to have ruled classic Maya cities like Palenque.

A mural by D. H. Xochitiotzin (1967–68) in the Tlaxcalan town hall pictures Marina as central to the meeting of Tlaxcalan chiefs and Spanish invaders.

his messengers relayed the news that Cortés, still on the coast, wanted to meet the great ruler. Moctezuma attempted to buy more time by sending excuses. He was too ill to travel so far. Moreover, the Spaniards should not come to Tenochtitlán either; the 200-mile journey was too rugged and climbed from the tropics up through deserts and snowy passes, from Moctezuma's friendly subjects on the coast to dangerous enemy territories in the Tlaxcalan highlands.

Moctezuma sent his discouraging words tempered with gifts of gold embellished with emeralds from Colombia and turquoise from northern Mexico, quills of precious feathers filled with gold dust, and yet more gold—one piece Cortés described as "a large gold wheel with a design of monsters on it and worked all over with foliage. This weighed 3,800 *pesos de oro*" (Cortés 1986:40). Of course, this gold dispelled any qualms the conquistadors might have had about their venture to "Yucatán"; as the Aztecs soon learned, "they hungered like pigs for gold." (León-Portilla 1962:51). These gifts, shipped to Charles V, emboldened Cortés who included with them his first letter to the Spanish emperor asking for his sanction.

> And, trusting in God's greatness and in the might of Your Highness's Royal name, I decided to go and see [Moctezuma] wherever he might be. . . . I assured Your Highness that I would take him alive in chains or make him subject to Your Majesty's Royal Crown.
> ■
> —*Hernán Cortés (1986:50)*

The March to Tenochtitlán

Before marching to Tenochtitlán, Cortés needed to attend to his enemies within the Spanish camp. A mutiny among his own men, followers of Governor Velázquez, was quashed and the culprits treated harshly: two Spaniards were executed and one had his feet cut off. In addition, agents of the Cuban governor had secretly landed near Veracruz: Cortés captured them and incorporated an extra 60 Spanish men and nine horses into his forces. And in his boldest act, he destroyed his own ships to banish any thought of retreat among his men. He told the Spaniards that one ship remained for those who wished to leave; after noting those who showed interest in escaping, he sunk that one, too.

On August 16, 1519, leaving a contingent behind to build a fortress in Veracruz, Cortés set out with 15 horsemen, 300 Spanish foot soldiers, 1,000 Indian carriers, numerous Indian hostages from among the nobility of Spain's newest allies, and an undetermined number of native warriors. Even with local guides to show him the best route, Cortés's march to Tenochtitlán was plagued by lack of water and firewood, hailstorms and bone-chilling cold, just as Moctezuma had warned. He was attacked by indigenous peoples and nearly routed. But on the whole he traveled with a certain degree of security. His allies on the coast were tired of the tyrannical Aztecs who "took their children to sacrifice," and they encouraged him to expect that other enemies of the Aztecs would embrace him in the interior, at Tlaxcala.

Along his route, Cortés was constantly observed by Moctezuma's messengers and allies. It took Cortés and his forces three months to reach Tenochtitlán; it took Moctezuma's messengers one and a half days by relay runners. At each advance, Moctezuma sent more gold, more precious feathers, more gifts, in the hope that the strangers would go away. He offered to pay tribute to Cortés's king, if only Cortés would turn back. When Cortés rested in Tlaxcala with the Aztecs' enemies, Moctezuma urged him on to Cholula, a sacred city in his own empire only 60 miles from the capital city.

> At dawn I came upon another large town containing, according to an inspection I made, more than twenty thousand houses. As I took them by surprise, they rushed out unarmed, and the women and children ran naked through the streets, and I began to do them some harm.
> ■
> —Hernán Cortés (1986:62)

Cortés marched into Cholula with his new Tlaxcalan allies. He had the Cholulan lords and their retinue rounded up and locked in the major temple. He ordered his men to kill them all. According to an Aztec account, "Then the slaughter began: knife srokes, and sword strokes, and death" (León-Portilla 1962:40).

Three thousand were dead in two hours, said Cortés; 5,000 to 10,000, say historians. Why Cortés committed this massacre remains unclear. He claimed Moctezuma had set a trap for him and his actions were in self-defense. Spanish eyewitnesses suggested Cortés wanted to make himself fearsome before marching into Tenochtitlán. He succeeded. The news traveled quickly to Tenochtitlán where, as the conquistador Bernal Díaz del Castillo said, "if we had a reputation for valour before, from now on they took us for sorcerers" (1928:181). The people were terrified.

Tenochtitlán

> . . . we did not know what to say, or whether
> what appeared before us was real, for on one side,
> on the land, there were great cities, and in the lake
> ever so many more, and the lake itself was crowded with
> canoes, and in the Causeway were many bridges at intervals,
> and in front of us stood the great City of Mexico, and we—
> we did not even number four hundred soldiers!
> ■
> —*Bernal Díaz del Castillo (1928:192)*

The 400 Spaniards marched into Tenochtitlán with 6,000 Indian allies, but they were still overwhelmed by the numbers of Aztecs who crowded to see them, covering the pyramids and temples, filling the lake with their canoes, and squeezing next to the conquistadors in the plazas. Tenochtitlán was greater than any city the Spaniards had ever seen. It was not simply large, it was dazzling—the Venice of the New World with canals for streets. An island metropolis, its great causeways, 30 feet wide, stretched miles across Lake Texcoco and bridges, wide enough for "ten horses abreast" (Cortés:103), spanned city canals. Beautiful gardens and the royal zoo and aviary adorned the city. The palaces were so large that a single one could house all the Spaniards, their horses, and attack dogs. Unlike any European city, Tenochtitlán was glistening clean, thanks to its good drainage system and nightly garbage collection.

Cortés approached Tenochtitlán at the invitation of Moctezuma, an invitation proferred against the objections of his advisers, who wished to attack. But Moctezuma's word was final. His despotic power was apparent in the pearl-and-feather-covered litter that transported him to meet Cortés, and in the retinue ritually sweeping the street where he would stand on gold-soled sandals. Cortés was the divine ruler's guest, yet he was understandably wary. Once inside the city, he and his soldiers could easily be "obliterated from all memory." So he took Moctezuma hostage.

With Moctezuma as their protector, the conquistadors remained peacefully in Tenochtitlán for six months. To avoid an uprising, Moctezuma had told his people not that he was imprisoned, but rather that he preferred to live with the Spaniards. He continued to rule and was escorted from the palace to perform official functions. Not deceived, the Aztec nobility became increasingly angry with the foreigners. The Aztec treasury had been sacked by the soldiers-of-fortune who melted down cherished art works into gold ingot—and still demanded more gold. They also made outrageous requests regarding religious practices, condemning human sacrifice and demanding that an image of the Virgin Mary replace that of the tribal god, Huitzilopochtli. Moctezuma warned Cortés he should leave.

Peace ended during the annual celebration in honor of the patron war deity, Huitzilopochtli. Cortés was absent: in response to the landing of Governor Velázquez's troops, he was marching to Veracruz. Pedro de Alvarez was in charge of the remaining 140 troops in Tenochtitlán. Alvarez claimed he mistook the dances and festivities in honor of the god as a prelude to an uprising. To forestall the Aztecs, he led his own surprise attack on the sacred plaza, sealing off the dancers and unarmed celebrants and slaughtering them.

> "Mexicanos, come running! . . . The strangers have mur-
> dered our warriors!" This cry was answered with a roar of
> grief and anger; the people shouted and wailed and beat
> their palms against their mouths. The captains assembled at
> once . . . Then the battle began. ■
>
> —*From an Aztec account (León-Portilla 1962:77)*

The Noche Triste

Cortés returned to Tenochtitlán having quashed Velázquez's attempt to replace him in Mexico. His own forces and stables were more than doubled by Velázquez's men who were promised their share of the bounty. The numbers would do him little good. Permitted to enter the city, he walked into a trap. The palace had been under seige for a month. Attacks were frequent; food scarce; retreat a necessity.

In a bid for time, Cortés asked Moctezuma to calm his people. According to the Spaniards, the ruler went to the rooftop and was killed by rocks hurled by his own people who failed to notice him. According to the Aztecs, Cortés, no longer finding any use for the emperor, had him stabbed to death. With Moctezuma dead, so was the calming voice that had aided the conquistadors in the early months of the conquest. Cortés asked for a truce and was derisively hooted down. Reported Bernal Díaz del Castillo, "we were staring death in the face."

On June 30, 1520, under the cover of darkness and with their horses' hooves muffled by cloth, the Spaniards tried to escape. Known in the histories as the *Noche Triste* (sad night), or the night that "greed overcame wisdom," the retreat was a catastrophe for them. The Aztecs had pulled up the drawbridges in the causeways and built barricades throughout the city to block their enemies' escape. Cortés led the charge, throwing portable bridges over the gaps in the shortest causeway. He made it to the mainland, but the weight of those who followed collapsed the makeshift bridges. With the Aztecs descending on them in the thousands, the Spaniards jumped into the lake and attempted to swim ashore, but the gold hoarded in their pockets sunk them in the hundreds. More than half the Spaniards and 4,000 of their Indian allies died. Forty-six horses were killed. It is said that Hernán Cortés wept.

The Final Conquest

Cortés survived because his Indian allies steadfastly stood by him. The Spaniards, reduced to a few hundred in number, were protected from the Aztecs by the Tlaxcalans. By May 1521 Cortés, strengthened by 50,000 Indian allies including the Texcocans, once part of the Aztec Triple Alliance, and buoyed by the arrival of new Spanish soldiers-of-fortune with their horses, cannons, and heavy guns, was ready to fight again. His strategy was to attack by ship as well as land, and his new fleet of brigantines, constructed in the intervening months, was carried through the mountains by 8,000 porters. Once at Texcoco by the lake, Cortés had the ships reassembled and was ready to lay seige on Tenochtitlán.

Cortés was aided by an unusual weapon: smallpox. "The illness was so dreadful that no one could walk or move . . . so they starved to death in their beds" (León-Portilla 1962:93). Tens of thousands of Indians, including Moctezuma's successor, Cuitlahuac, had died from it by May.

The Aztecs under the leadership of Moctezuma's 18-year-old nephew Cuauhtémoc fought ferociously nonetheless. The city was deprived of fresh water; the only food was lizards, weeds and dirt. People chewed leather to stay alive. Sickness was rampant, but the fighting continued for months.

Once inside the city, Cortés offered a truce to the starving survivors who replied they would rather die fighting. Cortés decided the only way to victory was to destroy Tenochtitlán. Cuauhtémoc was taken prisoner; years later he was executed by Cortés for allegedly conspiring against him. The city fell on August 13, 1521.

> These misfortunes befell us.
> We witnessed them in anguish.
> We lived through them with suffering.
> Broken spears and torn hair lie on the road.
> Houses are roofless, their walls now red with blood.
> ■
> —*Nahuatl Poem, 1528 (after Angel M. Garibay)*

Ruins of the Aztec Great Temple Complex surrounded by Spanish buildings in Mexico City. Only when some of the colonial buildings were destroyed in the 1980s did excavations reveal their Aztec foundations. Until then, it had been thought Tenochtitlán was totally destroyed

How Did the Spanish Succeed?

The relative ease of the Spanish conquest of Moctezuma's empire has baffled many. The Spaniards themselves claimed they were mistaken for the god Quetzalcoatl (feathered serpent), a god who opposed human sacrifice and who had, in the myths, been banished by evil deities, but who promised to return some day from the east. This captivating story often is repeated in histories of Mexico, and the Aztecs themselves championed it during the later colonial period as a symbol of their eventual resurgence. Yet scholars have recently challenged this theory. There is no such return myth for Quetzalcoatl in the accounts of Aztec religion least tainted by contact with the Spaniards. And for the Aztecs, as for other Mesoamericans, all gods, good or bad, required human sacrifice to be nourished.

Why, then, was Moctezuma so indecisive when others, such as the Yucatec Maya and even subsequent Aztec emperors, fearlessly fought, and defeated, the conquistadors? Aztec accounts repeatedly quote the emperor as being worried about the harm that resistance would bring to the elderly and children "who still crawl on all fours" (León-Portilla 1962:78). However, he clearly could not find a way to avoid war and

57

suffering in the heart of his empire. Perhaps he was defeated by circumstances, and as the Aztecs said: "He had lost his strength and spirit, and could do nothing" (León-Portilla 1962:36).

Another nagging question is how could so few conquistadors defeat so many Aztecs? The more lethal weapons of the Spaniards are often cited as the cause. European swords were made of steel, not obsidian; moreover, the Indian obsidian blades were sharpened to wound (for gathering captives for sacrifice), rather than to kill. The Spaniards' guns and cannons, too, were deadly—when not misfired. Despite such advantages, however, the Spaniards found the Mesoamericans formidable adversaries once they adjusted to the European weapons. They were nearly overwhelmed by the Tlaxcalans and were lucky to make their alliance. The Maya sent the first conquistadors scrambling in defeat from Yucatán. Not until the pre-Columbians divided, with some forming alliances with the Spaniards, did the Aztec empire suffer defeat.

Capital of New Spain

Two years after Cortés first marched on Tenochtitlán, the Aztec world was a smoldering ruin. The victorious Spaniards built their own capital over the ashes of Tenochtitlán (see page 57). Aztec labor constructed it. Aztec-cut stones formed the foundation. The government palace replaced Moctezuma's. Construction began on a cathedral next to the Templo Mayor. The first hospital of the Americas was founded at the spot where Cortés and Moctezuma first met. The pre-Columbian land became New Spain. The new city was called Mexico, after the Aztecs' name for themselves. In 1524 it counted only 30,000 inhabitants; not until the 20th century would its population once again equal that of Moctezuma's capital.

4

THE FOUNDING OF AN EMPIRE: SIXTEENTH-CENTURY MEXICO

The country we have won is ours . . .
∎
—*Hernán Cortés, 1521 (Thomas:543)*

While Cortés was conquering Tenochtitlán, no one in Spain paid the least attention; at the moment of victory over the Aztec capital, Cortés remained without official recognition from Charles V. Two years had already lapsed since the conquistador had sent his letter accompanied by Moctezuma's first gifts to Spain. But the Catholic king was too preoccupied with the Protestant Reformation and other European crises and too mired in local turbulence and petty politics to address the issues confronting him in the New World. The treasure from what was called "the new land of gold" did receive notice, however, as it traveled around Europe with the royal court.

With little preparation, Spain found itself ruler of a wealthy, civilized land many times larger than itself and far more densely populated. Spain might conquer such a kingdom as long as it had thousands of local allies. But how could it control and administer this empire? Indoctrinate it with Christianity and transform it into a European society? Yet all of this was accomplished in a matter of decades from a continent two months away by sea.

59

Conquest Beyond Tenochtitlán

While Spain dithered, Cortés was left to govern. Cortés normally would not have been the king's choice: conquistadors were just too independent to be trusted representatives of the Spanish bureaucracy. Because his popularity made him irreplaceable, however, Cortés received his commission in 1522, nearly a year after the conquest and about the length of time it took Charles to learn of it. Finally, the "Emperor . . . wrote him a letter, thanking him for the hardships he had undergone in the conquest, and for his service to God in casting down idols" (López de Gómara:329).

Cortés might easily have empathized with the Crown's distrust: he himself had trouble controlling his own soldiers-of-fortune. Their demands for more Aztec gold were nearly mutinous, though sometimes quite justifiable. After the royal fifth and Cortés's bounty (some said he stashed away three million pesos in gold), there was hardly any booty left over for everyone else. Soldiers received only one-fifth of the cost of their horses, and some were not paid enough to replace their ammunition. Rather than rolling in riches after the devastation of the conquest, the victors found that even food was in short supply. In an attempt to

New Spain in the 16th Century

discover more treasure, including the gold lost in the Noche Triste, the conquistadors tortured and maimed Cuauhtémoc and other Indian rulers, but to no avail.

Cortés exploited the restlessness of his men to best advantage. Using the Aztec tribute lists as a guide, he sent them off to other parts of Moctezuma's empire to find food and supplies and, of course, gold. When resistance was encountered, as it was initially in Oaxaca, Tlaxcalan and Aztec allies helped to settle matters quickly. A port was built at Veracruz, and other ports were established on the Pacific coast at places like Acapulco, in order to search for the yet-to-be-discovered route to the Orient. And trusted captains were charged with the conquest of independent regions and the peoples like the Tarascans to the northwest in Michoacán and the Maya to the south in Yucatán where they often battled for years before succeeding. While following the trail of the Fountain of Youth and other fantastic places, the conquistadors and their successors made their way to farflung parts of the Americas, such as what is now the U.S. Southwest. They crossed the Pacific Ocean to the Philippines and, eventually, created a New Spain that was three and a half times larger than Mexico is today.

The Mestizo Nation

> 13 August 1521, Tlatelolco—heroically
> defended by Cuauhtémoc—fell under the
> power of Hernán Cortés. It was neither
> a triumph or defeat; it was the painful
> birth of the mestizo nation that is
> Mexico today.
> ■
> —*Plaque on Aztec ruins in Mexico City*

The task of settlement required a different temperament from conquest, yet Cortés initially proved himself able to carry it out. To create European goods and commerce, he brought in the very first Spanish brood stocks—cows, sows, sheep, and goats—as well as seeds and mulberry trees for silk, vine cuttings, and sugar cane. He prevented his men from returning to Spain with their newfound wealth and, wanting families rather than just adventurers to settle, he advanced money to pay the travel costs of the conquistadors' wives. He encouraged others to marry indigenous women, and many conquistadors did just that, beginning the first legitimate *mestizo*, or mixed Spanish and Indian, families. Moctezuma's daughter Tecuichpo, baptized "Isabel," outlived her ruler-husband Cuauhtémoc as well as several Spanish captains; her daughter with Hernán Cortés, Lenor Cortés Moctezuma, more elevated by the powerful union of two worlds than tarnished by illegitimacy, was just one of her mestizo offspring. Most of the conquistadors' children, however, did not have such a romantic ancestry. Yet they all began what would become a most distinctive mark of Mexico: its mestizo majority.

The Encomienda

> The natives of these parts . . . possess such understanding
> as is sufficient for an ordinary citizen to conduct himself in a
> civilized country. It seemed to me, therefore, a serious matter
> at this time to compel them to serve the Spaniards . . . [yet] I have been
> almost forced to deliver the chieftans and other natives of these parts
> to the Spaniards in recognition of the services they have rendered
> to Your Majesty . . .
> ■
> —Hernán Cortés, 1522 (1986:281)

Settlement itself required economic incentives. In the New World, the greatest inducement was gold, but the most reliable one was the *encomienda* (land grants). The *encomienda* system, a thinly disguised form of slavery, granted entire towns and their Indian populations to an individual, the *encomendero*. Sometimes, depending on the grant, the natives were forced to relocate onto the land. The Indians owed the *encomenderos* tribute as well as free labor, and their labors usually supported the absentee Spaniards in grand style in faraway cities.

The *encomenderos* were supposed to Christianize and assimilate the Indians into European culture; exploitation and abuse were more common. With a few exceptions, the *encomiendas* reduced all Indians to the same level of impoverishment and cultural deprivation. In central Mexico, where *encomiendas* were extensive, the price of this forced acculturation was tragic: Indian homicide rates increased, as did alcoholism. In the Caribbean Islands, as Cortés himself had complained to the Crown, *encomiendas* had resulted in the annihilation of the indigenous peoples.

Charles V, wanting to directly control his new vassels and, as vicar of the church, wanting to protect them, outlawed the *encomienda*, but not before Cortés had distributed the lands among the conquistadors. Cortés's professed concern over *encomienda* did little to restrain his use of it. Nearly all the Indians in central Mexico had been distributed among the conquistadors by 1522. Cortés was most generous with himself: in

ALCOHOLISM

Mesoamericans fermented various juices to make mildly alcoholic drinks. Who could imbibe alcohol (only male adults and elderly women to warm their blood), how much (a few glasses), and when (in ritual celebrations) were regulated in Aztec society by severe penalties. A drunk's head was shaved in public, his house could be sacked and torn down. *Pulque*, made from an agave plant, was popular with the Spaniards, although Aztec nobles disdained it as plebeian, preferring their chocolate. After the conquest, when Indians died in alarming numbers, many Aztecs thought intemperate drinking of *pulque*, in the Spanish manner, might be the cause. By the end of the colonial period, Mexico City residents consumed enough *pulque* in a year to average 75 gallons each. *Pulque* cantinas continue to attract the poor in modern Mexico.

addition to vast tracts of land and many great cities, he "deposited" a million natives to his own care. It was said that nothing could stir up the conquerers more than the size of their grants. And nothing interfered more with Spain's control of its provinces since the *encomendero* had the right to all tribute and labor, not the Crown. The *encomienda* attracted settlers; it also created conflicts—and even Spanish rebellions—against both church and Crown when reforms were attempted during the 16th century.

Cortés Sidelined

Cortés was presumed dead while on a daring expedition to Honduras through uncharted territory in 1524–26. He had abandoned Mexico City in order to regain control of Honduras from a renegade conquistador (much like he himself was in 1519). Attempting to fill the political vacuum with themselves, enemies of Cortés spread rumors that the governor had been disloyal to the Crown and had cheated the royal treasury.

Cortés returned from the dead after almost two years away. The upstarts were hanged, but the Crown remained suspicious. Charles V, having wanted to place his own viceroy in Mexico for some time, accused Cortés of misconduct. Hoping to clear his name, Cortés returned to Spain in 1528 with an entourage of Mesoamerican nobles, ballplayers, and dwarfs, with jaguars and armadillos, gold and silver. He dazzled all of Spain and was elevated to the nobility and made marquis. He was not reappointed governor of New Spain, however. One of the wealthiest men in his time, Cortés begrudgingly retired to the periphery of Mexican politics as Spain imposed its bureaucratic will over its New World empire.

The Mendicant Friars Arrive

> Fray Marín de Valencia, the Pope's vicar, arrived in Mexico in the year '24, with twelve companions. Cortés received him with gifts, services, and honor. Whenever he spoke to them it was with cap in hand and one knee to the ground, while he kissed their robes as an example to the Indians who were to be converted.
>
> ■
>
> —*Francisco López de Gómara (331)*

In keeping with the conquistadors' creed of gold and glory but above all God, Cortés had smashed many idols and his chaplain had baptized numerous converts. But as Friar Motolinía, one of the first missionaries, put it, the conquistadors "were content to build their houses and seemed satisfied as long as no human sacrifice occurred in public" (Thomas). Unlike the conquerors, the emperor could not perform his duties half-heartedly. Charles V was granted extraordinary privileges by the papacy to head the Catholic church in all of Spain's domains because the conquest was seen as a sign of God's favor for the emperor: he alone was entrusted with all those souls. And Charles V proved himself a devout monarch.

Perhaps Cortés's most profound legacy was his recommendation to the Crown that the mendicant orders—the Franciscans, Dominicans, and Augustinians—be charged with the responsibility for the Indians' salvation. These missionaries, as opposed to the secular clergy, were educated individuals recognized for their devotion and respected for their vows of poverty. The religious orders and monastic life sustained them, not the charging of fees for services. Cortés believed their humble character would speed the conversion of the Mexican people. The emperor agreed.

The Franciscan volunteers arrived first in 1524. They quickly impressed the native population by walking barefoot from the Gulf coast port to Mexico City. Their simple dress and the self-inflicted suffering endured on their 50-day journey could not have contrasted more with the greed of the conquistadors. Nor could their thinking: rather than seeking fabled cities of unimaginable wealth, many of the friars saw the New World as an opportunity to create the monastic kingdom of pure charity—Thomas More's Utopia or Augustin's City of God. Their zeal was often fueled by the belief that Christianizing the Indians would create these ideal societies and thus pave the way for the second coming of Christ. The Crown, too, took its religious obligations seriously: when the first bishop, Juan de Zumárraga, arrived in 1527, he carried the title "Protector of the Indians."

The Spiritual Conquest

With millions to convert, the friars counted only in the hundreds, yet they remained undaunted in the task of spiritual conquest. They fanned out across the country—eventually they, not soldiers, would be the first to venture into new territories in the north in order to pacify the native

Sixteenth-century Church of Cuilapán in Oaxaca

populations. (They were also the first Europeans to see the Grand Canyon.) In Mexico they built their chapels atop pagan pyramids and established simple living quarters amid the most ancient cities of the Americas. Nine million people were baptized in the central region by 1537: Friar Pedro de Gante said it was not unusual to baptize 4,000 people in a day; Father Motolinía thought he alone baptized 300,000.

As the number of neophytes swelled, the friars needed churches, but the size required was well beyond any immediate building capabilities. So a uniquely New World architectural form was created: the open chapel, a solution especially amenable to religious practices of Mesoamericans who had always gathered in large open-air plazas. Over time, open chapels were replaced by enclosed churches and vast monastery complexes such as the one at Cuilapán. Using Indian labor, the friars built 50 such establishments by 1540 and, eventually, a total of 400 dotted the land from Yucatán to Michoacán.

The rapidity of conversion was no less astonishing than the Spanish conquest itself. Given that Mesoamerican religion profoundly permeated the native view of the world, from the creation of the stars to the planting of corn, it is hard to understand how it could be so quickly eradicated. In fact, there is abundant evidence that it was not.

Similarities between the religions facilitated conversion. Both cultures believed in an afterlife and a world created by god(s). The cross was a symbol for both, being also the symbol for the Mesoamerican world tree that linked the supernatural and earthly realms; the crucifixion of Christ was, for Mesoamericans, another example of their belief that sacrifice was needed for rebirth. Fasting, sexual abstinence, and even the ritual use of water, such as in Christian baptism, also resonated with indigenous practices. And both religions shared a ritual calendar that dominated the change of seasons and the march of the days. The Catholics honored their saints and the Mesoamericans their deities with religious processions, festively dressed idols, incense burning, music, and dance.

As the friars discovered, conversion often involved only the veneer of these similarities to Christianity: traditional beliefs and practices remained intact. It was one thing for the Indians to respect a new god so powerful as to have led the Europeans to conquer them. It was another to expect them to reject their own gods and not fear the consequences. Old ritual practices continued, most often in secret, although some were overlooked and even exploited by the priests—the dark-skinned Virgin of Guadalupe, for instance, conveniently made her miraculous appear-

Diego de Landa (1529–79). Although responsible for Indian torture and deaths during an inquisition, Diego de Landa also wrote the definitive work on Yucatec Maya customs, providing the key to decipherment of ancient Maya hieroglyphic texts that reveal the very Maya religion Landa hoped to repress.

ance to Juan Diego, a Nahua peasant boy, near the shrine of Tonantzín, Aztec earth goddess and mother of humankind.

In other instances, the vestiges of paganism proved intolerable: Friar Diego de Landa (see page 67), for example, was scandalized by the persistence in Yucatán of sacrificial rituals among his most dedicated converts. He instituted an inquisition into native idolatry in 1562, torturing the heretics and burning the Maya hieroglyphic books. He was ordered back to Spain: the Crown realized the Indians simply did not yet understand the true faith. From then on, Indians were exempt from the Inquisition.

Friars as Ethnographers

The priests understood that it was not just the Indians who required more thorough instruction. The friars needed a greater knowledge of native beliefs in order to eradicate them. From the beginning the fathers had been great linguists, learning the native languages and compiling dictionaries so that the catechism could be taught. Schools were opened for natives: one was a university for Indian nobles where they learned Latin so well they became the instructors for the Spanish settlers; others included the utopian communities established by Vasco de Quiroga in Michoacán where the Purépecha learned how to use their craftsmaking skills in order to be self-sustaining.

By the middle of the 16th century, the friars also became the first ethnographers, working in collaboration with the Indians and encouraging them to write about their own history and culture in their native languages. The most famous, Bernardino de Sahagún, working with a team of central Mexican nobles, compiled an encyclopedia of pre-Columbian Aztec life that described everything from sacred rituals to recipes for preparing hot chocolate. In the process, the nobles learned to write their own language, Nahuatl, in the Roman alphabet rather than in pictographs—a skill that greatly facilitated communication. On Sahagún's part, he left to posterity its greatest source of information on Mesoamerican life at the time of the conquest.

Mesoamerican Catholicism

Such collaboration did much to profoundly Hispanicize and Christianize many Indians. Once the native leaders changed, many of the commoners followed suit. The daily relation of the Indians with their land, the sacred landscape of their ancestors, and with their traditional communities, however, often remained untouched—the church seemed to think such "household" practices meaningless superstitions. In many instances, conversion only created what many anthropologists now call "Meso-american Catholicism," a reworking of Christianity that incorporated, and partially modified, the Mesoamerican world view, as can be seen in the distinctive imagery of this Nahua hymn:

> The roses, dark red ones, pale ones
> The red feather flowers, the golden flowers
> lie there waving like precious bracelets
> lie bending with quetzal feather dew.
> ■
> —*Indian hymn to St. Clare (translated by Louis Burkhart:210)*

Today most native-speaking Mexicans are devout Christians and many make pilgrimages to the nation's patron saint, the Virgin of Guadalupe. But most anthropologists believe the Virgin represents a powerful synthesis of the Christian and Mesoamerican beliefs: she is still called Tonantzín by the Nahua. Many such instances of a syncretic religion have been identified, including the performance of Ch'a-Chak rituals to the Maya rain god, common in years of drought. Perhaps the survival of such beliefs would not have been possible if the vibrant intellectual exchange between native and European had not ended until late in the 16th century when the friars lost much of their power to the secular clergy. Outside the cities, the Indians, who had often been officially separated from the colonists to keep them free of Spanish corruption, lost their only viable link to European ways. Without the friars and their investment in native education, the traditional communities themselves provided the daily context for religious observances.

Mid-Century Reforms

The remarkable achievements of Sahagún and other friars, such as Vasco de Quiroga, occurred during the middle of the 16th century. In what has been called the "golden age of Christianity," this was a period of unusual collaboration between the native population and the foreigners, from the Aztecs advising the new government on how to control the flooding of Lake Texcoco to programs that taught Indians European skills, such as blacksmithing and carpentry. There never was similar harmony among the colonists, the royal functionaries and the religious, however. The clergy wanted to protect the native population, of course, and provide them with salvation; the conquistadors wanted to work them like beasts of burden. But even among these factions, relations improved after the disputes immediately following the conquest.

INDIAN RESISTANCE TO CONVERSION

Not all Indians willingly participated in the new societal order. Armed rebellion did occur sporadically throughout the colonial period. The Mixton Rebellion in 1541 near Guadalajara was one of the most threatening: 100,000 native rebels rose against 400 Spaniards. They were defeated by 30,000 Aztecs, for the first time armed with Spanish guns. Native resistance to the religious and political conquest more often took the form of escape into remote regions—especially towards the end of the 16th century. Lacandons did just that, remaining unconverted and unassimilated well into the 20th century when logging operations and population pressures destroyed the Chiapas rain forest that had so long sustained them. The contemporary Tarahumara Indians of the Copper Canyon in northern Mexico, known so well by tourists, and the Huichol of the Colima plateau, famous for their peyote cult, are other examples. Their cultural survival also is threatened by environmental devastation.

A 20th-century Lacandon Maya Indian selling arrows at Palenque

The cooperative spirit certainly was promoted by two enlightened individuals during the founding of New Spain: Mexico's first viceroy (1530–50), Antonio de Mendoza, and its first bishop and archbishop (1528–48), Juan de Zumárraga. These two could not have carried out the enormous task of institutionalizing the power of the Crown and church in the conquered land more competently. Mendoza, the count of Tendilla and related to the royal house, had been a diplomat in Rome; Zumárraga, a true Franciscan in his poverty vows, was the executor of many royal commissions and a militant champion of Christian values (he risked his life challenging the abuses of natives by early officials). Mendoza was followed by another superb viceroy, Luis de Velasco (1550–64), who became known as "Father of the Indians." These three shared many Renaissance humanist views and each was scrupulous in implementing the emperor's policies. They set the best example for the future administration of the colony.

Their humanism, as well as that of the religious community, resulted in the passage of reforms that protected the native population. Both a papal bull (1537) and a royal edict called the New Laws (1542) settled the matter once and for all that Indians were human, capable of salvation, and worthy vassals of the Crown—principles that Bartolomé de Las Casas, bishop of Chiapas, had been lobbying for since he had witnessed the genocide in the West Indies. Indian slavery finally was outlawed.

The period of relative cooperation that permitted such radical reforms may have resulted, in part, from the low numbers of Spanish colonists. By as late as 1560, the Spaniards in New Spain probably numbered barely more than 20,000. Initially there was plenty of land and, usually, more than enough Indians to labor on the *encomiendas* or, at least, provide tribute to sustain the colonists in an acceptable manner. But as the Indian population declined catastrophically, the settlers' demands for native labor increasingly clashed with the reforming goals of the church and government.

The truth was that Indian labor was too much in demand. The church required, and trained, artisans to build and decorate monasteries and chapels. The government expected its *tequío*, or public service, too, for building town halls or repairing streets. And then there was the *encomendero*, whose sugar cane and cattle ranches had to be maintained. Although the Indians had provided tribute and labor to Mesoamerican rulers, the Spaniards had tripled the levels of Aztec tribute despite the catastrophic declines in population.

Depopulation		
	Oaxaca	Central Mexico
1519*	350,000	25 million
1568	150,000	3.6 million
1630	40,000–45,000	1 million or less

Never having been exposed to European diseases, the Indians had no natural immunity to smallpox, measles, typhoid, chicken pox, yellow fever, or mumps. At least seven major waves of these diseases had washed through the native population by 1600. Famine often followed because so few individuals were able to work the land. Added to the deaths caused by abuse, homicide, and cultural dislocation, the result was what some have called "possibly the greatest demographic disaster in the history of the world" (Denevan). No one understood the nature of infectious disease at the time: Friar Bartolomé de Las Casas thought the *encomienda* system was the work of the devil to depopulate New Spain; the Mixtecs, too, thought it was due to the supernatural and reverted to traditional curing rituals—called "witchcraft" by the church. By most estimates, the population decreased by 70 percent to 90 percent. Not until 1650 did the size of the native population begin to increase.

*There was no census until later in the century, when the native population already was decimated, so reconstructed estimates of population size at the time of conquest vary greatly. In this chart, the Oaxaca estimate is a conservative one from Ronald Spores; the Central Mexican figures by Cook and Borah are among the most generous for that massive region.

The Crown attempted to protect the Indians from further loss, swayed by economic reasons as well as arguments from the religious that the exploitative colonists were at fault. (Friar Bartolomé de Las Casas claimed that the Spaniards' abuses made the natives refuse baptism for fear of having to spend eternity in their company.) In addition to banning Indian enslavement, Mendoza lowered the amount of free labor and tribute permitted. To boost the economy, more African slaves were brought to New Spain. (No ban on their enslavement was considered.) Although these slaves somewhat reduced the settlers' need for workers, they also cost money—unlike the Indians. Twenty thousand had arrived in the colony by 1553, and although their numbers equaled that of the European community, they hardly made up for the millions of Indians lost to infectious diseases and abuse.

If restricted labor already was a cause for colonists to complain, the increased labor needs created by the first major mining strikes (1545–65) intensified the feeling. When, in 1564, the Crown tried to implement further reforms, it ignited treasonous ideas, especially since these reforms attacked the institution most sacred to the conquistadors' descendants: the *encomienda*. All *encomiendas*, it was ordered, would cease upon the death of the holder. No longer would the privileged status and wealth of *encomenderos* be inherited. Outraged, Alonso de Avila, son of a conquistador, argued for independence from Spain. He suggested the new Marqués del Valle, Cortés's son Martín, should be made king of the independent nation. And he thought armed resistance was in order. The talk didn't get much further before Alonso de Avila was arrested and beheaded along with his brother. The more fortunate Martín Cortés was exiled forever, and his stepbrother, the son of Cortés and Marina, was tortured. Others of the New World aristocracy were beheaded. But not only did all talk of rebellion end, so did any serious effort to eliminate the remaining *encomiendas*: eventually the practice would simply fade away.

Utopian Experiments End

As the 16th century came to a close, the conflicts took a different shape. The Renaissance humanism that had so imbued the mid-century exchanges between Europeans and the native population with tolerance (and even a tinge of mutual respect) ended with the more dogmatic promulgations of the Council of Trent (1563). Following the Council of Trent, many books, such as those by Erasmus, were banned in Spain, although they circulated freely in Mexico and were part of the catechism.

Charles V was dead, as were Zumárraga and Mendoza; the native aristocrats who had been educated in Mesoamerican traditions were dying out. The official onset of the Inquisition in Mexico in 1571 marked the final demise of this most idealistic religious period. Not only did the friars no longer attempt to create utopian Indian communities, but such work bordered on the heretical. Treatises by former archbishop Zumárraga were banned; Sahagún's work languished in archives until the 19th century. The early humanists were too often replaced by more corrupt individuals who saw the Americas as an opportunity to make a quick fortune or to hide their vices from European view. Even the clergy occupied themselves in building ever more ornate churches, replacing religious zeal with their own material comforts, and advocacy with authoritarianism.

MIXTEC CACIQUES THRIVE UNDER SPAIN

The *Codex Nuttall*, a pre-Columbian book, tells the story of the great Mixtec ruler, 8 Deer "Tiger Claw," in A.D. 1103. His descendants continued to rule in the Mixteca Sierra of Oaxaca well into the 19th century, whereas Moctezuma's dynastic line (more threatening to Spain) had lost the power to hold any office, however low, by 1565. In Oaxaca, the number of Europeans were fewer than in most parts of New Spain, never amounting to even 7 percent in contrast to 50 percent around Mexico City. The conquistadors could barely control Oaxaca City, which they founded; their influence was even less in the nearby rugged mountains, where they had sadly discovered during the conquest that "the terrain does not permit the use of horses." *Cacique* rights and territories were recognized in order to gain the Mixtecs' much needed cooperation. The indigenous economy, not *encomiendas*, became indispensable to Spanish society; the traditional communities and native political order remained intact, including class distinctions.

In the mid-16th-century *Codex of Yanhuitlán*, Don Gabriel de Guzmán, *cacique* of the Mixtec principality of Yanhuitlán and descendant of the

In this section of the pre-Columbian Codex Nuttall, *the Mixtec ruler 8 Deer (on right) undergoes a nose-piercing ceremony.*   (Drawing by Shannon Ernst)

The Mixtec cacique *Don Gabriel (on right) confers with a Spaniard, from the* Codex of Yanhuitlán. (Drawing by Shannon Ernst)

pre-Columbian ruler 8 Deer "Tiger Claw," meets with a high-ranking Spaniard. Below him is his Mixtec name glyph of 9 House. The Mixtec *caciques*, such as Don Gabriel, oversaw vast territories and functioned as they had for many centuries, except tribute was paid to the Spaniards instead of to the Aztecs. In return, the caciques received Spanish privileges: Don Gabriel was granted the gentleman's title of "don," a coat of arms, permits to raise livestock and the right to wear Spanish clothes, ride horseback, and bear arms.

The new king, Philip II reigned in these more severe times (from 1556 to 1598). Philip was more interested in the economy of New Spain than in the treatment of the native population. He was more sensitive to the jealousy of the settlers when Nahua nobles outdid them in schools than in attempts to enable the Indians to become fully realized vassals of Spain. The university was disbanded. Sympathetic to the colonists and their need for labor, Philip permitted the secular clergy, less educated and totally dependent on settlers' tithes, to take over from the meddlesome mendicant orders. The well-being of the native population became secondary to the need for a productive economy to sustain the Spanish empire.

Spain Flourishes

As the first century of European involvement in the New World came to a close, the potential wealth of the colony had already become apparent to all. Silver bullion weighted down the Spanish galleons—enough to pay for the entire cost of administering all the American colonies, with plenty left over for Spain. The China trade was established in 1564: silks and spices and porcelains from the Philippines arrived across the Pacific to Acapulco, and then, after being carried across Mexico to Veracruz, accompanied the silver in its transatlantic voyage. The galleons carried much of Europe's wealth. And Spain owned it all.

Piracy occasionally helped England and France to get their share of American bounty. Sir Francis Drake, for example, looted Spanish ships from the Pacific to the Caribbean with the full sanction of England. European powers also tried to colonize other parts of the Americas: for example, French Huguenots tried, but failed, to settle Florida. Wishing to protect his very lucrative domains, Philip looked for a port in California, sent colonizers to New Mexico, and Juan Ponce de Léon to Florida. He strived not only to secure the passage of his galleons but to guarantee the continued flow of New World tribute and exports.

New Spain Established

Before the end of the 16th century, a massive change had occurred: an indigenous civilization had been brought under the control of a European monarch. The wealth of a population of millions had been transferred to a few conquerors through *encomienda* and tribute; there was not a single aspect of the pre-Columbian culture that had not been transformed in the process: Indian writing had changed from pictographs to the Roman alphabet; ritual sacrifice had been eradicated, ribbons had replaced feathers in religious costumes, and once proud Mesoamericans who had believed their cities were the sacred centers of the universe, had been taught that the true center was far away in a foreign land. The very names of people and places had been changed: the sacred city of Teotihuacán was now San Juan Teotihuacán.

Until recently historians thought the viceregal and ecclesiastic control of native society obliterated preconquest institutions. Yet archival studies by historians such as Charles Gibson and James Lockhart have demonstrated that Spain's success lay in manipulating the native institutions to serve its own purposes. Replacing the imperial rulers of the Aztecs, the viceregal government achieved only an overlay of authority; under it and supporting it through trade and markets, farming and artisanship, tax collection and tribute, was a "Republic of Indians." Even the security of New Spain depended on the peacekeeping efforts and garrisons of native allies. In many regions, Spaniards relied on the old Mesoamerican political and social order, with Indian elites acting as intermediaries between their people and the foreign officials.

In less than 100 years after the conquest, viceregal government was fully developed and the Catholic church had sent its missionaries into most, if not all, recesses of the country. Spain's new government branch, the Council of the Indies, promulgated regulations to New Spain that affected everything from the location of a town church to the kind of crops that could be grown. But the forms of government and religion succeeded only because they took on a distinctly pre-Hispanic cast: Mexican in nature, the New World's institutions were as composite as its people were increasingly racially mixed.

The 16th century witnessed the formation of a new people and new institutions: a characteristic Mexican fusion. The bureaucracy of New Spain was in place and, as the century closed, Spain managed to remain the sole European power in this New World.

THE COLONY OF NEW SPAIN

Without the Indies or its trade, Spain would fall from its greatness,
because there would be no silver for your majesty, for the ministers,
for private individuals, for those holding . . . inheritances,
which all comes from the Indies . . .

■

—*Marqués de Varina, 1687*
(translated by Stein & Stein)

There were two Spanish perspectives in regard to New Spain. Those living in Europe thought the colony should be exploited to enrich the home country; and those living in the colony viewed the land as an opportunity to make money, enough to either recreate a genteel Spanish lifestyle in the Americas or to return across the Atlantic rich enough to enjoy the real thing. People of either view saw Mexico as a pot of gold to be melted and molded into their own treasure.

During three centuries of Spanish domination, the land was transformed by new crops and technologies and trade, new cities and ports, European art forms and crafts. Policies changed according to the fashions in Spain, as did the arts and cities and continuously evolving population. But Spain remained firmly in control of Mexico's economic and religious institutions. Its legacy has endured beyond the colonial centuries, leaving a poorly developed economy, a class structure based primarily on racism, and a too-common belief among officials that the governance of Mexico is an opportunity to enhance personal wealth.

The Capital

Spain's presence was concentrated in the colonial capital. Even before the pilgrims landed at Plymouth Rock, the avenues of Mexico City were

The heart of colonial Mexico City, with its cathedral, viceregal palace, and other administrative buildings, all constructed over the center of the Aztec capital (Courtesy of the Bancroft Library)

broad, parks and plazas were graced by fountains, and stately mansions were built of stone. Churches were numerous and imposing; the cathedral, magnificent. As one contemporary visitor said, "Besides these beautiful buildings, the inward riches belonging to the altars are infinite in price and value" (Gage:71). There were six hospitals (four for Europeans, one for Indians, and one for mestizos), even though surgeons were in fact no more than barbers and native curers were just as likely to be relied upon with no known disastrous effects. There were orphanage-schools for abandoned mestizos, Jesuit and Augustinian colleges, and the first university in the Americas, the University of Mexico, was founded in 1551—although centuries passed before a second one opened in Guadalajara. The city was abundantly provisioned, with foodstuffs from the surrounding countryside easily purchased at the huge outdoor market. Textiles and crafts came from New Spain; ivories and silks from the China trade, wine and olive oil as well as artists and paintings arrived from Spain.

Although the poor lived in squalor on the edges of the new city, it is no wonder that people of privilege found the city the only proper place

ENVIRONMENTAL CHANGE

The city floats in emerald circles,
Radiating splendor like quetzal plumes.
Around it chiefs are carried in canoes,
Veiled by a flowery mist.

■

—Aztec poem (recorded by Angel M. Garibay)

Mexico City was not an island for long. The series of lakes surrounding Tenochtitlán were drained over the centuries. Roads replaced the dikes; wheeled carts and mule packs the canoes. Gone were the waterbirds and fish that thrived in Lake Texcoco, gone the fresh water and *chinampa* agriculture that sustained the populace. Remaking Mexico City in the image of Spain, the Spaniards wreaked havoc on the environment. Initially, without the dikes, the city was repeatedly flooded in the 17th century. As the water levels fell, the central valley became increasingly infertile; today water shortages are severe.

to reside. The viceroy and his retinue resided here, creating an elegant court as the focus for European society. Here, too, resided the judges of the Audiencia who kept a watchful eye on the viceroy for the king. The seat of the other powerful authority in the Americas, the archbishop, was also in the capital along with an inordinant number of ordained priests. (Twenty-five percent, or 1,500, of the priests, both secular and mendicant, lived in Mexico City and another 1,400 lived in nearby Puebla, meaning that about half the priesthood of New Spain lived in central Mexico in 1650.) The capital and its environs were home to half the entire European population of the colony "who are so proud and rich that half the city was judged to keep coaches" (Gage:67). By the end of the colonial period, the city had as many racially mixed residents as Indians.

The capital reflected most of the wealth, power, and Spanish culture of New Spain. In 1800, with a population of 137,000—half that estimated for Tenochtitlán—it was the largest city in the Western Hemisphere and a symbol of European culture in the New World. The legendary city of Moctezuma had disappeared.

Regional Diversity

> Neither God nor his Majesty would have been served
> by the people of the provinces, as they are disorganized and
> have no head, and the land is sterile and has no products,
> nor has it silver or gold whereby his Majesty could be served.
>
> ■
>
> —*García López de Cárdenas, 1551*

Outside the capital, the impact of Spain and its settlers varied with the region. Viceregal control was as uneven as the distribution of settlements. Provincial administrators, called *corregidores*, existed in Spanish towns, such as Mérida in Yucatán; the *corregidores* were poorly paid and had limited authority, but they were notorious for finding ways to supplement their salaries. They oversaw and reported to the viceroy on the happenings in the municipality as well as in Indian settlements. These towns also had a local government separate from the royal *corregidor*. In the best of times local government officials were elected; when the Crown needed money, however, officials could buy their positions knowing that prestige and profiteering would amply reward their investment.

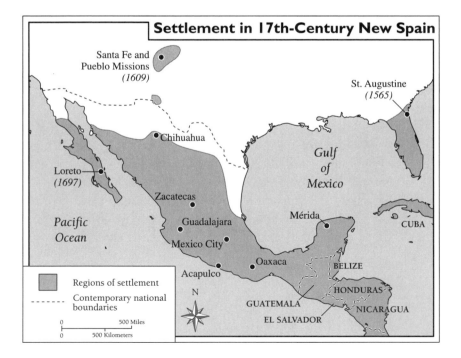

Settlement in 17th-Century New Spain

Santa Fe and Pueblo Missions (1609)

St. Augustine (1565)

Chihuahua

Gulf of Mexico

Loreto (1697)

Zacatecas

Pacific Ocean

Guadalajara

Mérida

CUBA

Mexico City

Oaxaca

BELIZE

Acapulco

HONDURAS

N

GUATEMALA

NICARAGUA

EL SALVADOR

Regions of settlement

Contemporary national boundaries

0   500 Miles

0   500 Kilometers

Colonial building in the provincial town of Pátzcuaro, Michoacán (Courtesy of the Mexico Ministry of Tourism)

Although such provincial towns were few and far between, all were organized according to royal decree: a main plaza dominated with the symbols of authority, the church and royal palace and town hall, and streets laid out perpendicular to the plaza in an orderly fashion. The 10 most important cities, such as Puebla, Oaxaca, and Guadalajara, were large enough to have cathedrals and grand palaces. Puebla eventually had a population of 100,000. The location of a town, the building of a church, and even the founding of a school were all regulated by the Crown through the Council of the Indies located in Seville, Spain. Although viceroys often ignored orders, claiming local conditions did not permit their implementation—"The law is respected but not obeyed" was the official response—the impact of royal edicts on the New World is unmistakable in the architecture of both provincial villages and regional capitals. More than 6,000 decrees governing life in the colonies were issued.

Hacendados often represented the only Spanish presence in many rural areas; and the mendicant fathers, though diminishing in number, continued to create missions in the hinterlands of the empire and to administer many of the 400 fortress monasteries they had built among their converts. Well into the 17th century, there were not enough parish

Provincial church in the Maya village of San Juan Chamula, Chiapas

priests to replace them, much less tend to the spiritual needs of the expanding colony. Given the thin layer of Spanish and church official-dom, an administrative system of *caciques* (native governors) was, of necessity, created to oversee the indigenous peoples and fulfill Spanish tribute and tax levies. The *cacique* system paralleled the town organiza-tion and reinforced the existence of traditional Indian communities.

The intensity and quality of viceregal control in a given area de-pended, at the very least, on the ratio of the density of Spanish settlers to the native populace. The Spaniards preferred to settle near large popula-tions of Indians who could support them. But they also preferred the regions that could most easily re-create life in Spain. The central high-lands, with their temperate climate suitable for Old World crops and livestock, were ideal. Here Spaniards settled in the greatest numbers, and most intensely affected the lives of the indigenous peoples as well as the land.

The tropical lowlands were too hot for the Spaniards, however, the vegetation unfamiliar, and the malaria too threatening. Sugar cane haci-endas were quite productive once Spain permitted the use of African slaves to work them. On the whole, the tropics were so unappealing that merchants didn't want to live in the ports of Veracruz or Acapulco; they simply set up tents on the beaches to await the arrival of the annual Spanish or Manila galleons. Yucatán was hot, too, but unlike Veracruz, it had more than enough Maya Indians for labor. But it had no silver mines or good soil for growing wheat, so the Spaniards settled it only sparsely, leaving most of the land to traditional Indian cornfields. Here Mayas with the desire to live independently could find refuge. English pirates, too, found good hiding places along the isolated Carib-bean coast.

The discovery of silver and gold could make any region attractive. The thinly populated northern regions would suddenly burst with activ-ity when a strike was made. Not only did golddiggers race to the frontier, but *hacendados* created ranches to supply them. After its great silver strikes, Zacatecas became the third-largest city in New Spain early in the 17th century; only the capital and Puebla were larger. It would be joined by other silver cities, Guanajuato, Taxco, and San Luis Potosí among them, changing what had been considered by the Aztecs to be barbarian deserts into wealthy enclaves.

The viceroyalty of New Spain administered a vast territory that ranged from Panama to California and included some Caribbean islands as well as the Philippines. A few regions, such as the Philippines, were

COMPARATIVE CHART OF SPANISH POPULATIONS*			
Region	Year	Total Population	Percentage of Spaniards
Mexico City	1794	104,760	50.3
Puebla	1777	71,366	25.6
Tlaxcala	1794	59,158	13.7
Oaxaca	1794	411,336	6.5
Yucatán	1780	210,472	7.9
New Spain	1810	5,764,731	18.6

* From Farriss:65

independently administered by *audiencias*. Some regions never were settled, leaving great territories to be usurped by other European powers (see maps on pages 81 and 99). Although some ports in California, essential stops on the China trade route, were settled in the 18th century, Baja California had only a few impoverished Jesuit missions. The colony in Santa Fe wasn't supported by any settlement in southern New Mexico, however, nor did any chain of Spanish villages connect it with California. Even where there were settlements, communications among them could be difficult and resources nonexistent. These areas were barely integrated into New Spain, which administered them. As Friar Alonso de Benavides (1630) described life in the New Mexican pueblos, 1,800 very long miles from the capital, "five and six years were wont to pass without royal officials bethinking themselves about us . . . and god only knows what it costs to remind them."

Spain Regulates the Economy

The colony of New Spain was to be managed for the benefit of Spain. All traded items had to be approved by Spain and sent on Spanish ships—a severe burden given that the Spanish galleons sailed in protected convoy only once a year. Commerce with foreign governments was prohibited. Protectionism was unquestioned policy, preventing the free development of industries that competed with those in Spain. Usually items for domestic consumption were permitted—from wheat and mutton to handpainted majolica ceramics, while royal monopolies on gunpowder, silk, mercury for mining, tobacco, and cochineal guaranteed considerable income for the Crown and its merchants.

The Hacienda

Initially the Spaniards had taken from the Indians whatever they could sell abroad and what they needed for their own comfort and sustenance, relying on the indigenous patterns of agriculture and industry to support them. Bishops were happy with mitres made by Aztec featherworkers; settlers found they could convert the native dye, cochineal, into Europe's most fashionable red tint—used also to dye the uniforms of the British redcoats worn against American independence fighters. Other native products made their way around the world: vanilla-flavored chocolate became the drink of Spanish royalty; maize found immediate popularity in Africa and the Middle East. The tomato and peanut, however, took longer to gain popularity. Tobacco took off more than any foodstuff: within a century, it was distributed and grown around the world.

The systems of tribute labor and *encomienda* that had at first sustained New Spain were inadequate once royal edicts had limited their scope and once the number of settlers grew. Also, as wealthy as the *encomienda* had made some Spaniards, it required great numbers of Indians to be productive, numbers that epidemics made unrealizable. Tribute had its limitations as well, if there were not enough Indians to contribute—and besides, the Crown wanted most of the tribute for itself. By the end of the 16th century, these early institutions no longer were adequate to supply the colony with foodstuffs, or support the more recent settlers.

The Spaniards were forced to become involved in shaping the economy of New Spain, and they shaped it to their Old World tastes. With Indian depopulation, there was less resistance to Spanish takeovers of land. Small estates were sometimes legitimately purchased and sometimes granted by the Crown; they also were seized from the Indians. In pursuit of the Spanish ideal of gentlemanly land ownership, many small plots were consolidated into huge estates called haciendas. Instead of indigenous maize and turkeys, wheat was planted and European livestock bred. Friars introduced the first olive groves and vineyards, but these eventually were prohibited by a monopolistic Spain that exploited the captive market for its own wines and oils.

At first, the cattle, sheep, and goats grazed primarily in the densely populated central areas, exhausting formerly rich agricultural lands. The raising of livestock carried such prestige in the home country, however, that it was a preferred occupation in the New World: not only was there profit in exporting hides to Spain for leather but considerable status as well. Because cattle grazing didn't require a lot of workers, the hacienda owners with their silver spurs and wide-brimmed hats, and the chap-protected *vaqueros* (cowboys) soon found their more proper niche in the less populated grasslands near the mines of the north, where "Texas" longhorns thrived. Herds of 150,000 roamed the frontier regions. One family ranch extended over 11 million acres.

Debt Peonage

Despite the introduction of plows and pack animals into New Spain, the agricultural haciendas flourished only where there was sufficient Indian labor. Under the New Laws, the *hacendados* had to appeal to Indians to work their land by paying them. Even under the continued *repartimiento* system, the "tribute" labor required for public works and the demonstrated needs of the colony, there was pay involved, if sometimes only a pittance. The natives could be forced into *repartimiento* for only a limited number of days each year, and each day was to begin at dawn and end before dusk so that the work didn't disrupt the Indians' own farming in support of their families. Such was the new, more humanitarian *repartimiento* system promulgated by Spain.

Practice, however, was another matter. The restraints on exploiting Indian labor were rarely observed—their lack of implementation provides, instead, a typical example of the discrepancy between royal word and colonial deed. The local *corregidores* made much of their income through their management of *repartimiento* labor in favor of the local *hacendados*. The abuses became so bad that agriculture was eliminated from the labor drafts under *repartimiento* in 1630. The *hacendados* learned that few Indians would voluntarily work for scandalously low wages. A solution was soon found, however, and along with it a new form of enslavement: debt peonage. Indians, promised generous sums of money paid in advance, were enticed to work on the estates. Many found it impossible to work off their debts, especially when they were forced to buy food and goods at inflated prices at the only nearby store: the one owned by the *hacendado*. And it wasn't unheard of to rig the accounts in the *hacendado*'s favor. Not legally permitted to leave the hacienda with outstanding debts, the Indians were forced to work until their deaths. Their debts were inherited, unfortunately, bringing other family members into peonage.

THE MIXTECA AND COCHINEAL

In the Mixteca Sierra change was drastic, but under native control. Thanks to powerful *caciques* such as Gabriel de Guzmán who was introduced in the last chapter, the Mixtec never gave up the right to their traditional lands, though they did use them in ways that were profitable to Spain and its settlers. Two Spanish enterprises were silk production and sheep grazing—the Mixteca Sierra was the only region where Indians owned more sheep than the Spaniards. And even when the silk industry died out at the end of the 16th century (due to competition from the Far East), the native red cochineal dye enabled the Mixtecs to flourish for centuries more.

Cochineal, tiny insects that live on prickly pear cactus, were cultivated, then dried and crushed to produce the dye. Cochineal had been traded by the Mixtecs in pre-Hispanic times and paid to the Aztecs in tribute. Under Spain, production increased dramatically for the burgeoning textile industry in Europe, and the dyestuff became the most valuable export after silver and gold. Some said the Mixtecs—at least the Mixtec *caciques* and *cacicas* (women chiefs, who were among the wealthiest individuals in all of Oaxaca)—were wealthier under Spain than their preconquest ancestors had ever been. By controlling their own lands and the production of major commodities, the Mixtecs were unusual among indigenous communities in that they never labored directly for the Spaniards, who were too few to take control beyond tribute and tax demands. Through the Mixtecs' participation in the colonial economy, Oaxaca became one of the most important regions in New Spain, and by 1797 its capital was the third largest city.

Mining

I went to a mine called the Trinity . . . Respecting its wealth, persons worthy of belief who know the region [of Pachuca] told me that in ten years this mine has produced forty million pesos, with nine hundred to a thousand men working daily.

■

—Gemilli Carreri, 1697
(reported in Charles Cumberland:84)

Agriculture was New Spain's primary economic endeavor: maize production alone often exceeded silver in total value. Yet it was the mines, not the corn, which preoccupied the Crown. Gold, and especially silver, were produced in extraordinary quantities. During the colonial period, the equivalent of $2,250,000 worth of silver and gold were extracted. In the 18th century, Mexico produced as much silver as the rest of the world combined. Spain gained so much wealth from the mines—it received approximately 20 percent of the value of all precious metal production in taxes, fees, the royal *quinto* (or fifth), etc.—that it foresook its own moral principles in regard to them. Even after *repartimiento* officially ended for farm labor, it was condoned for the mines despite the high death rates. For 12 hours a day, workers descended into the damp and dangerous mine shafts—the one called "the mouth of hell" in Guanajuato was 2,000 feet deeper than any mine in the world—returning with 200, even 300, pounds of ore on their backs. Working conditions led to labor unrest and rebellions, and the mines had difficulty meeting production schedules. Eventually market forces, not the Crown, eliminated *repartimiento* labor in the mines: rising prices for silver encouraged the mining companies to pay adequately for much needed skilled labor. Once properly paid, workers were in plentiful supply.

The Social Classes

A social caste system based primarily on race existed in New Spain and was reinforced by law. At the pinnacle was the white ruling class, comprising 1 million of the entire population of 7 million by the end of the colonial period. Distinctions were made among the whites, however. Preferences were given to those born on the Iberian peninsula of Spain (*peninsulares*), even though the vast majority returned to Spain after serving their terms of office. In fact, their lack of engagement in New Spain was the reason for their royal preference. To preserve their absolute loyalty to the Crown, viceroys and other royal officials usually served limited terms, often no more than five years, and they were banned from owning property (though some managed to make a considerable fortune during their terms) or marrying in the colony without special permission (though fewer than 10 percent were women).

These *peninsulares* ranked higher than Mexican-born Spaniards called *criollos* (creoles): the pale-skinned children of conquistadors and permanent settlers found a guaranteed high position in society regardless of how lowly their ancestors' status had been in Spain. However, creoles could not hold royal office, because the Crown suspected that their place of birth tarnished their loyalty.

RACIAL COMPOSITION OF NEW SPAIN 1810		
	Number	Percentage
Indians	3,676,281	60
Whites		
Peninsulares	15,000	0.3
Creoles	1,092,367	18
Mestizos	704,245	11
Mulattoes/zambos	624,461	10
Black	10,000	0.2
Total Population	6,122,354	
Based on Meyer & Sherman: 218		

Only whites were permitted to wear European silk finery, ride horses, and be called *damas* (ladies) and *caballeros* (gentlemen). So important was it to pretend to be pure white, and so unlikely was that to be the case in New Spain, that the Crown would certify all Indian or African blood "extinguished" in a family—for a fee.

Beneath the Spanish upper stratum were the peoples of color. Spain developed an elaborate terminology for what it perceived as 16 relevant permutations of European, African, and American peoples—mulattos (African and white), and zambos and coyotes (Indian and African), among them. The African slaves often labored under the worst conditions in the tropics and the mines, but as personal property they seldom were concentrated together in sufficient numbers to maintain a separate group identity. One runaway slave, Yanga, established a stronghold of 80 individuals near Veracruz; after defeating royal troops, he forced the viceroy to recognize their freedom, permitting them to establish the town of San Lorenzo de los Negros. On the whole, the numbers of African slaves diminished over the years to 6,000 by 1800, as they either escaped to remote Indian regions or bought their freedom (permissible under Spanish law). The number of individuals with some African heritage, that is mulatto or zambo, was over 600,000.

And, of course, there were the more numerous mestizos, a group that would continue to grow throughout the country's history. Immediately after the conquest, both church and Crown encouraged intermarriage; under the more rigid colonial society, they simply looked the other way in regard to concubinage—mestizos often were the illegitimate children of Spanish men and Indian women. The mestizos predominated where the Spaniards did: in central Mexico. Although legally lower than the whites, they were subject to the same taxes and military duties even if they were not granted the same privileges. Their treatment varied. Some, born to the famous, such as Cortés's illegitimate son, were treated as aristocracy. Others were ranchers and soldiers on the frontier; and still others, in a social intermediary role, supervised native laborers for Spanish overlords. Many were simply poor and considered inferior. Some found their greatest opportunities as vagabonds and thieves who prowled the countryside.

Below the mestizo but above the slaves and with protections not granted to the Africans were the Indians, the largest class of all. Although considered wards of the Crown and church, Indians suffered abominably whether because of debt peonage or mine labor. At least one half of Indian children died in their first year; 75 percent died in early infancy. Excluded from formal education, their lot became that of illiterate and abjectly poor laborers and peasants. Of course, there were interesting exceptions, and the harshness of their fate varied according to region and position in native society. In fact, the pre-Columbian class structure, divided between a ruling native aristocracy and commoners, survived the centuries in many traditional villages and was inadvertently reinforced by viceregal recognition of local *caciques*.

CACIQUE AND COMMONER IN THE MIXTECA SIERRA

Caciques, chosen from the Indian nobility, inherited their position. In the flourishing Oaxaca region of the Mixteca Sierra, they also inherited wealth. Cacique Guzmán of Yanhuitlán, descendant of the pre-Columbian leader 8 Deer, had 980 acres of farm and grazing land, and many houses and animals—more than owned by any Spaniard—and a salary of 400 pesos plus the tribute due him from his people for the administrative services he rendered. By contrast, most commoners left only a shack, a small piece of land, and a few animals to their descendants. Some among the Mixtecs accumulated a bit more: the 1710 will of Domingo Ramos left farmlands, an adobe house, a storage chest with key, a bed, a skirt, a quilt, 21 mares, cloth, some silver, and what appears to be a pre-Columbian preference for green feathers—nearly 1,200 of them. (Spores 1984:116)

The Church and Culture

In Spain, the religious orders were primarily charged with education, just as they were in the conversion of the peoples of Mexico. Their responsibilities also included the first generation of creoles, whose conquistador fathers were mostly uneducated. The high status of creoles in New Spain required that they be educated, and the religious community taught them in seminaries and colleges; in Spanish communities of any size, the Jesuits and Augustinians provided primary school education. During the colonial period, the University of Mexico granted 4,000 undergraduate degrees and 1,000 postgraduate ones, training the doctors, scientists, priests, and lawyers of New Spain.

Creole education (and primarily that of the males) became the only educational preoccupation of the established colony. By 1800 there were only 10 primary schools in New Spain. Indian schools, even the famous Franciscan college of Santa Cruz de Tlatelolco where Aztec nobles were taught theology and rhetoric, did not last beyond the 16th century. Mestizos and Indians were banned from most professions including the law, although like much else in colonial life, there were always exceptions.

Even in the trades, there was considerable discrimination. Initially the friars had taught Indians how to paint Renaissance murals from copy books and had trained them in European trades: blacksmithing, tailoring, carpentry. And they had engaged them in constructing the first church with a true vault. As time went on, the whites took control of the trades and often permitted only themselves to rise to the rank of master craftsman.

The skill of the artisans in New Spain, even when they weren't granted master status, can best be judged by the quality of the approximately 12,000 churches built during the colonial period (see pages 93 and 102)—most of them finely frescoed or carved, all adorned with elaborate altarpieces and silver chalices, and fitted with lavishly embroidered vestments. Their style varied according to the fashions in Spain, beginning with the Renaissance and Spanish plateresque style of the 16th century and evolving into 17th-century baroque. Although European artists provided inspiration for the colony—such as the Spanish painting tradition of Francisco de Zubarán and Bartolomé Murillo—the peninsular styles were often interpreted according to the colony's own needs and preferences. The open chapels of the 16th century (see page 65), for example, and the exuberant ultrabaroque style, called *Churrigueresque*, is another local development that resulted in some of the finest buildings in 18th-century Mexico. Such artistic bounty, sustained over several centuries, was the work of thousands of anonymous artists, both Indian and mixed race.

The church was not only the educator of New Spain, but also the great patron of colonial art. And it had the money to sustain such

The old Basilica of the Virgin of Guadalupe (c. 1700). Patron of Mexico and the favorite of the poor, the Virgin's shrine attracted 10 million pilgrims in 1995. It is one of the most important shrines in Christendom. (Courtesy of the Mexican Ministry of Tourism)

creative and lavish outpourings, having been the beneficiary of royal land grants and church tithes as well as bequests from everyone from Mixtec *caciques* to wealthy creoles. It would eventually own half the land in Mexico.

> There are no more devout people in the world toward the Church and clergy. In their lifetime they strive to exceed one another in their gifts to the cloisters of nuns and friars. Some erect altars . . . worth many thousand ducats . . . others at their death leave to them two or three thousands ducats for an annual stipend.
> ■
> *—Thomas Gage (1648:70)*

Because of the church, Mexico was left the legacy of two of its greatest colonial painters. Miguel Cabrera (1695–1768), a mestizo born in Oaxaca and abandoned to an orphanage, became the most popular baroque painter in Mexico (see page 95) and a favorite of the archbishop. His contemporary, Juan Correa (c. 1645–1716), son of a freed African slave and a mulatto physician from Spain, was one of the most prolific painters of his age, contributing many works to the Mexico City cathedral. Given Mexico's artistic heritage, it was appropriate that when the Academy of San Carlos was established in 1785, it granted admission to artists of all races.

The introduction of the printing press in 1537 enriched the cultural life of the colony. Even though there was no newspaper until 1805, weekly gazettes and literary reviews were published. Fifteen thousand books (all passing the Inquisition's censorial review) were printed in Mexico during the colonial period. The first book published was a bilingual one in Nahuatl and Spanish by Bishop Zumárraga; others were written in a total of nine different native languages, and most books were devoted to religious topics. Books were imported as well, and Juan de Palafox y Mendoza (1600–59), who served both as bishop of Puebla and viceroy, collected a personal library of 43,000 volumes, the largest in the Americas.

The cultural life of Mexico City created two outstanding literary figures: Sor Juana Inés de la Cruz (1651–95), the great Mexican poet, and her friend Carlos de Sigüenza y Góngora (1645–1700), an historian, scientist, mathematician, and poet. The latter wrote an ode to the Virgin of Guadalupe and a history of pre-Columbian civilization, yet, like most of his class, held the native peoples in contempt.

The friars introduced sacred music into the colony from the earliest days, by training the Indians for the church choirs (and exempting them from tribute when they participated) and teaching them to make Euro-

SOR JUANA INÉS DE LA CRUZ

Born in Mexico and of illegitimate birth, Sor Juana was the first great poet of the post-conquest Americas and one of the most esteemed baroque poets in the world, as well as an early champion of women's rights. Her beauty and genius for learning made her a favorite of the viceregal court, but instead of marrying she joined a nunnery—the only institution in that era in which women could devote themselves to intellectual pursuits: "for it seemed to me no cause for a head to be adorned with hair and naked of learning," wrote Sor Juana in "La Repuesta" (translated by Margaret Sayera Peden:30).

In an age when most girls were taught needlepoint and ladylike deportment, Sor Juana composed all kinds of poetry (including some in Nahuatl and others in the language of nearby African slaves), wrote plays (one based on Greek and Aztec mythologies), and essays (in one, "La Repuesta," she defended the right of women to education and culture). Today she is an icon of Mexican culture and an inspiration to contemporary writers.

Portrait of Sor Juana Inés de la Cruz painted by Miguel Cabrera in 1750

pean instruments. The Indians not only made the instruments and performed, they also composed church music and recorded it on choirsheets. Later in the colonial period, creoles composed chamber music and operas (Manuel Zumaya's *La Partenope*, performed in 1711, was the first). Every element of society enjoyed more popular music, from the African marimba and Spanish-introduced fandangos and guitar ballads to Indian festival dances and flute-and-drum music. Wrote Thomas Gage in 1648, "I dare be bold enough to say the people are drawn to their churches more for the delight of the music than for any delight in the service of God."

The Spanish Legacy

By 1700 New Spain had been transformed from the land of the Aztecs and Maya to that of an exotic European colony. Cochineal dye was produced near fields of grazing sheep, wheat spread through the central highlands, and cornfields were everywhere. The people, too, were increasingly mixed: Africans with Indians and Europeans along the coasts; Europeans and Indians in every town. Indian myths and language infused the poetry of even the highest classes. The wheeled cart slowly replaced human carriers and canoes; the burro took the burden off native carriers. The Catholic domain was, nonetheless, a cultural patchwork: at its most rural recesses, indigenous traditions remained unassimilated, contrasting with the Spanish cattle ranches and European cities. The Spanish caste system spread illiteracy, racism, and official corruption through the land, setting one group against the others.

Although most indigenous peoples were reduced to illiteracy, the Yucatec Maya scribes continued their pre-Columbian tradition of recording the events of their people in books of the katuns. The books, written in Yucatec but no longer in hieroglyphs, were kept secret from the Spanish world throughout the colonial period. Sometimes the words are unforgettable reminders of the changed world of the indigenous peoples of Mexico:

> Then the Indians had no sickness; they had no aching bones; they had no burning chest. They had no abdominal pain; they had no consumption; they had no headache. At that time, the course of humanity was orderly. The foreigners made it otherwise.
>
> —Book of the Chilam Balam of Chumayel, *17th century (translated by Ralph Roys)*

THE BOURBON REFORMS AND INDEPENDENCE

1700–1821

The condition as conquerors of a conquered land, makes them
[the Spaniards] the first inhabitants, the preferred and the privileged
of all America; and woe to us, woe to the peninsula, and woe to the
Indies the day we lose our ascendancy, source and sole shield of
obedience and subordination.

■

—Merchants Guild of Mexico to the Spanish Cortes, 1811
(translated by Stein & Stein:57)

The Enlightenment brought changes to New Spain in the last century
of colonial rule. A new faith in science and reason led the Bourbon
monarchy to modernize the administration of the colonies and to squeeze
out yet more profits for Spain. As the century progressed to embrace both
the American and French revolutions, increasingly radical ideas filtered
into New Spain—ideas about social equality and self-governance. After
a long and destructive battle for independence, the Spanish colony would
become the free country of Mexico.

The Last of the Spanish Hapsburgs

In 1700, the Hapsburg control of Spain's monarchy ended. Given the
devastated condition of the empire, the end should have come sooner.
Too many battles—and too many defeats—had bankrupted the country
and resulted in the loss of considerable European territory. The former
war machine had become so pitiful that soldiers ran from battle. The

nation chosen by God to rule the New World, suffered English, French, and Dutch colonies on American soil.

For all its monopolies and protectionism, Spain was broke. Its preference for precious metals had led the empire to ignore its industrial development—a plentiful silver supply had made it too easy to purchase manufactured products from the rest of Europe. War, not investment in the nation's economic infrastructure, drained the treasury and forced

CAN EK, 1697

AMaya dynasty, said to descend from the ruler of the great Yucatec city of Chichén Itzá, ended around the same time as the Spanish Hapsburgs. The Itzá, having fled to the remote Petén jungle, reestablished themselves on the islands of Lake Petén Itzá, now in Guatemala. Their numbers swelled to 25,000 with Maya refugees from Spanish rule. These Maya painted their bodies red and black and tattooed their faces—all forbidden by the early friars. They built stone temples and colonnaded palaces, they worshipped the old gods, followed rituals dictated by their hieroglyphic books, and lived under the rule of the Can Ek dynasty that demanded, and received, tribute from Mayas in Spanish-controlled areas of the Yucatán peninsula. After 200 years in the New World, the Spaniards finally forged a trade route through the region. They captured the last Can Ek and destroyed the Itzá kingdom of Tayasal—their guns being as effective against feathered-decorated spears as they were under Cortés. The last Mesoamerican ruler became a symbol of resistance, his name taken by future Maya rebels. An eyewitness account describes Can Ek:

> The King Can Ek was well adorned, a crested crown of pure gold sat on his head and great golden discs covered his ears with dangles . . . Gold rings adorned his arms and fingers. His tunic was pure white with blue borders; a cloak hung from his shoulders, immaculately white with blue border and fringe and cinched with the wide black belt of an Itzá priest. . . . And the cape had hieroglyphs for his name that meant "Twenty-Serpent-Star."

> ■
> —El Manuscrito de Can Ek (*Grant Jones 1991: 40–41*)

Spain to borrow. In the end, two-thirds of its silver bullion went to pay off debts in foreign European banks. Spain had become a third-rate economic power.

In an enlightened age, Spain was intellectually stifled by the Holy Office of the Inquisition. In time of tolerance and scientific understanding, it was ruled by feeble-minded Charles II (1665–1700), called "The Bewitched." With his death in 1700, the Spanish Hapsburgs, too, came to their grueling end.

Bourbon Reforms

Although most courts in Europe could make some claim as to their right to rule Spain, it was the French dynasty of the Bourbons that maneuvered Philip V (1701–46) onto the throne and successfully kept him there through the War of the Spanish Succession (1701–13).

To make their trading empire more efficient, the Bourbons streamlined the viceregal administration of New Spain, replacing 200 provincial *corregidores* and local mayors with 12 regional *intendentes*. The *intendentes* were well paid and experienced administrators—quite able to collect

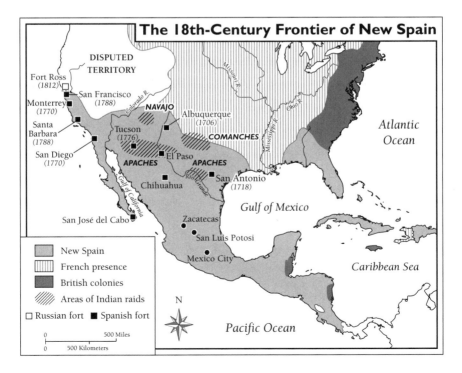

The 18th-Century Frontier of New Spain

the taxes and tribute owed to the Crown. In an effort to preserve the frontier areas of New Spain against additional foreign encroachment —the Russians had ships in California waters; the French were in Louisiana—the Crown developed the first professional army of New Spain and established a colony in San Francisco and missions in Texas. To increase the volume of trade, it broke up old monopolies, permitting more ports to compete with Veracruz and Acapulco (such as Campeche and Progreso in Yucatán) and allowing direct trade among the various New World Spanish ports. The number of Manila galleons increased by two annually. Also some taxes were lowered to encourage silver mining.

Such modernization had its greatest impact under Charles III (1759–88). Silver production, assisted by new technology as well as royal incentives, rose from 3.2 million pesos in 1700 to 27 million pesos in 1804. Gold production tripled. Cochineal production also increased, becoming the second most valuable export and employing 30,000 Mixtecs. Agricultural products, especially sugar cane, increased in export value. And royal monopolies on domestic production of tobacco and *pulque*, the native alcoholic drink, further increased revenues. Tobacco revenues alone were greater than those from mining; those from *pulque* equaled all Indian tribute. At Veracruz, the more liberal trading policies attracted up to 500 ships in one year.

The reforms worked for Spain because the Bourbons sent able viceroys to Mexico. The rule of Antonio María de Bucareli (1771–79) was marked by peace and exceptional prosperity. Another great viceroy, the count of Revillagigedo (1789–94), created the first public transportation system and lowered the crime rate in the capital by lighting the streets.

REVENUES FROM NEW SPAIN 1786–1789	
	Peso Value
Tobacco	16,000,000
Sales tax (includes silver)	15,500,000
Royal grant: silver and gold	9,000,000
Coinage	6,000,000
Pulque	3,500,000
Indian tribute	3,500,000
Customs duty	3,000,000

Source: José Miranda, et al, *Historia de México* (Mexico 1971:263) as presented in Meyer & Sherman (1983)

The Impact on New Spain

Spain's concern was always Spain . . .

■

—*Charles C. Cumberland (95)*

The world's trade flourishes at the expense of the peoples of America and
their immense labors, but the riches they draw from the bosom of the
fertile earth are not retained.

■

—*Memoir to Viceroy of Mexico, 1723*
(translated by Stein & Stein)

The reforms made Mexico the most prosperous of all Spain's colonies.
And they made Spain wealthy. But they also had adverse repercussions
in the colony. Many of the reforms benefited *peninsulares* and, indeed,
increased emigration from Spain. This class of aristocrats expanded, at
the expense of the creoles. The regional administrators were all from
Spain, save one, and, worse, they replaced creole local officials. The
pulque and tobacco monopolies increased prices on locally consumed
products and displaced those who had haciendas producing them. The
demand for productivity created more hardships for those who labored,
and Indian tribute to the Crown was more vigorously collected.

In 1810, New Spain produced 75 percent of the profits from all of
Spain's colonies. Yet Spain reinvested little of the monies, the bulk of
which went to Europe or toward the administrative costs of other
colonies. The end result was an economy as undeveloped as that of
backward Spain. There were few manufactured goods. The roads that
existed were better for pack animals than coaches—and there were too
few of them. Many whites, living like the landed gentry of Europe, owned
vast tracts of land, but too often worked very few acres. The land of vanilla
and chocolate and cotton had to import these items because their
production was so neglected. The country was regulated to an extreme:
a ranchero needed a permit to slaughter his cattle for his own dinner
table. Cattle and sheep roamed everywhere, in countless numbers, yet
there was not enough wool or fresh beef.

Not only did waste and overregulation and corruption still exist after
the Bourbon reforms, the racist class system remained undisturbed
despite the egalitarianism of the Enlightenment. While the economy
prospered in the Bourbon years, the wealth remained concentrated
among the white population. Yet more than 80 percent of New Spain was
nonwhite by the end of the century, and the squalor that most were

CHURRIGUERESQUE ARCHITECTURE

Churrigueresque church facade in Zacatecas

The Mexican baroque style of the 18th century is the great cultural legacy of rich creoles. The silver barons could afford to fund the construction of entire churches, and one, José de la Borda of Taxco, offered to pave the road from Veracruz to the capital in silver coins if the pope would agree to visit. The cities they graced with their mansions, gold altarpieces, and churches are part of Mexico's artistic heritage. Historically preserved and protected, the cities— among them Guanajuato, Querétaro, Puebla, and Zacatecas—today attract considerable tourism.

destined to suffer couldn't have contrasted more sharply with the opulence of the ruling class: in 1784 300,000 Mexicans died from either famine or diseases related to malnourishment.

The Creoles

Despite problems with the economy, the creoles were not rebellious. They were conservative and supported the monarchy. And no wonder— as dependent as the economy was on Spain, it made most creoles fabulously wealthy. Only the galling inequities in their treatment by the Spanish festered.

Given their number in the colony, the *peninsulares* were disproportiately wealthy. Yet the creoles did very well. Count Regla, a mining baron and creole, was the wealthiest man in 18th-century New Spain; over 30 years, the net profit from his silver mine in Pachuca alone was 15 million dollars. Count Bassoco, like 50 other fabulously rich creoles, received his noble title after a generous contribution to the Crown—in his case, a gift of 200,000 pesos. Count Valenciana, although not the richest of the rich, earned 1 million pesos each year just from his famous silver mine in Guanajuato. Merchants and ranchers made their fortunes, too. In the north, *hacendados* had immense landholdings for their herds. The Sánchez Navarro family estate—the largest in the New World—was about the size of Portugal. The creoles traveled and studied in Europe and took on the high styles of that continent. They built ornate palaces for themselves at home and contributed to the building of entire Churrigueresque churches.

Wealth didn't entirely satisfy the New World aristocracy: resentment of the privileges of the *peninsulares* intensified. Phenomenally rich, many creoles were like royalty themselves with their own mining and ranching kingdoms. They increasingly took pride in their Mexican heritage: their Spanish was peppered with Indian words, their chicken with chile. And they called themselves "*americanos*." The condescension of the Spanish-born toward these provincials rankled—especially when a *peninsular* originally came from the lower classes, as many did.

By mid-century, the Holy Office of the Inquisition could no longer keep out the pervasive ideas of the European Enlightenment—ideas about human rights versus the divine rights of kings, about liberty and social equality. Yet here the creoles were treated like second-class citizens in their own country; the highest church and government positions were not open to them. A creole village priest, for example, could make as little as 100 pesos, in contrast to a *peninsular* bishop's 100,000. The Bourbon reforms brought no new social and political opportunities—even at a time in which the United States gained its independence from Britain (1776) and the French Revolution (1789) overthrew the Bourbons.

Political Ferment

The creoles wanted more control over the future of New Spain, but few had any interest in upsetting the society that had so amply rewarded them. There were critiques of Spain—of the brutality of the conquest and centuries of colonial enslavement; there were satires on the more absurd aspects of Spanish rule. There were even foreign agitators, from newly independent France and the United States, who tried to bestir the Mexicans.

Only a few conspired for independence. Military officers, kept out of the highest ranks, and small merchants and bureaucrats gathered in "literary" societies that were fronts for their plots. Among the most radical were some parish priests who, finding themselves in the poorest regions, tended their Indian parishioners with the care of the most humanistic 16th-century friars.

Most creoles, however, realized that their privilege and prestige resulted from the imperial system. They were satisfied to tinker with the colonial system, maintaining their loyalty to the Spanish monarchy but demanding equality with the *peninsulares* or, better yet, their replacement by the creoles themselves.

The non-privileged classes heard little or nothing about the Enlightenment. Their own lot was itself enough to foment rebellions—and they did occur, but usually were not organized well enough to spread beyond a local community. By the 18th century the Indian population was once again on the increase, intensifying frictions over land use. On the whole, the native peoples were so downtrodden that some Spaniards deluded themselves into thinking they were naturally servile. Economic growth encouraged some Indians to leave their traditional communities in order to participate in the broader society and some managed to do well, taking on Spanish customs and language. Even the *caciques* took on more

CAN EK REBORN

One Indian rebellion was led by the shaman Jacinto Canek, who took the name of the legendary Maya leader (see page 98). He was crowned king, he said, in order to lead his people out of their servitude through armed revolt against the Spaniards. His message appealed to many in Yucatán and terrified the white population until royal forces entered Canek's village in 1761 and killed half of the 1,200 armed Maya assembled there. Canek escaped, but was later captured, tortured to death, and cremated. Some rebels were drawn and quartered; others, after being flogged, had one ear cut off to mark them. Canek's village was razed in the hope that, like the leader himself, no trace of the event would be left.

Spanish customs and were expected to be, at the very least, bilingual. Frequently employed as mediators or merchants within the traditional communities because of their bilingualism, these Indians were often the worst oppressors of their own people.

Many *castas*, or mixed-race individuals, were able to find more remunerative work and responsibility in the expanding Bourbon economy. The caste system prevented them from being truly assimilated into the society, however. At times light-skinned mestizos and mulattoes "passed" as whites; others successfully bribed priests to register their children as creoles; still others maneuvered into the trades, the clergy, and the burgeoning militia. For most, their color meant a lifetime of resentment and exploitation.

The increasing numbers of nonwhites living free, out of debt peonage and slavery, would have made natural allies for the more liberal creoles— if they had so wished. For most creoles, the entire class system could be endangered by such alliances, and so there was little interest in organizing broader protests.

Despite the lack of fervor for independence, political events in Europe made radical change a necessity. Charles IV (1788–1808), far from the wise monarch his father had been, permitted the plunder of the colonies. In 1804 the charitable funds of New Spain, belonging to the church and used not only to help the poor of Mexico but also to give credit to creoles, were taken for the royal treasury to pay off European war debts. The church had to call in all mortgages, destroying some creoles financially; clergy no longer were able to respond to even the most disastrous circumstances of needy parishioners. The church was already festering, because Charles III had expelled the Jesuits in 1767 and confiscated all their property, closing schools and frontier missions.

Charles IV was destructive of Spain, too, where uprisings led him in 1808 to abdicate in favor of his son, Ferdinand VII. The turmoil continued when Napoleon forced both Spanish Bourbons, Charles and Ferdinand, into exile and placed this brother Joseph Bonaparte on the throne in 1808. Various rival governments, or *juntas*, in support of the Spanish monarchy took charge in areas outside Napoleon's control. Without the monarchy, the Mexican creoles thought they should rule themselves; the *peninsulares* believed otherwise. The tug of war in both Spain and Mexico created instability: Mexico had four viceroys in just two years. Worse, the policies of the Spanish juntas were despotically conservative in regard to the colonies: they ordered the arrest in the Americas of anyone agitating for reform; the Holy Office of the Inquisition became a spying arm of the government, rather than an enforcer of religious standards; and important individuals were arrested and deported. The creoles no longer hoped that their political fortunes would improve through peaceful means. By mid-1810, creoles in every major city had formed secret societies in opposition to the government.

Miguel Hidalgo

> My children . . . will you free yourselves?
> ■
> —*Father Miguel Hidalgo y Costilla, 1810*

In 1810 when Miguel Hidalgo gave his famous *Grito de Dolores*, the cry to action that is reenacted on September 16 in Mexico today, he gave creole leadership to the disorganized stirrings of the mestizos and other *castas*, to the Indians and other disenfranchised masses of Mexico.

Considered the father of the Mexican nation, Miguel Hidalgo y Costilla (1753–1811) was born to a creole family on a hacienda in the province of Guanajuato where his father was manager. He was sent to a Jesuit College in what is now Morelia, but his education was soon interrupted by the expulsion of the Jesuits. Having learned a lesson in imperial whimsy, Hidalgo enrolled in another college and received his degree from the University of Mexico in 1774. He was ordained as a priest in 1778. Eventually he became rector of the prestigious college of San Nicolás in Morelia, founded by the 16th-century utopian Vasco de Quiroga. Like Quiroga, he studied Indian languages, but unlike Quiroga he soon was investigated by the Inquisition (1800), and although nothing against him could be proved, he lost his position: he was too much a child of the Enlightenment, reading banned literature, questioning church dogma—and keeping a mistress. He ended up in the village of Dolores, where he tried to improve the economic well-being of his parishioners. It was in Dolores that he met others who would become the martyrs of independence.

Hidalgo belonged to a secret society in Querétaro that included Ignacio Allende and Juan de Aldama, both officers in the army; a former *corregidor* of Querétaro and his wife, the Mexican patriot Josefa Ortiz de Domínguez; a postal clerk; and others. Until his famous proclamation catapulted him into the position of leadership, Hidalgo was a minor figure in the central Mexican "Committee of Correspondence" conspiring for independence. His particular group gathered arms for an insurrection set for December. But when, on September 13, 1810, Josefa Ortiz de Domín-

Father Hidalgo with torch of independence in Carnaval de Ideologías *(1937–39), a mural painted in the Guadalajara Government Palace by José Clemente Orozco*

guez let out the news that royal officials were arresting those involved, the uprising prematurely went forward.

Receiving the news, Allende, Aldama, and Hidalgo managed to meet at the small town of Dolores. They decided to go forward with the insurrection. In the predawn hours of September 16, Hidalgo tolled the bells to call his Indian and mestizo parishioners to church. His cry for independence went well beyond narrow creole interests; he attacked the conquistadors' confiscation of Indian land and declared an end to tribute. Later, Hidalgo would also declare an end to slavery. He gave the rallying cry in the name of the dark-skinned Virgin of Guadalupe. In response to his "Viva Guadalupe!," his parishioners are said to have shouted "Death to the *peninsulares*!"

The ferocity of the rebellion unleashed in Dolores caught everyone by surprise—even Hidalgo, who suddenly was swept to the forefront of the movement. He had naively thought the mere threat of insurrection would lead everyone to the reasonable position of agreeing to independence. Marching under the banner of the Mexican Virgin of Guadalupe, his forces swelled with the oppressed, armed only with the peasant's machete, the miner's pick, the bow and arrow, and, occasionally, a gun. By the time he captured what is now Morelia, his forces numbered 60,000—and thousands more were fighting with Allende farther north. More poor joined Hidalgo at Morelia, until their numbers swelled to 80,000. Instead of well-disciplined soldiers led by army professionals, the insurrection was fought by a barely controllable mob and an overwhelmed priest. Said Lucas Alaman, an eyewitness, "The pillage was more merciless than if done by a foreign army" (1943: vol 1, 403).

The insurrectionists swept through the countryside, confiscating land and livestock—some ate the first beef of their lives. Wherever resistance was met, they attacked viciously. In Guanajuato the hundreds of frightened *peninsular* families who had gathered together in the granary were slaughtered. And even though 2,000 rebels were killed by royalist guns and grenades, they kept fighting. After their victories, towns were sacked, markets stripped of food, baroque mansions looted of silver. The capital remained untouched, because Hidalgo, fearing the worst bloodbath imaginable, didn't invade despite Allende's urging; historians believe such an invasion could have achieved independence early in the fighting. Yet in just over a month the rebels controlled much of central Mexico, from Guadalajara and Zacatecas to the Pacific and Gulf coasts.

Despite their stunning victories, the insurgents soon suffered major setbacks. The royalists, under General Félix Calleja, regrouped and regained Guanajuato and other cities. Calleja fought mercilessly and executed innocents as gruesomely as the revolutionaries did. In March 1811, Hidalgo and Allende were captured in Texas and returned to Calleja. Both were executed, and their decapitated heads were hung from the granary walls in Guanajuato for 10 years as a macabre warning to the public.

José María Morelos

The popularity of the Independence movement diminished. Some poor were content to work the land they had "liberated." Creole support plummeted: fearful of the attacks on personal property and of slogans promising social change, the privileged shifted their allegiance. They realized only too well that for the masses, there was little difference in appearance between the *peninsulares* and themselves—and little difference in their exploitation of workers.

Central Mexico & Towns of Independence

Most of the fighting occurred near the provincial cities of central Mexico where creoles predominated with their mines and haciendas.

Not surprisingly, the movement that continued was under the leadership of a mestizo, the priest José María Morelos y Pavón, who had been recruited to the cause by Hidalgo. A military genius with clear political objectives, Morelos brought together a fighter force that included students and peasants, military officers and Indian *caciques*. Each wore the badge of the Virgin of Guadalupe who, in addition to being the protector of the poor, had become the symbol of a free Mexico. Morelos organized his soldiers into small bands well trained in guerrilla warfare. Gradually, they won enough territory, from Oaxaca to Tampico, to encircle and isolate the capital.

In 1813, Morelos convened a constitutional convention to govern the liberated territories and alarmed the creoles and clergy alike with his politics. He advocated the end of the caste system as well as equal rights for all regardless of race; he even recommended that church lands be redistributed among the poor. In independent Mexico, he said, "the only thing that will distinguish one American from another is vice and virtue" (Herrejón:133–34). Spain itself would champion such liberal ideas in a decade, but the conservative creoles found them thoroughly objectionable. Moreover, Morelos extolled not European culture but rather the preconquest past, laying the foundation for a unified, and uniquely Mexican, nation.

> Spirits of Moctezuma, Cacamitzin, Cuauhtémoc Xicotencatl, Calzontzin! Take pride in this august assembly and celebrate this happy moment in which your sons have congregated to avenge your insults!
>
> ■
>
> —*José María Morelos, 1813 (translated by Charles Cumberland)*

The royalist forces under the ruthless General Calleja once again succeeded in winning back cities. To guarantee a firm hand during the war, a revived Spanish monarchy made Calleja viceroy. Morelos was captured and executed in 1815, nearly ending the struggle for independence. Only a few continued the fight: Guadalupe Victoria (the *nom de guerre* of Félix Fernández), hiding out in the mountains above Veracruz, and Vicente Guerrero on the Pacific slopes. Most defected; others were pardoned. By 1816 the fighting was so sporadic that Spain felt safe enough to replace Calleja with a more moderate viceroy, and by 1819 offered amnesty to the insurgents.

Independence

By 1820 Spain again controlled all the Mexican cities and most of the territory. Yet in a short time, with barely any bloodshed, Mexico would be independent. Under threat of a military coup, the restored Spanish monarchy was forced to function under a liberal constitution, which recognized the sovereignty of the people. The constitution permitted free speech and open trade and clipped the powers of the church and its vast properties—a common anticlerical position of the Enlightenment. Although Morelos was long dead, his specter seemed to haunt Mexican conservatives.

Finding Spain too liberal, the creoles, even the most conservative, opted for independence. They were supported, and partially funded, by the church. Their modus operandi was a military coup, and their chosen leader was Agustín de Iturbide, a greedy and vain individual who had resigned from the royal army when accused of corruption. The creoles' goal was to institute a constitutional monarchy with a member of Europe's royalty who would preserve their privileged position in Mexican society.

The creoles convinced the viceroy to reinstate Iturbide in order to defeat Vicente Guerrero once and for all. Iturbide took his army to the state of what is now Guerrero and, instead of going to war with him, negotiated with the rightly suspicious Vicente Guerrero to join forces to fight for independence. On February 24, 1821, they signed the Plan of Iguala, a platform permitting all of Mexico's factions to agree. Above all, it declared independence for all people, whether of Indian, European, or African descent. In addition, it stated that the nation would be governed by a constitutional monarchy, headed by either King Ferdinand of Spain or some European prince. It also declared that the state religion would be Catholic, and no other, and guaranteed the properties of the church. Lastly, it stated that all citizens could be employed in any position without distinction other than merit. Iturbide came away with the necessary document for independence; he also managed to confiscate a silver shipment for Manila into his own safekeeping.

The plan appealed to conservatives and liberals alike. The viceroy, realizing that the army and most municipal officials supported the Plan of Iguala, resigned. Spain, forever hopeful, sent as a replacement Juan O'Donoju, a liberal Spaniard of Irish descent. He quickly realized that independence was to be a reality and met with Iturbide to ratify the plan. Iturbide negotiated one modification in what then became the Plan of Córdoba: in the event that a European prince could not be found to rule, an appropriate Mexican could be monarch.

On September 27, 1821, Iturbide marched into the capital with Vicente Guerrero and Guadalupe Victoria at his side. After too many years of wars and atrocities, Mexico was independent from Spain.

7

YEARS OF CHAOS
1823–1876

Somber events engulf us. Although the revolution
is over, its consequences keep us exposed to grave
perils; various parties, some swollen by
triumph, others bitter over defeat, divide our
reborn society . . .

■

—El Aguila Mexicana, *1823 (quoted in Stein & Stein:130)*

Mexican hopes that independence would bring a modernized economy and more egalitarian society were not realized in the next century. Instead, the legacy of the battle for independence was the increased importance of an unscrupulous military and a bankrupt treasury.

Feuds and class differences that had been matters of life and death during the fighting—between aristocratic creoles and mestizos, between liberal anticlerics and the church, between monarchists and republicans, and rich and poor—remained unresolved. Worse, none of the social reforms hoped for by the masses fighting the war were instituted.

In its first 40 years, Mexico had more than 50 governments. Sometimes two or three different factions claimed the office simultaneously. One year there were as many as five changes in the presidency. The newly independent nation was ruled by military coups d'etat, not a constitution; graft, not government. Taking advantage of the unsettled political situation, foreign governments intervened.

These disturbing times have left the Mexican consciousness with one of its greatest heroes, the first Indian president, Benito Juárez, as well as a fully developed distrust of its northern neighbor, the United States, to whom half of Mexican territory was lost. It also defined, though did not fully end, the power struggles between the church and the modern secular state.

Emperor Iturbide

A significant misfortune for the new nation of Mexico was to have the disreputable Iturbide as its first leader. Joel Poinsett, a minister from the United States, described him as "distinguished for his immorality" in a society riddled with corruption. After staging an unruly demonstration in support of himself in the streets of the capital, Iturbide was able to bully the creole-dominated congress into making him the emperor of Mexico.

Iturbide was to govern a fledgling but enormous nation, covering 1.73 million square miles from California through Central America to Panama (see map on page 99). Its borders with the United States to the north and Belize to the south were not clearly demarcated, however. And not all its territories had participated in the War of Independence: some Central American governments had to be encouraged with the threat of invading troops to remain part of Mexico. Ferdinand VII of Spain had not completely accepted his expulsion and managed to keep troops on a fortress island in the Veracruz harbor. The United States was territory hungry, and both Great Britain and France were seeking special trade concessions.

As his first concern for leading such a vast nation plagued by so many foreign policy issues, the pompous ruler devoted himself to making elaborate plans for his coronation a few months later on July 21, 1822. A French baroness, former couturier to Napoleon, was hired to design costumes for the new emperor. A court etiquette was issued, outraging republican factions who deemed it inappropriate to be forced to kiss Iturbide's hand. A bankrupt nation issued new coins engraved with the emperor's portrait.

Economic Legacy

Iturbide and his creole supporters had thought that replacing the *peninsulares* in government would automatically rectify the ills of the Mexican economy. The profits would remain in Mexico, in creole pockets, and the taxes would support the new government. They had overlooked the 75 million peso debt the country had incurred during the War of Independence. They hadn't factored in the loss of gold and silver currency the *peninsulares* would take with them as they fled the country.

The mines themselves, near the primary battlegrounds for independence, were flooded and the machinery damaged, requiring considerable capital to return them to working order. Textile mills were closed because banditry and bad roads prevented the transport of cotton. Haciendas had been burned and sacked. Returning soldiers couldn't find jobs: as many as 20 percent of adult males were without work.

The colonial economy was destroyed. The first Mexican empire nonetheless lavished money on Iturbide, granting him a million-peso bonus. Congress appropriated 80 percent of its revenues—more than the viceroyalty had spent during the independence wars—for the emperor's cronies, the military. Nothing was invested in restarting the economy: not even the bloated military made an effort to open the roads for commerce. The country was at an economic impasse. When short of funds, the government attempted to borrow them, incurring more debt. When even those funds were insufficient, loans were decreed from the church or money confiscated from citizens.

It didn't take long for Iturbide to lose support. The devastated country-side could not properly provision the cities. The congress was outraged by Iturbide's arrest of enemies and censorship of the press—so the emperor dissolved it. Some creoles, embarrassed by Iturbide's excesses, wanted a European prince installed as monarch, but many a confirmed monarchist joined the republican side. When a military coup forced the emperor to abdicate his majestic office only eight months after coronation, Mexico's debt was as remarkable as the disarray of its government.

General Santa Anna

Mexico learned from the Iturbide interlude to distrust monarchies. A republic, governed by an elected congress and president, was established under the Constitution of 1824—a document that would be repealed and fought over, but returned to over time. Much to the chagrin of the monarchists and centralists, this federalist constitution divided the Republic of Mexico into 19 states and four territories (excluding the provinces of Central America, which declared their own independence in 1823). Catholicism was the state religion and the only permitted religion. There were free press and free speech. Indian tribute was abolished, in law if not always in deed. By 1829 slavery was officially ended, too. In reality, the new political order had minimal impact on the majority of Mexicans who lived in rural isolation and for whom voting rights mattered little because they were illiterate and, often, did not speak Spanish.

The 1824 Republic

Even under the republican regimes, military heroes of the Wars of Independence with no administrative experience, were elected to—or grabbed—the presidency. The first president, for example, was the rebel leader, Guadalupe Victoria. Uneducated, uncontrollably jealous of rivals, and unable to inspire the republic, he nonetheless did manage to continue the bad economic policies of the empire by spending more money on the military than revenues could sustain. Many of these military bosses, called *caudillos*, kept their politics more local, ruling the countryside with their band of armed adherents and ready to make trouble when their interests weren't served. They would usurp the power of all but a few presidents.

The most remarkable figure in this turbulent period was General Antonio López de Santa Anna (1794–1876). Repeatedly president of

Mexico, yet disgraced almost as often, exiled, and, in the end, executed for treason, Santa Anna's political life spanned the first critical decades of Mexican Independence. His opportunistic vascillation between liberal and conservative causes, his constant engagement in military coups and

Antonio López de Santa Anna, a creole born in the state of Veracruz, quickly found his niche in the military. Both as president and from behind the scenes, he controlled and disrupted Mexican politics from 1824–1855 and in the process made himself a millionaire. (Courtesy of the Bancroft Library)

foreign confrontations (he called himself the liberator of Mexico), his fine-tuning of political corruption, personified this era of anarchy.

Santa Anna first walked onto this historical stage under Iturbide. He was commander of Veracruz, charged with eliminating the sole remaining Spanish troops on an island fortress in Veracruz harbor. Instead, he declared against the unpopular Iturbide and formed an alliance with the old independence rebels, Guadalupe Victoria and Vicente Guerrero. After seeing the emperor depart Mexico, he returned to Veracruz to expel the Spaniards from their fortress in 1825.

Again and again Santa Anna issued pronouncements against various regimes. In 1829 he defeated 3,000 Spanish soldiers who had landed in Tampico on the Gulf coast in order to reconquer Mexico for Ferdinand VII. Finally he himself was elected president in 1833—he would hold office a total of 11 times—but instead of governing, he retreated to the sanctuary of his Veracruz hacienda and let his vice president, Valentín Gómez Farías, take care of the boring day-to-day details.

Church Power Confronted

Gómez Farías typified the more liberal element of the creoles. An anticleric, he subordinated the church and seized its properties for the greater welfare—an action that would repeatedly bring conservative reaction throughout the century. Like Morelos before him, Gómez Farías considered the wealth of the church wasteful: indeed, its wealth was estimated at 180 million pesos when the total annual Mexican budget was only 13 million. The church was powerful, its clergy numerous, yet most priests resided in the cities, leaving themselves open to charges that they inadequately administered to the faithful in smaller towns and rural areas. Since the church was responsible for educating the populace, their absence from the countryside also contributed to illiteracy, legitimizing the call of liberals like Gómez Farías for secular education.

Gómez Farías also tried to bring the military under greater state control. He attempted to reduce its size and to eliminate its exemption from civil trials. In doing so he took on at least one too many powerful groups. President and General Santa Anna bestirred himself from his hacienda and once again proclaimed. This time he marched against his own vice president, dismissed the congress, suspended the federalist constitution, and assumed dictatorial powers in 1834.

A charismatic figure, Santa Anna was able to contemptuously disregard the constitution and desperate needs of his country. While the

Mexico City During a Counterrevolt

Fanny Calderón de la Barca, the English wife of a Spanish diplomat, visited Mexico during the Santa Anna years and recorded her lively impressions in a diary. Here is her description of the capital during Santa Anna's military coup of 1840:

> . . . The chief danger to those who are not actually engaged in this affair, is from these bullets and shells, which come rattling into all the houses. We have messages from various people whom we invited to come here for safety, that they would gladly accept our offer, but are unwilling to leave their houses exposed to pillage, and do not dare to pass through the streets. . . . We were astonished this morning at the general tranquillity, and concluded that, instead of having attacked . . . the government was holding a parley . . . Innumerable carriages, drawn by mules, are passing along, packed inside and out, full of families hurrying to the country with their children and moveables. Those who are poorer, are making their way on foot—men and women carrying mattresses, and little children following with baskets and bird-cages. (234–36)

conservatives and liberals feuded over matters of substance, the president assumed the pomp and excessive show of a sultan. Having lost his leg in battle, he had it ceremoniously interred and enshrined in the presence of the entire cabinet and diplomatic corps. His greed and graft knew no limits during his last presidency when, assuming the title "His Most Serene Highness," he raided the treasury to finance lavish balls and build an opera theater as ornate as any in Europe. His blatant disregard for the well-being of the nation culminated in the act that would bring about his final downfall: he sold the Mesilla Valley, 30,000 square miles in southern Arizona and New Mexico, to the United States (where it was called the "Gadsden Purchase") in 1853 to pay for his extravagances.

The Alamo
Santa Anna's legacy to his nation was more than corrupt government. His role in the battle for Texas resulted in great territorial losses to the

United States. Not only did the president command the troops at the decisive battle of the Alamo, his policies precipitated the crisis. As a dictator, Santa Anna's sympathies were most naturally with the centralists. After the suspension of the federalist constitution in 1834, Mexico was reorganized into larger territories more directly under the control of the president. Various parts of the country, including Texas, agitated against these centralists shifts and had to be pacified by the army.

In the hope of limiting U.S. expansion into its colonies, Bourbon Spain had encouraged the settlement of Texas by favorable land-grant policies. The primary beneficiaries were Anglo-Americans from the United States who brought their slaves to till the fertile land and cultivate cotton. In exchange for nearly free land and initial tax exemptions, these settlers agreed to become Catholics and assume Mexican citizenship.

The land-grant system did at least part of what Spain expected: it settled Texas. Eventually, the immigrants outnumbered the Mexicans by more than 20,000 to 4,000. However, assimilation into Hispanic culture did not occur, and Anglos continued to speak English and practice the Protestant faith; cultural conflict between the groups were not uncommon. Centralism, however, incorporated Texas into a much larger, purely Mexican province, so that Anglo culture and economic interests were made subservient.

Before the outbreak of open rebellion, Mexico had seen the problems brewing in Texas. Mexico hoped that a by-product of outlawing slavery in 1829 would be to make Texas less attractive to U.S. citizens—it did allow Anglo-Texans a temporary exemption, however. In 1830, Mexico closed its borders to new immigrants but like today, the frontier between Mexico and the United States was extremely porous. Mexico also increased its customs duties on exports, greatly affecting Texan trade with the United States. There was also the threat of U.S. annexation: some private armies had already attempted to invade Texas. To protect its borders and territorial integrity, Mexico assigned more military units to the region.

Stephen Austin, son of the founder of the Anglo colony, protested both centralist policies and new customs regulations. Liberal Mexicans and U.S. politicians alike encouraged him to throw off the dictatorship of Santa Anna. When the Mexican government learned Austin was advocating separation under the name of the Lone Star Republic and encouraging Texans to arm themselves, President Santa Anna sent army reinforcements. When Austin forced their surrender and departure from Texas, the president himself led 6,000 troops to Texas.

> . . . zealous in the fulfillment of my duties to my country, [I] declared that I would maintain the territorial integrity whatever the cost . . . Stimulated by . . . courageous feelings I took command of the campaign myself, preferring the uncertainties of war to the easy and much coveted life of the palace.
>
> ■
> —*President Santa Anna, 1835 (1969:49–50)*

The rebel Texans, including Davy Crockett and Jim Bowie, barricaded themselves into the old Franciscan mission of the Alamo in San Antonio. General Santa Anna laid seige for several days. On March 6, 1835, his soldiers attacked the seemingly impassable walls and faced the heavy artillery of the Texans. Hundreds died while others broke through the walls. Government forces greatly outnumbered the Texans, and the government won, leaving not a single survivor.

A few weeks later another Mexican general surrounded the town of Goliad, forcing the Texan forces of Colonel James Fannin to surrender. Both sides understood that the Texans' rights as prisoners of war would be respected. But upon learning of the incident, Santa Anna ordered their execution as pirates.

More than the slaughter at the Alamo, the death of 365 prisoners galvanized public opinion in the United States. Supplies were sent. Volunteers joined the Texans. Within weeks, Sam Houston was in a position to strike back. The Mexican army was defeated, and Santa Anna was taken prisoner.

The peace treaty Santa Anna signed promised that all hostilities would cease and the Mexican army would withdraw south of the Río Bravo (as the Rio Grande is known in Mexico). Santa Anna, not at the moment stimulated to "courageous feelings," also signed a secret treaty that promised to arrange recognition of Texas as an independent republic in exchange for his personal freedom. An outraged Mexico refused to recognize either treaty.

Mexican-American War

From 1836 to 1845, Texas remained independent. Turbulent domestic politics and military revolts as well as a French invasion and the bubonic plague made any intervention too difficult. Yucatán, too, declared its independence, and Mexico concentrated its armies there from 1839 to 1842. But when President John Tyler introduced a joint resolution to the

U.S. Congress for the annexation of Texas, Mexico could ignore its northern frontier no longer and was brought to the brink of war.

More than Texas was at stake. The Lone Star Republic, now the 28th state, falsely claimed its western border to be the Rio Grande, which doubled its size. The additional territory included the heart of the old colony of New Mexico around Santa Fe and half of what is now Colorado. The United States, under President James K. Polk, not only claimed the disputed territory, but also wished to add California and the remainder of New Mexico to the package; these he was willing to purchase, however: $5 million for New Mexico, a minimum of $25 million for California. A total of 1 million square miles of territory was at stake.

When Mexicans learned that Polk's representative, George Slidell, was coming to Mexico to negotiate such an offer, they were indignant. Their national identity was at issue. Vast territories would be lost.

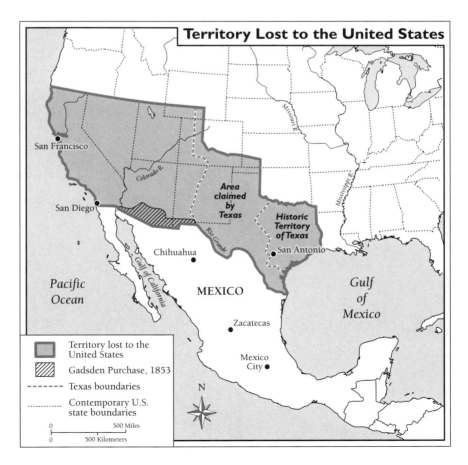

Territory Lost to the United States

Legend:
- Territory lost to the United States
- Gadsden Purchase, 1853
- Texas boundaries
- Contemporary U.S. state boundaries

0   500 Miles
0   500 Kilometers

Newspapers threatened rebellion if the government accepted the terms. While the Mexicans fulminated, Polk considered a declaration of war over the disputed territory. He decided to wait for an incident to justify such an act, and it came on May 9, 1846. General Zachary Taylor, leading his forces into the Mexican territory disputed by Texas, encountered resistance from the Mexican army. Sixteen of Taylor's soldiers were wounded or killed. Just enough for Polk to go to Congress for a declaration of war, disingenuously claiming that Mexico had invaded U.S. territory.

Instead of devoting itself to the awesome responsibility it confronted in the north, the Mexican army engaged in presidential politics. Finally, after a coup, General Santa Anna was installed again in office. By then, U.S. forces were already well organized. General Stephen Kearny marched on Santa Fe where he met no resistance. Leaving forces to occupy New Mexico, others went south to Chihuahua while Kearny headed for California. By the time Kearney arrived, California had already been taken by the navy under John Sloat and John Fremont. There had been little resistance. In Chihuahua, the Mexicans resisted but were poorly armed.

At Monterrey, however, General Taylor met the forces of General Pedro de Ampudia who was able to stall Taylor's advance by several days. Then Santa Anna arrived with a hastily assembled army of 20,000. The initial battle of Buena Vista was a stalemate: the next morning, fighting should have resumed. Instead, Santa Anna inexplicably began his return to Mexico City. Mexico's northern territories were lost.

Invasion of Mexico City

Mexico's losses were too great for its leaders to simply end the struggle. While they debated what to do, the United States under General Winfield Scott led the battle to the capital. Landing at Veracruz, Scott cleverly cut off the well-armed troops in the old island fortress by landing above the city and surrounding it from the rear. He then bombarded the helpless residents and ignored all appeals to let innocent women and children leave. A total of 6,700 shells bombarded the city. Civilian casualties were double that of the military. Veracruz finally surrendered.

Scott marched towards Mexico City. Santa Anna tried to cut him off but was either outmaneuvered or rejected by the citizenry who didn't want their cities devastated like Veracruz had been. The capital tried to prepare itself, but the old conflicts rendered a unified effort impossible.

Some thought the city was impossible to defend and that peace should be negotiated. Provincial leaders refused to contribute to the corrupt central government, and congress was reluctant to give the general the support he requested given his recent failures in battle.

The U.S. forces were well drilled and well supplied, and they outnumbered the Mexican troops. But on August 20, 1847, during the battle of Churubusco on the outskirts of the capital, the Mexicans fought hard. Even after intense hand-to-hand combat exhausted them, they refused to give up. Scott, believing the Mexicans defeated, asked for their surrender. Santa Anna used the negotiations to buy time and reinforce his position. Resuming the battle at Molina del Rey, 4,000 Mexicans were killed and wounded, 1,000 Americans. Scott marched on.

There was only one fortification of the city left: Chapultepec Castle. The castle, surrounded with land mines, was occupied by a military academy and defended by 1,000 soldiers and young cadets. Scott ordered the castle stormed on September 13. The land mines didn't explode, and the invaders were able to scale the walls. The cadets joined in the struggle, choosing death over surrender. It was the last battle. Santa Anna retreated and went into exile. Under the resultant treaty of Guadalupe Hidalgo (February 2, 1848), Mexico lost its vast northern territories (See map on page 121). As something of a compensation, the loss included less than 2 percent of the population and no known natural resources (until the San Francisco gold rush only months later corrected this misimpression). In exchange for its territory, Mexico received $18 million, less than half its annual budget.

For Mexicans, the U.S. invasion of the "Halls of Montezuma" is symbolized by the young cadets, called the "heroic children," or *Niños Héroes*, who died fighting at Chapultepec Castle on September 13, 1847. The cadets are immortalized in the street names of nearly every town. Statues depict their martyrdom throughout the republic, but none is more monumental than the one at the foot of Chapultepec Castle where it is said one cadet hurled himself wrapped in the Mexican flag. These battles would become a part of the new national consciousness, inevitably tinged with Yankeephobia.

Neo-colonialism: Mexico at Mid-Century

By the mid-18th century, Mexico was exhausted and humiliated. More than half of its territory had been lost to the United States, a country the liberals had admired and aspired to emulate. Apaches attacked northern settlement, and rebel Mayas almost took control of the entire Yucatán Peninsula in the Caste Wars (1847–49). In central Mexico, revolts and counterrevolts had created thousands of army deserters for whom banditry was the only means of support. The continuous upheaval had destroyed a considerable amount of property, some belonging to foreigners whose governments then demanded compensation. This situation created its own ludicrous results in 1838 when war with France followed Louis Phillip's demand for $600,000 in payment to a French chef for the pastries devoured by hungry Mexican soldiers in the city of Puebla. Mexico couldn't pay, so France sent its warships. (And Santa Anna came to the rescue once again, defeating the French troops in Veracruz.) The chaos made Mexican soil fair game for every adventurer: a Frenchman tried to create paradise lost in Sonora; an English pirate claimed Baja California.

With no peace, Mexico had made little progress since gaining independence. Foreign investment—British, French, and U.S.— had revived the mining industry, however; production had increased to the levels of the late 18th century by 1855. Here and there, especially in the increasing number of foreign-owned mines, more modern technology was introduced. For the future of Mexico, the problem would be that the creoles didn't invest their wealth in commerce and industry, leaving later Mexicans to struggle with the problem of foreign ownership of national resources.

MIXTECA SIERRA AND COCHINEAL

With independence, the Spanish elite who had exported cochineal left Oaxaca. During the decades of political turmoil, Oaxaca's economy became isolated from the rest of Mexico. By mid-century chemical dyes had destroyed the European market for cochineal. The Mixteca in the highlands of Oaxaca, so long favored by circumstances, fell on more difficult times. The number of aristocratic Mixtec *caciques* fell from 45 in 1700 to only eight. Then, noble titles were outlawed after independence, so that Mixtec *caciques* officially lost theirs along with the creole counts. A few continued to inherit their wealth, but they no longer were politically powerful. Even the family of the aristocratic *cacique* Gabriel Villagómez, descendant of the great 8 Deer "Tiger Claw," sold some of his estates.

THE MAYA CASTE WARS, 1847–49

In Yucatán, near the ancient city of Chichén Itzá, the Maya found the time had come, as foreseen by their prophets, to reclaim their land from the *dzul* ("whites"). They had been armed by Yucatecan creoles in a war for independence from Mexico, and they had been promised better conditions, which were not forthcoming. At the very moment Mexico was preoccupied in Texas, numerous villages joined together under the divine direction of the Maya-Christian cult of the Speaking Cross. They succeeded in battling the *dzul* practically into the sea. Those whites who remained were packing to leave Mérida, their last stronghold, when the Maya suddenly abandoned the fight in 1849. Sighting clouds of winged ants, the traditional sign of the first rain, the Maya had returned to plant their corn fields so as not to offend the gods of the *milpa*. The *dzul* fought back and by 1855 had regained their lands and control of central Yucatán. The rebel Maya retreated to the undeveloped Caribbean section on the peninsula where they maintained an independent state under the cult of the Speaking Cross until the beginning of the 20th century.

But mining, the one bright spot in the economy, functioned despite the obstacles. All commerce was impeded by the lack of transport. Apart from mule paths, there were three roads in deplorable condition; in 1860 there were only 15 miles of railroad tracks when the United States had 30,000, and bandits added to the expense of any commerce. A thriving national economy and unified people could hardly result from such circumstances. Marketing domestic products beyond the local level was next to impossible, although the textile mills in cities rapidly developed. On the international market Mexico continued to export raw products (92 percent of which were silver and gold) for foreign manufactured goods, remaining as industrially undeveloped as under Spanish rule but even poorer.

In principle, free trade with many nations—the United States, Britain, France—was an improvement over colonial times. It also provided the government with one of its few sources of taxable revenues, but custom duties became so high that smuggling often replaced sanctioned trade. There are no measures of the trade and production in this period; the chaos extended to official record keeping. Taxes proliferated—on windows, dogs, on *pulque* cantinas—and still Mexico defaulted on its loans.

There was a tax on every adult male, but even that tax was undermined by the wars, poverty, and social decay: population levels stagnated.

Despite the language of social equality found in the constitution, some historians argue that conditions for the poor actually worsened. At the very least they did not improve. The aristocratic creoles took on greater airs in replacing the *peninsulares*: most Mexicans they considered worthless rabble. Access to the best positions and to wealth remained open to very few. Indian lands were increasingly gobbled up by hacienda owners. Miners had to work four days in order to earn enough to buy a sack of corn. Entire families, children included, needed work to survive, yet work was too frequently unavailable. Sometimes the poor were not properly buried because they could not pay the church fee. Educational opportunities were as scarce as any route to improvement; at best, one in 10 Mexicans was literate. The society remained so unchanged—despite years of war and devastation in the name of human rights—that many called the first century of independence the "neo-colonial" period.

Cultural Life at Mid-Century

The barbaric European overlooks nothing.
He breaks, fells, and annihilates
With an army of fury.
It's his pleasure to convert
Cities into desert wastes.
(What honorable deeds!)
■
—Ignacio Rodríguez Galván "Profecía de Guatimoc," 1839
(after John Lloyd Read 1939:59)

The creole failure to modify the social order was not for want of ideas. The intelligentsia agitated for change, arguing for the elimination of debt peonage and for improved schools. In this post-independence period, romantic poets and writers searched for a uniquely national identity; they attacked some of the most central tenets of the European-focused creoles. Mexican civilization began with its pre-Columbian heritage, they argued, not with the barbarity of the Spanish conquest: Mexicans were Americans, not Europeans. Even the spelling of "Méjico," they argued, should be changed to the more Indian "México." A literary society, the Academia de San Juan de Letrán, included the best playwright, Fernando Calderón (1809–49), whose works satirized Santa Anna, and the foremost poet, Ignacio Rodríguez Galván (1816–42). Rodríguez's most famous poem, "Profecía de Guatimoc," is dedicated to the Aztec emperor, Cuauhtémoc.

In art, sculptors like Pedro Patiño Ixtolinque found patriotic subjects in pre-Columbian rulers and heroes of independence. These historical themes were echoed in paintings and woodblock prints, and in the search for a national identity, the native landscape of volcanoes and tropical exuberance, Indian ruins and Catholic churches. These beginnings of a national art lost their impetus, temporarily, when Santa Anna hired all European teachers for the Academy of San Carlos. Outside the academy, however, provincial artists, such as José María Estrada (active 1830–60), Agustín Arrieta (1802–74), and Herme- neguildo Bustos (1832–1907), left an enchanting legacy of local life in their portraits and still lifes.

The Liberals and Benito Juárez

Adversity discourages none but the contemptible.
■
—Benito Juárez, 1867 (Smart:276)

In 1855, the Liberal Party chased Santa Anna and the Conservatives out of government. The country, fed up and desiring a government that might unify the nation, gave an unusually broad base of support to the liberals in the armed struggle known as the Revolution of Ayutla. Based on the principles promulgated in the Constitutional Convention of Ayutla (March 1, 1854), they were committed to free and honest elections, free public education, the separation of church and state, and a federalist republic as delineated in the Constitution of 1824.

The liberals were members of the younger intelligentsia. Some were poets, such as Guillermo Prieto. Some were Renaissance men, such as Melchor Ocampo who was a naturalist as well as the translator of French political works and a student of Indian languages. All had been active in politics: Prieto had been jailed by Santa Anna; Ocampo had been gover- nor of Michoacán. Many were exiled by Santa Anna to Louisiana, where they formed a revolutionary group. Numerous liberals were mestizos and other peoples of color who had worked their way through the ranks of the army or had managed to obtain an education.

The most famous leader, and certainly the individual most indicative of a new social order, was Benito Juárez (1806–72). A Zapotec Indian who is often described as the Abraham Lincoln of Mexico, Juárez was born in a hamlet in the highlands of Oaxaca. Orphaned at the age of three, he had the good fortune, when going to the city of Oaxaca at 12 years of age, to work for a Franciscan friar who paid for his education. Upon graduating from law school, Juárez entered politics and eventually became governor of Oaxaca where he was recognized for his honest management of the state. Like other liberals, he was later exiled by Santa Anna.

Portrait of Benito Juárez *(1871), by José Escudero y Espronada in the National Museum of History, Mexico City*

The Reform Laws

The new Liberal government, with Juárez as secretary of justice, targeted the church and military for its most controversial reforms. The Ley Juárez eliminated the special exemption the clergy and military received from standing trial in civil courts—even for crimes such as rape and murder. As they had in reaction to previous attempts at change, conservative creoles, clergy, and militia rallied themselves into a frenzy. Although forced to install a new president, the liberals remained in power.

But the new president also antagonized the conservatives by promulgating the Ley Lerdo (1856). This law, acceptable to the moderates for the revenues it would generate, required all institutions, both religious and secular, to divest themselves of property not used in their normal operations. States would keep the governor's mansion and office buildings, for example, but all other properties would be sold at public auction. For the church, with its vast holdings beyond its churches and monasteries, the losses would be particularly painful.

The next reform sensibly gave the state the power of registering births, marriages, deaths, and the like, instead of the church. In the Ley Iglesias it also deprived the church of the right to set its own fees: no longer could the poor be forced to pay for receiving the sacraments. All these reforms were incorporated into the new Constitution of 1857, along with freedom of speech and press, freedom of education and, for the first time in Mexico, freedom of religion. Only this last article was defeated by the Catholic church.

There were disastrous consequences of the Reform Laws. One was the effect of the Ley Lerdo on traditional Indian villages. Although the independence hero Morelos had argued for something akin to the Ley Lerdo, he had wanted to redistribute church properties to benefit the poor. Nothing of the sort occurred under the liberal Reform Laws, because only the wealthy could afford to buy the properties. And included in the auctioned properties were *ejido* lands, the communal farms belonging to the Indian villages. Under the republic, the separately functioning Indian communities had been outlawed—after all, free and equal Indians could vote along with non-Indians for the municipal government. The Indians, however, rarely gained office even when they constituted the majority. Communal Indian lands were absorbed by the larger municipality and, under Ley Lerdo, were sold to pay off state debts. The aristocratic *caciques* were thereby deprived of the last vestiges of their political power and Indian communities lost their voice in Mexican affairs. Ley Lerdo not only created larger estates for the rich, it severely

129

undermined the autonomy so long enjoyed by indigenous peoples in more remote areas, such as Oaxaca and Yucatán. For this reason, the liberal reforms have been called "the second conquest."

Another result of the reforms was war. Anticlericalism had been resisted by the church since the struggle for independence, and the church reacted once again. The wealthy were threatened with excommunication for purchasing church property. Those who swore allegiance to the constitution also would be excommunicated. Pope Pius IX entered the fray, declaring the Mexican constitution "null and void" in regard to the "Most Holy Religion." The state required an oath of support from its civic officials, and those who worried about the consequences with the church lost their jobs. In this devoutly Catholic nation, the church and Mexican state polarized the entire society.

The Reform War: 1858–61

Once again Mexico found itself incurably divided into two camps: this time the issue was the proper function of the church in Mexico. The army declared the conservative General Félix Zuloaga, president. Many liberals escaped north to Querétaro where Benito Juárez was declared president.

THE MIXTECA SIERRA

Although the glory days of the Mixtec aristocracy passed with cochineal, geography continued to protect the Mixteca villages from the ravages experienced by other traditional communities of Mexico. Despite the Ley Lerdo, the region retained most of its communal lands. Sugar cane had replaced cochineal in Oaxaca as the profitable cash crop, but *hacendados* had little interest in growing it in the mountainous Mixteca Sierra. As one Mixtec village appealed to the government in its effort to be exempted from the law:

> we lack lands that are called "plough lands" since the places where it is not steep hillsides are rocky and cut by ravines.
>
> ■
>
> —*Eusebio López, Mayor of Nuyoo, 1856 (quoted in John Monaghan:264)*

A war ensued. The clergy and military supported Zuloaga. But some Indians did, too, such as the Yaqui in the north, because the liberal's Ley Lerdo had deprived them of their *ejido* lands. Others were convinced that the Zapotec Juárez would have their best interests at heart.

Mexico was again at war, this time for three years. Many noncombatants were treated brutally. The conservatives shot doctors who treated liberal soldiers; the liberals abused priests who wouldn't administer to them. Thousands of innocents were wounded. Haciendas were burned, and churches were used as stables. The war continued until the liberals defeated the conservatives, marching into Mexico City on January 1, 1861.

French Intervention: Cinco de Mayo

Juárez was elected president. The treasury was empty. Juárez declared a two-year moratorium on payment of foreign debt—some of it outstanding since Iturbide's time. The Europeans, who had had their citizens wounded or killed and their silver shipments stolen, were driven to action. France, England, and Spain, with the pope's blessing, agreed to a joint occupation of the customs house at Veracruz. Without interfering with Mexico's right to govern itself, they intended to garnishee the receipts to pay off their loans.

Close to 9,000 foreign troops landed in Veracruz in 1862. It soon became clear that the French had designs on Mexico that extended beyond the repayment of loans. In fact, Mexican conservatives in exile had been agitating in Europe for the installation of a monarch. France, under Napoleon III, had agreed. Spain and Britain withdrew their troops in protest. And 6,500 French soldiers marched towards Puebla with the intention of occupying Mexico. On May 5 (the famous date of "cinco de mayo" in Spanish), the Mexicans routed the French in Puebla under the leadership of General Ignacio Zaragoza and Brigadier General Porfirio Díaz. It would be a year before the French could resume their march.

More Anticlerical Reforms

Such a long-awaited victory against at least one of Mexico's many foreign invaders became a rallying cry for the nation, except for the conservatives, who thought that only through the reinstitution of a European monarchy could authority—and peace—be achieved. Aristocratic creoles aided the French troops. Conservative guerrillas assassinated liberals in the countryside, including such luminaries as Melchor Ocampo.

Priests used their Sunday pulpits to support the French and advocated the overthrow of the Juárez government.

The Reform Laws had most affected the clergy, and they had been sharpened during the Reform War, when new laws were issued that clearly made the church subservient to the state. All church properties had been confiscated. Monasteries were closed. Public religious displays were curtailed. Now, in an attempt to end what he perceived as the traitorous influence of the church, Juárez decreed that the religious were forbidden to wear their vestments in public and threatened imprisonment to any priest fostering disrespect for the government and its laws.

Juárez's efforts, however, didn't stop the French government from creating the second empire in his country. With the United States embroiled in its own civil war, Napoleon realized he could proceed unchallenged. Thirty thousand additional troops were sent to Mexico. Puebla was taken after a two-month siege that reduced its populace to eating rats. The Mexican army was decimated. Juárez, realizing he didn't have the troops to defend Mexico City, evacuated the capital and withdrew the government to the north, establishing it near the U.S. border in what is now El Paso.

Maximilian and Carlota

In consultation with Napoleon III, arch-conservative Mexicans selected the Austrian archduke, Ferdinand Maximilian of Hapsburg as the vehicle for restoring themselves and the church to power in Mexico. Maximilian stipulated that he must have the support of the Mexican people before he took the throne of Mexico, yet the eager conservatives failed to perceive his liberalism. And the ill-fated Maximilian believed their cynical assertions that a plebiscite of the Mexican people had resoundingly approved him as emperor.

Maximilian and his beautiful wife Carlota, the Belgian princess born as Marie Charlotte Amélie Léopoldine, were both romantics and youthful in their innocence—he was 32 and she only 24. Embracing Mexico and all things Mexican, they disappointed the Europeanized conservatives. Endorsing the Reform Laws, they scandalized them. As foreign interlopers, not even their liberalism and idealism could prevent them from being enemies of Juárez; as monarchs, the republican government in exile could only plot to overthrow them.

The second Mexican empire endured for only a few years. Arriving in Veracruz on May 28, 1864, Maximilian was forced to surrender three years later. On June 19, 1867, he was executed by the Juaristas. In those years, the French constantly were fending off the guerrilla attacks of the liberals. They managed to pacify only parts of central Mexico, and in 1865 they captured Oaxaca from Porfirio Díaz. But the struggle was unceasing. At one point the army deceived Maximilian by claiming Juárez had given up and had withdrawn to the United States. Arguing for summary execution of all remaining republican agitators, they were granted permission by the emperor—who thereby sealed his own fate.

In the capital, the royal couple established their court at Chapultepec Castle but did not isolate themselves. They received the people weekly to learn about their concerns and toured the countryside to acquaint themselves with their realm, which they found quite beautiful. When it was suggested that a marble arch should be dedicated to Carlota, Maximilian thought one commemorating Mexican independence would be better. He outlawed debt peonage, and he granted communal lands to Indian villages that had lost them under the reforms. Yet none of these sympathetic acts could redeem the foreigner in the eyes of most Mexicans.

No sooner did the U.S. Civil War end, than President Lincoln threw his support behind Juárez. Having fought its own war of independence, the United States had declared in the Monroe Doctrine that the Americas were off limits to European colonization. Juárez was permitted to purchase arms, and 3,000 Union soldiers joined his army. The United States advised the French to leave, and Napoleon, also under pressure in Europe, recalled his troops in late 1866.

With the French army gradually withdrawing, Maximilian found he had few choices left. The conservatives no longer approved of him; the liberals never would. He considered abdicating the throne. Carlota convinced him to remain while she traveled to France and then to Rome to secure support. But neither Napoleon nor Pope Pius IX, who was disgruntled that church lands had not been restored, was willing to help. Carlota went insane and was institutionalized in Europe.

By the end of 1867, the Juaristas had recaptured much of northern Mexico and Oaxaca. Most of the French had withdrawn. Maximilian still considered abdication. Instead, as a gesture of his Hapsburg pride, he joined the last French troops in the city of Querétaro. The Juaristas surrounded them. Maximilian resisted for 100 days. His entourage arranged for his safe escape; he refused, finding it more dignified to stand his ground and surrender.

Juárez ordered that Maximilian be tried for violation of Mexico's sovereignty and, when found guilty, executed. Mexicans, both men and women, implored him not to kill the well-meaning emperor. Presidents and monarchs from around the world appealed to him for clemency. Juárez, however, could not forget the executions of his own men ordered by Maximilian nor the 50,000 Mexicans who had died fighting the French. He followed the letter of the law. Maximilian faced the firing squad.

The Restored Republic, 1867

While the story of Carlota and Maximilian has captured the imagination of filmmakers and romance writers, the reality for Mexico of this quixotic interlude was not so inspirational. The nation was saddled with Maximilian's war debt, which Juárez refused to pay. The economy was even more deeply disrupted and local *caudillos*, or political bosses, had more power than ever. The foreign debt in 1867 was 375 million pesos in contrast to 56 million in 1850. There wasn't a peso in the treasury.

Although the war against the French defined a new sense of nationalism, the anarchy had intensified regional autonomy at the expense of federal control. Thirteen years of war had destroyed the conservative army that always had been ready to stage a counterrevolt; yet many ambitious *caudillos* were included in the liberal army. And the underclasses—Indians, shop keepers, laborers—had been asked to fight the French, empowering them in a way that they had not experienced since Hidalgo.

Having temporarily quieted their conservative opponents and having moved the church out of politics and education, the liberal party had to control its own internal divisions. The middle class thought the large landowners (also members of the party because of the windfall property obtainable through the reforms) should take their fair burden of the taxes. Instead, many *hacendados* paid no more than landless workers. The poor thought there should be a major redistribution of the *hacendados'* land. The rifts were there, but while Benito Juárez was alive, the party united behind him.

The Juárez Presidencies, 1867–76

> Until Juárez took control, Mexico never was governed.
> ■
> —*Justo Sierra, 1867*

Under Benito Juárez, Mexico finally experienced a period of extended political stability and peace. As a civilian president, he stood in marked contrast to the military heroes who had dominated politics since independence. In 1867 he was elected to his third term as president: the first one that would not be interrupted by war.

Juárez's popularity in no small part helped prevent the usual military coups, but he also had to juggle many competing interests in the liberal party. To keep the *hacendados* behind him, Juárez granted them absolute privileges over their domains—no small matter when some, such as the Terrazas family, owned properties in the north the size of a state and when the injustices of debt peonage had yet to be eliminated. The middle class was pleased with the increasing number of positions in the government bureaucracy and the growing number of public schools in the cities, from fewer than 2,500 in 1857 to over 8,000 in 1874.

The liberals were basically satisfied with Juárez's public policies as well. Although the federalist state had become more centralist, the elections were more open than they had ever been, if not totally free of state tampering. The press was free and, indeed, intellectuals such as Ignacio Altamirano (1834–95), an Indian historical novelist, didn't hesitate to criticize the president. The anticlerical reforms remained intact, though no one contested the church's quiet procurement of new urban properties. And congress was strengthened as a branch of government.

There were serious problems, however. To control the military and to save the treasury money, Juárez dismissed 40,000 of the 60,000 soldiers who had fought the French. Many *caudillos* were furious, expecting more spoils from the war; some plotted against Juárez—including the hero of Cinco de Mayo, Porfirio Díaz. The unemployed soldiers added their numbers to the bandits already plaguing the countryside, making all travel unsafe and attacking rural towns and haciendas.

The land problem, exacerbated by the Reform Laws and Juárez's favorable policies for *hacendados*, was an explosive issue for the Indians —one that would divide the country just as the church had done. Juárez was sympathetic to certain checks on debt peonage, but congress overruled him. Indian revolts were increasing, squatters frequently took over hacienda land until federal soldiers arrived. Famine, such as that in 1869, further inflamed the situation. Some estimate that one fifth of the population was dispossessed, scavaging for food in the countryside or begging in the city streets.

Peace, however, and a conscientious government, enabled some improvements in the economy, especially in the area of transportation. A railroad was built between Veracruz and the capital; roads were upgraded for stagecoach travel. A police force, called the *rurales*, provided increased security on the roads, which facilitated commerce. Commerce did improve. Although cochineal had become inconsequential, hide exports were 20 times greater than during the viceroyalty, and Yucatán profitably exported sisal, or *henequén*, for making rope and cordage. Lumber and coffee became major exports, too. Yet gold and silver retained their number one position, especially with the opening of new mines in northern regions such as Chihuahua.

Mexico attempted to attract both foreign settlers and foreign investment. Given its recent history, however, Mexico was considered a poor risk. Some capital found its way to the mining and textile industries. European immigration was encouraged in the hopes of gaining skilled labor and increasing the population. With so many deaths due to war and high infant mortality, Mexico's population remained under 9 million in 1874—only 2 million more than at the end of the colonial period. Yet by 1876 a mere 25,000 Mexican residents were foreign born.

Stable Juárez Period Ends

In 1871, Juárez decided to seek a fourth term—against sound liberal principle. He appeared an absolutist rather than the constitutional president he had been. It was a hotly contested election with three candidates: Juárez, General Porfirio Díaz, and Sebastián Lerdo de Tejada, chief justice of the Supreme Court. No one won a majority, so congress decided the matter in favor of Juárez. Lerdo came in second. Díaz, like so many military *caudillos* before him, proclaimed himself in revolt. Few joined him and Díaz was defeated—temporarily.

On July 19, 1872, Benito Juárez died of a heart attack. As chief justice, Lerdo succeeded him as dictated by the Constitution of 1857. In the next election Lerdo was chosen for president over Díaz by a massive majority and continued the progressive policies of his party. In a few years he had further increased the number of primary schools and had contracted for more railroads. He also connected all the provincial capitals by telegraph wires. Less popular was his diligent implementation of the Reform Laws, closing convents and confiscating church properties.

Foundations of the Modern State

Until the French invasion, it would have been hard to discern more than factionalism and wars and their disruptive effects on the population in 19th-century Mexico. After the French intervention, Mexico became a more unified nation, and when Juárez died in 1872 the country had at least experienced a constitutional and democratic government. Progress had been made in separating religious and civil authority, and Lerdo had continued upholding the laws of the constitutional republic. General Porfirio Díaz, however, would reverse the course that had been so painfully set.

THE PORFIRIATO DICTATORSHIP

1876-1910

Don Porfirio's slogan was "Bread and the
Club": bread for the army, bread for the
bureaucrats, bread for the foreigners, and even
bread for the Church—and the club for the common
people of Mexico and those who differed with him.
■
—Lesley Byrd Simpson (1962:258)

For 34 years Mexico was ruled by a man who fought his way into power on the slogan of "no reelection": Porfirio Díaz. This dictator left an extraordinary legacy. He attracted foreign capital and modernized the economy. Cities were beautified and the countryside rid of banditry. His most exceptional legacy, however, was the Revolution of 1910. Because all he achieved was at the expense of the Mexican people, he is considered the villain in 20th-century Mexican history. It is not his statue that graces village squares, but rather that of Francisco Madero, who stood against him for democracy; it is not Díaz who rides the white horse in Mexican muralist art, but rather Emiliano Zapata who fought for the return of peasant lands. These events, the Porfiriato dictatorship and the Revolution, have defined contemporary Mexico.

No Reelection

Since independence, the uncompromising factionalism of Mexico had benefited the military. First, it created Emperor Iturbide. Then His Most Serene Highness Santa Anna. With Juárez the country took a breather from generals, if not from war. And finally the political process of pronouncements and revolt favored yet another *caudillo*, General Porfirio

Díaz (1830–1915). Díaz, a mestizo born of a Mixtec Indian mother, was from Juárez's state of Oaxaca. He went through a similar educational process as Juárez but never finished law school. After joining the army, he became a national hero of the liberal cause during the battle of Cinco de Mayo. Later he liberated the capital, as well as Puebla and Oaxaca, from the French and took up a position in congress under Juárez.

Initially Díaz tried to get himself elected president legitimately, arguing that Juárez and Lerdo, by seeking reelection, were despots not democrats. After losing, in good *caudillo* fashion, he proclaimed against the government and led an armed revolt on the principle of "no reelection." The idea was quite popular with the middle class, because—when extended to municipal and state elections—it meant that a lot more people would have a chance at office. Against Lerdo, Díaz succeeded in toppling the government. And during his first term (1876–80) he unified the country behind him when the United States, under President Hayes, encroached on Mexican territorial sovereignty by permitting its soldiers, who were in pursuit of Apaches, to cross into Mexico. Díaz held firm, despite threats of war by the United States, and gained considerable popularity by standing on principle.

But Díaz would soon be found to hold few principles so strongly as to defeat his own interests. The Constitution of 1857 stood. Why bother to create the controversy that would be aroused by repealing it when it could simply be ignored? So compelling was the principle of no reelection, however, that Díaz arranged for a stand-in candidate his second term. After his third, no one dared complain, but to maintain a facade of legality, the law was changed to permit unlimited terms at every level. All other officials, local and federal, were handpicked by Díaz and held their positions as long as they were in favor. And when they were not in favor, they more often than not were assassinated by Díaz's personal police called the *Bravi*. Elections continued throughout the Porfiriato; but because the outcomes were always known in advance, few bothered to vote.

Pax Porfiriana

> There are no drunken riots . . . little thieving . . .
> The least disorderly action, even loud talking
> in the streets, causes prompt arrest . . .
> ◼
> —J. Hendrickson McCarty, 1888

Given the decades of Mexican anarchy, Díaz's ability to forge a strong centralized Mexican state is a testament to his political toughness as much as it is to Mexico's exhaustion. Díaz faced the usual disruptions in the countryside during his first term. There were peasant uprisings, Apache raids, and more than one revolt by a regional chief. By expanding the rural police force, the *rurales*, Díaz quickly put any such trouble down. And he did so ruthlessly. Under Díaz, the *rurales* included notorious bandits who were permitted to murder anyone and justify their acts by the Ley Fugo: "Shot while trying to escape." Operating outside the constraints of any due process, the *rurales* were known for their fearlessness against presumed enemies of the regime. Well paid by Díaz, their loyalty was unquestioned. Order was achieved.

Díaz used more than repression in consolidating his power. He was a political wizard capable of conciliating and co-opting the various factions of the middle and upper classes. The army, for example, was appeased by a larger budget and new weapons at the same time it was decentralized and depoliticized by the simple expedient of assigning soldiers in smaller battalions to different regions on a constant rotation. In a classic Díaz maneuver of balancing one group against another, he created several militia groups, such as the *rurales*, to compete with the army. The church was satisfied that Díaz did not actively enforce the Reform Laws, permitting them to build up their properties and wealth and to reopen their schools. Although the anticlerical constitution was technically still in effect, Mexico under Díaz encouraged the clergy to expand in number from the 500 under Juárez to 5,000.

The middle class, the intelligentsia, the petty *caudillos*, and the haughty creoles supported Díaz because he brought them increased prosperity. He did so by doing all the right things to attract foreign capital and know-how. First, his Pax Porfiriana enabled commerce to resume unimpeded. Second, he stabilized the government by buying off the various factions. And third, but no less astonishing, he gradually put the government on a sound financial footing. Continuing Juárez's policy of streamlining the government, Díaz brought in professional financiers such as José Yves Limantour to manage the budget. By 1894, the budget was balanced; in 1910, there was a comfortable surplus.

Modernization

In 1876 Mexico was basically the same feudal society as during the viceroyalty, and while rigid social stratification had yielded to permit more people of color into the ranks of power, most of the population was unskilled and living in peonage. Three-quarters of the society was rural.

Only in the cities was there any sophistication. Modernization was practically nonexistent: oxen, not tractors, plowed the fields, and most silver was extracted with 16th-century technology. Mexico City, which was regularly flooded during the rainy season, was less capable of building dikes and ditches than Aztec Tenochtitlán. The ports, even Veracruz, were in need of dredging. Instead of trains, burros and human carriers (used since pre-Columbian times) transported goods.

Díaz believed modernization would come only with foreign capital and the emigration of skilled Europeans. Government policies, such as special tax and legal exemptions, were implemented. Laws were passed not only permitting investors to profit from the products they extracted, but granting them subsoil rights that had previously been reserved for the government: a boondoggle for investors in the case of metals and petroleum.

With domestic peace and a sensible budget, Mexico was deemed one of the most creditworthy nations in the world. Foreign loans were readily available and were repaid in a timely fashion. Investors liked the welcoming attitude and privileges offered to them. Hydroelectric plants were built. Steam and water power became available for modern machinery —5,500 textile mills and cement factories, sugar and flour refineries, and

Citlaltépetl *(1879), a painting by José María Velasco in the National Museum of Art, Mexico City*

141

IMPORT AND EXPORT GROWTH DURING THE PORFIRIATO				
Millions of Pesos	1877	1890	1900	1910
500				XX(488)
450				
400				
350				
300				
250			XX(@275)	
200				
150				
100		XX(@110)		
50	XX			

Source: Estadísticas Económicas del Porfiriato: Comercio Exterior de México. Mexico, 1960

breweries were the result by 1902. Telephones and telegraphs linked the nation. The first steel mill in Latin America produced 60,000 tons annually from Monterrey, which was fast becoming the industrial capital of Mexico. The British built a six-mile tunnel through the mountains that protected the capital from flooding. Foreign monies and technology dredged the harbor of Veracruz and improved ports such as Tampico, Manzanillo, and Maza-tlán: foreign trade increased nearly tenfold during the Porfiriato. Silver and other metals were more easily extracted with new technology: silver production quadrupled, gold increased from 1.5 million pesos in 1877 to 40 million 11 years later; copper became a major export.

The greatest impact on Mexico was the completion of a rail network of more than 15,000 miles by 1910. Subsidized by the Mexican government, the railroads were constructed by foreign companies and owned by foreign banks. Around 1908, Mexico took a controlling interest in most of them to form the National Railways of Mexico—many claimed it overpaid to appease foreign interests. The tracks radiated from the capital to major cities such as Guadalajara, Puebla, Monterrey, and Oaxaca; they connected the coasts from the Pacific to the Gulf and linked the major ports with production centers and Mexico City with its Guatemalan frontier. Initially, the lines extending to the Texan border at El Paso and Laredo and from Guaymas on the Pacific to Nogales, Arizona created considerable concern. Mexicans feared, after the losses in the Texas wars, that the railways would simply facilitate a U.S. takeover of the rest of Mexico.

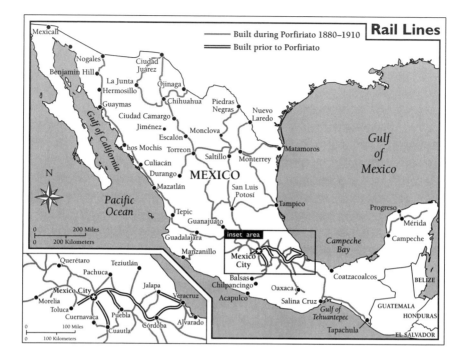

Rail Lines

Built during Porfiriato 1880–1910
Built prior to Porfiriato

The railroad network had its gaps—for example Yucatán was not connected at all. Yet it unified much of Mexico and helped Díaz control the various regions with a stronger arm: troops could arrive quickly to any problem area. But above all, the railroads enabled the Mexican economy to develop more rapidly than ever before. For the first time, cotton arrived expeditiously and affordably to the textile mills and silver to the smelters and ports. Shipping costs were lowered so much by rail transit that what had cost $67 to ship in 1877 cost only $3 in 1910. The trains created a profitable domestic and export market for agricultural surpluses: farm exports, sisal, and goat hides, for example, generated more than 100 million pesos, up from 7 million.

The Gilded Age

The impact of a strengthened economy and a modernized infrastructure on Mexico cannot be underestimated. Those who benefited from the economy—most of the middle and upper classes—gained a new sense of pride in their country. European governments gave honors to Díaz.

Visitors from abroad extolled the nation's progress. With peace, the population grew to more than 15 million, and the population of Mexico City finally exceeded the population of Aztec Tenochtitlán at 470,000.

Most of the population growth was in the cities, especially Monterrey, Chihuahua, and Durango in the more industrialized north. But smaller towns such as Salina Cruz, now reachable by train, also blossomed. The commerce brought a construction boom and an expanding middle class that resided mostly in the cities. Government workers and school teachers, skilled artisans and professionals, clergy and petty army officers increased in number and income; initially from the lower classes, they now could afford indoor plumbing, some fashionable clothes, and meat a few times a week.

Mexico was more confident, but not so much so that it didn't borrow European culture and fashion. The literati studied the classics. Cities such as Guanajuato and Mérida built magnificent Belle Epoque opera houses, importing Italian marble and artisans to create them even though Mexico had marble and skilled artisans of its own. The upper classes sent their children to French universities, joined French cultural societies, and assumed the latest French fashions (see page 147). The bishop of Mérida was transported in a jewel-encrusted carriage from Paris. An opera by Gustavo Campo on Nahuatl poet and king Nezahuacóyotl was entitled in French, not Spanish.

For all its pretense at progress, the Porfiriato did little to improve educational opportunities. The middle classes in the cities and women found schooling more accessible, but higher education remained almost exclusively the preserve of the elite. Rural areas, predominated by poor peons and Indians, were even less well served. The number of schools did double; the number of teachers almost did too, although they were paid no more than a housemaid. Yet the population doubled as well. The national illiteracy rate was 80 percent.

In the mid-19th century, Fanny Calderón de la Barca despaired that "the women of the landed class were condemned to a life, the vapidity of which makes us yawn at the very thought." Their education was neglected; most were as illiterate as they were gracious and kind. During the Porfiriato an increasing number of women were educated for the professions. The first woman graduated from the medical school in Mexico City in 1887 and a commercial school for women was opened to great demand in 1903. A feminist group, the Admiradoras de Juárez, was founded in 1904.

Intellectuals and artists were able to pursue their interests as long as they did not criticize the dictatorship. Some journalists and newspaper publishers found this difficult: Filomena Mata was jailed 34 times for the independence of his publication. The period did produce sophisticated literature in the modernist tradition, which eschewed politics for a purer art-for-art's-sake aesthetic. Amado Nervo (1870–1919) was the most talented and prolific writer, best known for his first novel, *El bachiller* (1895). Typical of the age, he resided in Paris. Historians produced scholarly studies of the long-past (hence politically safe) colonial period, such as Joaquín García Icazbalceta's (1824–94) biography of Bishop Zumárraga. Justo Sierra (1848–1912), Díaz's minister of education, wrote *México: su evolución social*, an interpretive history of the nation.

Positivism was the dominant intellectual movement and the one that rationalized Díaz's dictatorship. This philosophy, also borrowed from France, originated with the emphasis on scientific thinking in the philosophy of Auguste Comte. Positivists, called *científicos* in Mexico, controlled the highest governmental positions. They argued that the country's problems could be solved by the application of statistics and sound thinking. Rational policies and social order would bring the nation

Porfirio Díaz and the Científicos *(1957–60), a mural by David Alfaro Siqueiros in the National Museum of History, Mexico City*

to the level of Europe and the United States. This thinking was never more effective than in Minister Limantour's handling of national finances. However, the policies were less "scientific" when a dash of Social Darwinism was added to preserve the privileges of creoles and the ruling class, who argued that only they were fit to govern. Mexico wasn't ready for democracy, Justo Sierra said from the Ministry of Education. And the indigenous masses, inferior according to these *científicos*, would never be ready.

European tastes predominated in art, setting back the national themes that had prevailed after independence, especially during Maximilian's reign. The capital's most elegant avenue, the Paseo de la Reforma, had been designed by Maximilian, but was not sufficiently European for aristocrats of the Porfiriato. It was redesigned to look more like Paris's Champs-Élysées and lined with statues, many commissioned from abroad. Don Porfirio also found little in national art appealing. The Mexican entry at the Paris World Fair of 1889 was neo-Greek in style and flanked by sphinxes. The dictator appointed a director of the Academy of San Carlos who agreed with his preferences and who brought in many other European instructors to "civilize" local tastes.

Fortunately, fashion didn't dictate all art of the period. Many artists continued to seek a Mexican style. José María Velasco (1840–1912) and José Guadalupe Posada (1852–1913) created works that are among the finest examples of art. The soft grandeur of Velasco's Mexican landscapes (see page 141) derive from the academic tradition. In fact, Velasco was an instructor at the academy and one of Diego Rivera's early teachers. By contrast, Posada (see page 147) was trained as a printer's apprentice. He created his expressive and often fantastic engravings for street gazettes; his illustrations of folk ballads and his political satires and amusing *calaveras* (skulls) for Day of the Dead editions were meant for popular audiences. The Daumier of Mexico, Posada created what is considered the earliest example of the modern Mexican art style that predominated after the Revolution.

Foreign Dependency

> The North American, the foreigner, had prospered
> in Mexico, but not its native sons.
> ■
> —*Regis Planchet, 1906 (quoted by Charles C. Cumberland)*

Just about everything in Mexico was foreign owned. There were more than 1,000 mining companies: 85 percent were American and a few of

La catrina *(1913), metal cut by José Guadalupe Posada in the National Museum of Prints, Mexico City, satirizes the French fashions of the Porfiriato.*

them, such as Daniel Guggenheim's American Smelting and Refining Company and Anaconda Copper Company, operated many different mines in most of the states in northern Mexico with a total value of some $12 million. Petroleum was first drilled successfully in 1901 by Edward Doheny, a Californian who owned 600,000 acres along the oil-rich Gulf coast; when he sold his wells to Standard Oil Company, they were producing $1 million of oil a week. A second dominant producer of Mexican oil was the Briton Sir Weetman Pearson, later Lord Cowdray. Many banks were in foreign hands, too, as well as most industries.

The foreign firms gave job preference to their own nationals and even in Mexican-owned firms, the manager was often a foreigner. So prevalent was this practice that Mexicans rarely made their income from management, but rather as intermediaries for foreign investors with the government. Although European companies included Mexicans on their boards and in other capacities, American firms rarely did. And in a practice that would lead to conflict, foreign workers doing the same job as a Mexican usually earned much more.

The economy was fueled by foreign trade. Although Mexico was becoming somewhat industrialized, especially in the north, it exported

THE ANTIQUARIANS—A DIFFERENT KIND OF INVESTMENT

Not all foreigners came to Mexico for aristocratic balls or to make a fortune. Many Europeans and Americans wished to know more about the ancient ruined cities. Edward Thompson, U.S. consul in Mérida, used his spare time to investigate the Maya ruins of Yucatán for the Peabody Museum of Harvard University. In 1894, permissive Mexican land policies enabled Thompson to buy the Hacienda Chichén, 100 square miles of land that happened to include the ruins of Chichén Itzá, a pre-Columbian city of 50,000 inhabitants in A.D. 880. Thompson devoted himself to the study of the ruins and befriended his Maya workers, who permitted him to observe rituals and dances which they said were preserved from ancient times and could be seen carved in the walls of Chichén.

primarily raw, not manufactured materials—just as it had in colonial times. The economy depended on the strength of European and U.S. demands for these products. For most of the Porfiriato, Mexico benefited from an expanding U.S. economy. The potential profits from foreign trade had transformed the agricultural sector into producing cash crops. Yucatecan *hacendados* found that sisal alone brought such incredible profits on the world market that they planted nothing else. The states of Chiapas and Tabasco, too, had little diversification, gambling on the world market for their coffee and rubber exports to keep the wealthy wealthier. In the north, where the economy was more diversified with mining and industry, cash crops such as chickpeas and profitable animal grazing dominated agriculture.

The Land Grab

[One of Mexican agriculture's] greatest drawbacks
is that the whole country is divided into immense
haciendas or landed estates, small farms being rarely
known . . . Some of these estates comprise square leagues
instead of square acres in extent and are said to
have irrigating ditches from 40 to 50 miles in length.
■
—D. A. Wells, 1887

By 1910 only 2 percent of the population held title to land and 3 percent of the properties covered 58 percent of Mexico. Nearly 70 percent of those titles had been acquired since the reforms of Ley Lerdo in 1867. Yet seven out of 10 Mexicans were farmers; most were forced into debt peonage in order to survive.

Under Díaz, two policies concentrated land in the hands of the privileged. The first, the Ley Lerdo, had not been extensively implemented in regard to Indian community lands under Juárez. Now it was ruthlessly implemented. The second was the vacant lands survey in which allegedly untitled or "public" lands were surveyed and put up for sale; in total, surveyed land constituted the size of California and was sold to Díaz favorites and the surveyors themselves for a pittance. Worse, it was often confiscated from the legitimate owners.

Under either policy, when an Indian had been deprived of land, there was little hope of rectifying the injustice. Yet some did try. If Indians could find the money and wherewithal to file a complaint in court, they not only rarely won but sometimes were fined by judges for daring to besmirch the name of the *hacendado* or gentlemanly surveyor. When land wasn't taken under the guise of the Ley Lerdo or survey, it could be taken by cutting off the water supply. Or by force. The Yaqui Indians of Sonora, for example, after holding off the army in bloody battles for years, finally were routed and sold as laborers to *henequén* plantation owners in Yucatán where they were forced to work in chains. Their fertile lands went to the American Richardson Company.

Hunger

In 1910 only 10 percent of Indian communities held land. The landowners held vast territories. When the arable lands weren't devoted to cash crops for export, they often lay fallow. When hungry Indians asked to rent such land in order to grow their subsistence corn and beans, they too often were refused. Despite a 50 percent increase in population, Mexico produced less maize in 1910 than in 1877. Mexico failed to be self-sustaining in wheat, too, even though this grain was favored by the upper classes. Economists estimate that there were on average two pounds of maize available daily to each Mexican at independence; a century later, in 1910, there was less than a pound —including imported grains. The price of the little maize that was available cost twice as much, and beans, now an export crop, cost six times more. Wages, however, remained the same throughout the 19th century. Mexicans were starving.

CASH CROPS IN TWO REGIONS

Called "green gold," the Yucatán's *henequén* crop represented the most extreme consequences of commercial agriculture. It was so lucrative to grow the fibrous sisal for international cordage that cattle were killed in order to use the pasture to grow more *henequén*. In fact, so many animals were killed that serious meat shortages were created, even for the wealthy. And *hacendados* encroached on traditional Mayan *milpas*, too, with near impunity, so they could plant yet more sisal.

Finding themselves dispossessed, the Maya repeatedly rebelled against the *hacendados*, creating serious labor shortages. When the military arrived, they fled toward the less developed Caribbean where other rebel Maya congregated in what is now the state of Quintana Roo. Those who didn't escape were forced to work the sisal fields, slaves in all but name. When synthetic cordage was developed after World War I, the *henequén* market collapsed along with the Yucatán's economy.

In contrast to Yucatán and the rest of Mexico, the Mixteca Sierra—and indeed all of Oaxaca—managed to retain most of its communal lands not just during the Reform Period but throughout the Porfiriato. Historians are uncertain of the reason, but some believe the continued absence of a large wealthy *hacendado* class meant few were in a position to buy up the lands. Also, with the loss of cochineal and with erosion caused by overgrazing, there was no cash crop that especially attracted foreign monies to the area.

Survival of the Fittest

> The white is proprietor; the Indian, proletariat.
> The white is rich; the Indian, poor, wretched . . .
> The white lives in a magnificent town house; the
> Indian is isolated in the countryside and lives
> in a miserable shack . . . two different people in
> one land; what is worse, two people to a certain
> degree enemies.
> ■
> —*Francisco Pimental, 1865 (translated by Stein & Stein)*

The circumstances of the poor masses were dreadful during the Porfiriato. The shameful state in which most Mexicans were forced to live is reflected in equally dismaying statistics. Sixteen percent of Mexicans were homeless. Of those with shelter, half lived in hovels that the government census deemed unfit for human habitation. Sanitation was nonexistent: public baths were rare, and a bar of soap cost 25 percent of the basic wage. Hungry, the poor were beaten to work under onerous conditions—regardless of the provisos against forced labor in the 1857 constitution. In both factory and hacienda the masses labored seven days a week, 11 to 12 hours a day. Not surprisingly, the national life expectancy in 1910 was 30—in contrast to 50 in the United States. In some rural, predominantly Indian areas 800 out of every 1,000 people died before reaching their first year; the national average was bad enough, at nearly 450 per 1,000.

Peasant uprisings became common. All were put down mercilessly with the support of those profiting from the Porfiriato. When confronted with the embarrassing reality of the mortality statistics, the privileged had a ready answer: the Indians were to blame. It was their innate laziness, not the lack of food and wages (most were paid in chits at the company store, not cash), that made them poor workers. It was their stupidity, not their lack of education, that made them illiterate. Alcoholism, they said, not hunger and poor sanitation, caused their early deaths.

Indians, the *científicos* claimed, held back the progress of Mexico. In the age of Social Darwinism, pseudo-science glossed over blatant racism: the Indians were inferior, and there was no way to improve their lot; no education or training would enable them to farm better; no wage increases would improve their work; and no improved housing, nutrition, or sanitation would improve their health. So said the *científicos*.

European Immigration

Most of the population increases were in cities. In many regions there were severe labor shortages. But European laborers and small farmers were preferred, not Indians. Díaz embarked on a program to encourage immigration. The *científicos* believed increasing the number of Europeans would add intelligence and energy to the labor force. Citizenship was made easy, and "vacant" lands were available at low prices so that the Indian presence could be "diluted." Although Europeans were preferred (to diffuse the influence of the North Americans as well), Mexico failed to attract them. Mexican wages and working conditions could not compete with the appeal of the United States, where an average of 3,500 Europeans arrived daily in 1907. Most who did take advantage of the welcome were Americans, half of whom were illiterate drifters looking for a handout. In perhaps the worst racist policy since the colonial caste system, Díaz and his *científicos* managed to insult most Mexicans in order to attract just over 100,000 foreigners.

Growing Nationalism

After 1900, the results of Porfiriato policies culminated in increasing dissatisfaction and rising opposition. In a surge of nationalism Mexicans, from northern *hacendados* to factory workers, were resentful of privileges granted to foreigners but not to them. The wealthy Madero family of Coahuila opposed an American company's attempt to monopolize water rights. Young professionals saw only foreigners in the management positions they wanted and only 60-year-olds in the government of the aging Díaz. Small businesses couldn't get bank loans. Workers saw Americans gain the best jobs in factories.

In this atmosphere of growing resentment, an increasing number of liberal publications found their voice. One, *Regeneración*, published by the Flores Magón brothers attracted enough attention to land the brothers in prison and eventually to self-exile in the United States. But from there they continued to publish—despite an assassination attempt ordered by Díaz—and received support from young Mexican intellectuals in their call for freedom of the press and better conditions for the poor. They wanted an end to child labor, an eight-hour work day, and the redistribution of uncultivated land.

A more serious challenge to the regime came from industrial workers who went on strike for equal pay with foreigners, thus disrupting the Pax Porfiriana. Some of the strikes, involving thousands of laborers, received national attention—and brutal repression. In 1906 striking textile workers in Veracruz, who had the audacity to request that Díaz arbitrate, were massacred.

To aggravate matters, the U.S. press called for the annexation of Mexico, and the U.S. government realized Mexico's worst fears when it militarily intervened on behalf of its business interests in Guatemala and the Caribbean. Mexicans wanted Díaz to reverse his favoritism of the United States. He tried, but not openly, and thereby gained no political advantage at home. Meanwhile he offered to Great Britain government oil contracts that formerly went to the United States, thereby gaining the enmity of his northern neighbor.

Economic Depression: 1907–08

Material progress had secured support for the dictatorship among the middle and upper classes. In the last decade of the Porfiriato, however, the economy faltered. First, inflation became a serious problem when foreign investment tripled and when Díaz adopted the gold standard for currency. Real wages fell. And a depression (1907–08), triggered by a slowing U.S. economy, caused layoffs and further reductions in wages. A bad harvest caused food prices to increase. In Chihuahua, for example, wages decreased 20 percent as basic living expenses increased 80 percent.

In the midst of its first economic crisis, the laissez-faire policies of the Porfiriato did little to provide relief. In fact, the government made matters worse by increasing taxes on the middle class in an effort to keep its treasury full. The foreign banks made credit tighter: many of the upper class defaulted on their loans. Everyone was affected by the catastrophe. For the first time, national (not just local) opposition groups formed advocating the violent overthrow of the dictator.

"No Reelection" Revisited

In 1910 Díaz was 80 years of age and running for reelection. Foreign investors and supporters had been uneasy about his successor for some time. To guarantee a peaceful transition after his death, the *científicos* had urged him to run with a vice-presidential candidate as early as 1904. This time there was discontent among so many sectors of society that opposition grew to his running for office at all. Three national opposition groups formed; two of them advocated a violent overthrow of the regime.

Díaz made the mistake of telling a U.S. reporter that Mexico was ready for democracy and that he would not stand for reelection in 1910. In fact, he had no intention of retiring and was surprised when the article, "Thrilling Story of President Díaz, the Greatest Man on the Continent," reached Mexico. His opponents took Díaz's remarks to mean they could support other parties and candidates without fear of reprisals from the dictator, even if he himself ran.

Díaz maneuvered the most serious contender into a position abroad. He left the diminutive Francisco Madero from Coahuila alone, however, thinking that the northerner was a harmless idealist. Madero was disenchanted with Díaz's dependence on foreign capital and, like most wealthy individuals from the border states, he especially disliked the growing influence of the United States. Nationally known for a book he had written on presidential succession (which basically flattered Díaz), Madero argued that Mexico should return to the Constitution of 1857 with free elections, a free press, and an independent judiciary. He formed the Anti-Reelectionist Party, but social reforms in land and working conditions were not part of his platform.

Much to Díaz's surprise, Madero was enthusiastically received as he campaigned throughout the country with his call for "No Reelection." Even some *hacendados* in the north, angry that Díaz had supported calling in their defaulted mortgages during the depression, threw their support behind Madero. Increasingly concerned by his opponent's visible popularity, Díaz trumped up charges against Madero and had him temporarily imprisoned. The dictator and his vice president were reelected, of course, and Madero, escaping to Texas, claimed that the results of the 1910 election were fraudulent.

Centennial Celebration: 1910

I consider general revolution to be out
of the question as does public opinion
and the press.
■
—*Karl Bunz, German envoy, 1910 (translated by Frederick Katz)*

On September 16, 1910, Mexico celebrated the centennial of its independence. Emissaries from around the world arrived in Mexico City to honor the success of the young nation and to pay homage to the dictator on his 80th birthday. Amid the glitter of the month-long celebrations, Díaz seemed at the apogee of his power. The city was festively hung with lights, too bright for most to notice what all the poor saw as an omen in the dark night sky: Halley's Comet. With the poor rounded-up so as not to offend visitors' sensibilities, few could imagine that in seven months Don Porfirio would be forced into exile.

The government spent 20 million pesos, more than the entire education budget, on lavish celebrations to impress the world with its prosperity and cultural sophistication. Operas were performed under a glass curtain designed by Tiffany. Plays in French were attended by all. At one ball alone, 20 carloads of imported French champagne were consumed. With only European waiters (or European look-alikes), no one would be reminded that Mexico was the land of Moctezuma rather than Cortés. In what has been called surreal illogic, Díaz arranged for a costly exhibit of Spanish art in a building especially constructed for the purpose as part of the independence celebrations. Mexican artists, led by the painter known as Dr. Atl (1875–1964), scraped together several hundred pesos to stage their own protest exhibit in the corridors of the Academy of San Carlos.

A hundred years after independence, Mexico was right to celebrate its modernization. The railroads and telegraphs, the international commerce, did much to unify a nation that had previously been fragmented. The political peace did permit the nation several decades in which to grow more confident in itself.

But there were other Díaz legacies: racism, xenophobia, starvation. The repressive and exploitative manner in which Díaz achieved modernization was about to exact its toll on Mexico with 20 years of war and even more of political turmoil. Peace and progress belonged only to the upper classes and had been achieved at the expense of the masses. The Porfiriato only too naturally led to the Revolution. A hundred years after the call for independence, Mexico was again at war with itself.

THE REVOLUTION OF 1910

1910-40

> The Revolution . . . was an explosion of reality.
> ■
> —*Octavio Paz, 1961*

The most devastating civil war in Mexican history produced contemporary Mexican society. In the 10 years of its military phase, between 1910–20, as many as 2 million people may have been killed, or one out of eight Mexicans. Trains were blown up, haciendas were burned, and corruption prevailed. Yet the Revolution created new political structures and produced the Constitution of 1917. It destroyed the privilege of the creole and gave birth to the mestizo nation. It ended feudalism and peonage and created labor unions and redistributed land. It gave birth to Mexican heroes like Emiliano Zapata and Lázaro Cárdenas and Mexican artists like Diego Rivera. The Revolution gave Mexicans a sense of national pride and a deeply held appreciation for their own culture, called *mexicanidad*.

The Beginning

A century after Hidalgo's declaration of independence, Francisco Madero (1873–1913) declared himself provisional president of Mexico from the safety of San Antonio, Texas. A member of the upper class, Madero typified his era by having been educated in both Paris and the United States. His family owned large estates as well as a smelting factory and mines. Liberal in his thinking and actions, Madero provided schooling and medical care for his workers and peons. Much like Hidalgo, he seemed to have little understanding of the forces he was about to unleash.

Like Hidalgo, he thought political, not social, change would rectify the nation's problems. He had previously opposed unseating Díaz by violence, but now realized that honest elections were impossible under the dictatorship.

In October, Madero issued his Plan de San Luis Potosí calling for Mexicans to rise against tyranny on November 20, 1910, after 6 P.M. His call to arms was vague enough to appeal to everyone with a complaint against the Porfiriato. On the appointed day small guerrilla forces sprung into action throughout much of Mexico. Like the *caudillo* revolts of the Santa Anna epoch, these poorly armed groups were inspired by local leaders and, except for local members of Madero's Anti-Reelectionist Party, were not coordinated with each other. The fighters were teachers, mechanics, merchants, and miners; and they were the unemployed, the soldiers of fortune, and bandits. They were creoles who received too few favors from Díaz and the *científicos*. They were *hacendados* like Madero, who were concerned with electoral reform and foreign influence. Living off the countryside, the revolutionaries found plenty of support among the peasants, who quickly swelled their ranks. The radical and liberal, wealthy and poor, no matter their differences, united against Díaz.

Díaz tried to defeat them. He sent the army; he sent the *rurales*. He did quash the rebellions in most regions. But in the state of Chihuahua, he had no success. Chihuahua had long been simmering under the despotic hand of Luis Terrazas and his family. Terrazas was the richest man in Mexico, made more rich and powerful by Porfirio Díaz. He personally owned 50 haciendas and ranches that covered 7 million acres; his son-in-law, Enrique Creel, owned nearly another 2 million by himself. They owned mines, banks, telephone companies, textile mills, and meat-packing plants. Family members were governors, state legislators, and senators. Nothing happened in Chihuahua without their permission.

The revolutionary movement in Chihuahua grew under the leadership of a former mule skinner, Pascual Orozco, Jr. Joining him was the cattle rustler, Pancho Villa. Orozco had lost his business because Terrazas did not favor him. Pancho Villa had escaped from debt peonage. Both understood what was at stake in changing the established order. And there were many on the outs with the Terrazas clan. The Chihuahuan rebels successfully routed a large contingent of the federal army and took control of most of the state.

In February 1911 Madero crossed the border into Mexico to join forces with Orozco and Villa: he would be the political symbol; they would be his army. It turned out to be a fragile alliance between civilian and military authority, one easily broken by strong personalities and military might. Unfortunately, it would typify the problems of governance in Mexico for the next decade.

Victories in Chihuahua reignited the rebellion in other states—Coahuila, Puebla, and Morelos—and soon revolutionaries like Emiliano Zapata controlled most of the Mexican countryside. On May 8, Orozco and Villa captured the first large city, Ciudad Juárez. The rebels, against Madero's orders, defeated the army and occupied the city as their provisional capital. Other cities in the north and central Mexico were soon in rebel hands.

Federal troops began deserting. Madero's supporters demonstrated in the capital. Newspapers attacked Díaz. Businesses faltered. President Taft sent U.S. warships off Veracruz to express displeasure at the continuing civil war. Díaz finally realized his situation was hopeless: an armistice was negotiated and signed on May 21.

The news spread though the streets of Mexico City. Mobs of people gathered in front of the National Palace shouting for Díaz to resign. The dictator responded as he always had—with force. Two hundred demonstrators were gunned down. He did resign on May 25, 1911, and surreptiously slipped away to Paris. An interim president was appointed until an election could be arranged.

President Madero

Madero has unleashed a tiger; let's see if he can control him.
■
—*Porfirio Díaz, 1911 (quoted in Meyer & Sherman)*

Madero marched into Mexico City to the joyful cheers of mobs of Mexicans. In a matter of months, he had swept away the Porfiriato, and yet he would find it difficult to satisfy the aspirations of most of those who greeted him in the capital that day.

The most agile and charismatic leader would have stumbled, and Madero was neither. He appointed family members, some quite conservative, to important posts and left them to undermine the reforms he advocated. He invited charges of corruption against his government by giving out contracts to his family businesses. Most importantly, he didn't fully understand the injustices requiring redress: early in his presidential campaign he had said that Mexico needed liberty, not bread. He thought the battle was over with a free and open election. He naively agreed to disband the revolutionary army.

Meanwhile Porfiriato conservatives were still active. Foreign businesses required profit. Workers demanded better conditions. And Emiliano Zapata, recognizing that Madero's victory did nothing for his cause, never stopped fighting for the return of peasant lands in the south. Workers struck for better conditions, but despite good intentions, Madero did little more than disperse the strikers. There were many factions Madero needed to appease, but he satisfied few. When he announced his support of a tax on idle land, those fighting for land redistribution were as disappointed as any foreign investor.

Many *caudillos* declared against him. Unfortunately for Mexico, they would continue declaring for the next decade, sometimes for their political principles but just as often out of envy and personal pique. The factions fought not only the Porfiristas, they fought each other. Against Madero, the first to proclaim was his former commander Orozco. Another was President Díaz's nephew. And there were others. He put them down with the assistance of Victoriano Huerta, who would later turn out to be traitorous.

Events overtook Madero and the fledgling democracy he instituted. Too kind to execute conservatives who had risen in arms against him, Madero imprisoned most of them in Mexico City where they proceeded to join forces. On the morning of February 9, 1913, they mysteriously gained release from prison and led their troops to the National Palace. Indifferent to the plight of the capital's residents, they brought their battle to the heart of the city. Madero responded with General Huerta in charge. For 10 days, called the *Decena Trágica*, the city suffered machine-gun fire and shelling, looting, and panic and hunger. Civilian casualties were in the thousands.

Madero demanded to know from his general when the fighting would stop. The next day it did, because Huerta had switched sides. The American ambassador appointed by President Taft, Henry Lane Wilson, in the interest of protecting American business investments, had negotiated the resolution of the battle. Throughout Madero's term, Wilson had meddled and even called for Madero's resignation—especially when the president decided to tax oil production. In a shameless instance of dollar diplomacy, Madero was arrested, forced to resign, and murdered. General Huerta became president.

The Social Revolution

The real Mexican Revolution didn't begin until the Madero regime ended. Until that point, most political changes had fulfilled the democratic values of the liberal middle class. Fighting had not been so drastic as to disrupt the economy. *Científicos* and foreign interests had influential allies in the Madero government.

With Madero's death the revolution intensified and swirled through the country like a tornado touching down to wreak havoc on the people and the economy while destroying enemies. Then feeding on its destructiveness, the violent winds would find new enemies—over and over again. For seven years, the factions would realign themselves, splinter, and gust ahead. When the dust settled in 1920, Mexico's institutional and intellectual underpinnings would be drastically changed from the preceding centuries. And the people who occupied the positions of power would be those who had been held in silence so long.

The breakdown of the racist class system that had presided in Mexico since the conquest can be seen in the personal histories of the revolutionary leaders, many of whom became presidents of the republic. Unlike previous Mexican power brokers, most were either mestizos or Indians from rural areas and many were poor. Pancho Villa (1877–1923), the most colorful of the revolutionaries, was uneducated and was 25 years old before he could sign his name, yet he taught himself to read during a stint in prison. A bandit by trade, he was called Mexico's Robin Hood by the U.S. press. He fought the Revolution, he said, for land reform and "so that every Mexican child could go to school" (Guzmán:393). Yet his impetuosity and cruelty—he gave free reign to Rodolfo Fierro, "the Butcher"—were as legendary as his daring and brilliance as a cavalry leader.

Emiliano Zapata (1879–1919) was a small landowner and horse trainer who had battled in court against the injustices of Díaz's land reforms to no avail. He was a trusted leader of his Morelos village and spoke the Nahuatl of his mostly Indian followers as well as the Spanish of politicians. In his Plan de Ayala, which called for the return of land illegally seized under Díaz and for the expropriation of lands, woods, and water from monopolists for the "majority of Mexicans who own nothing more than the land they walk on" (Meyer & Sherman: 515), he articulated the agrarian issues that would be central to the Revolution, issues that he would die fighting for under the banner *Tierra y Libertad* (Land and Liberty).

Although Zapata and Villa forced the basic issues of social reform, neither would assume political power. Others would, from similar back-

Detail of Emiliano Zapata, *mural (1929) by Diego Rivera* (Cortés Palace, Cuernavaca)

grounds of poverty and political oppression. Victoriano Huerta's mother was a Huichol Indian, his father a mestizo. Although he made his way up through the army ranks by keeping the peace for Díaz against the Yaquis in the north and the Maya in Yucatán, he was never truly accepted by the elite society of the Porfiriato. Alvaro Obregón was a mechanic and small rancher who had witnessed the awful confiscation of Yaqui lands in his home state of Sonora. Plutarco Elías Calles was an impoverished school teacher who didn't own a pair of shoes before he was 16 years old. Lázaro Cárdenas had only three years of schooling and, at the age of 12, was the sole supporter of his family. He joined the Revolution when he was a teenager.

The Defeat of Huerta

The array of personalities and shifts of power in Mexico is dizzyingly intricate. Yet the individuals and their causes—or lack of them—are well known to every Mexican schoolchild. Madero is the symbol of democracy; Zapata the symbol of peasants' land rights. Pancho Villa is the fearless leader of the cavalry charge. Movie stars clamor to play these war heroes; novelists describe the dehumanization of the long struggle; artists paint U.S. capitalists meddling in Mexican affairs; war songs have become Mexican folk songs. The events are integral to contemporary Mexican nationalism.

The first political setback of the Revolution began with the opportunist Huerta. He defied the constitutional rights the Madero revolution had fought for and created a dictatorship (1913–14) with Porfirista support. With surprising shrewdness for a man who was not often known to be sober, he held on to the presidency for 17 long months—repeatedly using political assassination against those who criticized him. Huerta couldn't assassinate, however, the new president of the United States, Woodrow Wilson, who refused to recognize his government of "usurpers" and who recalled Huerta's ally, Ambassador Henry Lane Wilson. But he could use renewed European support to threaten U.S. business interests.

What would destroy Huerta were the revolutionary armies that sprang up against him and the support they received from Woodrow Wilson. Outraged by the murder of a compatriot, Venustiano Carranza, a conservative governor of Madero's home state, pronounced against Huerta on a platform similar to Madero's and formed the Constitutional Army of the North, declaring himself the "First Chief." Other chiefs in the north, including Pancho Villa, Alvaro Obregón, and Plutarco Calles, signed on for the fight even if they were disgruntled by Carranza's presumptuousness in naming himself their leader. President Wilson permitted arms to be shipped across the border to them; payment was made with cattle stolen from the Terrazas clan. Emiliano Zapata had never stopped fighting and although he remained independent of the Constitutional Army, he forced Huerta to fight in the south as well as the north.

The revolutionary struggle resulted in the total militarization of Mexico. Huerta closed all businesses on Sundays so civilians could receive military training. The trains were preempted for military personnel, and the federal army grew from 50,000 to a quarter of a million troops. When the number of volunteers was inadequate, the poor were rounded up—outside a cantina, inside a jail—and tied up in a wagon for transport to the field. Huerta's programs supplied fresh recruits when they were most needed and were continued by others throughout the Revolution. One-third of the budget went to Huerta's army.

WOMEN IN THE ARMY: SOLDADERAS

The army of the north, whether riding hard on the prairies or commandeering the trains, was like a massive migration of people. Women joined their husbands, often foraging for food and nursing the wounded, but also as *soldaderas* (women soldiers), slinging a rifle over one shoulder, a child on the other. When the federal government tried to banish women from its army, the troops threatened revolt.

Yaqui Indian soldier of the Revolution
(Courtesy of the Bancroft Library)

> Popular among the troops was
>   Adelita
> The woman the sergeant adored
> Because she was as brave as she
>   was pretty
> So even the colonel respected her.
> ∎
> —*"Adelita," a revolutionary folk song*

Initially, Huerta was successful against the revolutionaries. In the south the Zapatistas were driven into the mountains, and their village supporters were placed in concentration camps. In the north Carranza and Villa were pushed back. By 1914, Huerta controlled two-thirds of Mexico, the ports, and the vast majority of its population. The war effort was paid for by forced loans on businesses and taxes on oil—and church support that revived the old anticlericalism of the Juárez reform war. Debts were permitted by banks thanks to the financial backing of Great Britain and Lord Cowdray's Mexican oil interests.

Huerta's successes were reversed by the infusion of U.S. military aid in 1914. The competition over oil between Britain and the United States combined with the anti-Americanism of Huerta, moved Woodrow Wilson to openly support Carranza and his Constitutionalists. These armies of the north began taking cities from Huerta at the same time Zapata and his bands of guerrillas took over more areas in the south. The United States then intervened with its warships along the Gulf coast, attempting to force Huerta to resign.

The United States effort backfired when marines landed at Veracruz and thereby almost united all of Mexico behind Huerta. This insult to Mexico's sovereignty forced even Carranza and Zapata to denounce the invasion. Wilson agreed to permit some South American countries to mediate while he imposed an arms embargo at the port of Veracruz. The Constitutionalists, still supplied from the northern border, gained considerable ground in the fighting. In negotiations, Britain and the United States resolved their own disputes. The Huerta government was bankrupted and isolated. Huerta sailed into exile on July 20, 1914. On August 15, Obregón led the first troops of the Constitutional Army into the capital and Carranza, as First Chief, proclaimed victory for the revolutionaries. The Porfiristas had been defeated once again.

Anarchy

> With Carranza's whiskers
> I'm going to weave a hat band
> To put on the sombrero
> Of his better Pancho Villa
>
> ■
>
> —*"La Cucaracha," a revolutionary folk song*

Having successfully united against Huerta, the revolutionaries rediscovered their differences. Villa and Zapata had been confiscating and redistributing haciendas during the fighting. Carranza, a political reformer but not a social activist, disapproved. Too autocratic to listen to the other side, Carranza could not understand that elections, especially when they usually were rigged, were not the overwhelming concern of most of those who had been fighting—a change in the social order was.

There were personality clashes, but also class differences in the divide. Mostly Indian peasants had fought with Zapata under the symbol of the Virgin of Guadalupe, soldiers wearing sombreros and white peasant clothing who had been deprived of both land and water. Villa's army, the largest and most professional in the Revolution, was more diverse but included many who had gone hungry—peons, cowboys, and miners. Although these revolutionaries attracted their share of intellectual supporters, most of the middle class had supported Carranza. As Villa said to Zapata in their historic meeting in Mexico City, the Carrancistas "are men who have always slept on soft pillows. How could they ever be friends of the people, who have spent their whole lives in nothing but suffering" (Quirk: 135).

In October 1914 the various military factions gathered at the Convention of Aguascalientes to select a provisional president. Villa controlled the outcome, which meant that a puppet president, rather than Carranza, was selected. The result was five more years of war.

> Villa? Obregón? Carranza? What's the difference? I love the revolution like a volcano in eruption; I love the volcano, because it's a volcano; I love the revolution, because it's a revolution.
>
> ■
> —The Underdogs, *Mariano Azuelo, 1916*

Each faction claimed its own capital, provisional president, and issued its own currency. But Carranza, based in the port of Veracruz and near the foreign-owned oil fields, was able to get an infusion of munitions and mount the strongest army. Obregón, siding with Carranza, defeated Villa in 1915 in the famous battle of Celaya with only half the number of Villa's 20,000 troops. Of the Villistas 4,000 died, 5,000 more were wounded, and 6,000 were taken prisoner. Obregón claimed fewer than 200 dead among his soldiers. By 1916 Villa was forced to retreat to the Chihuahuan hills where he had begun as a cattle rustler. But he remained a dangerous threat to Carranza, raiding towns and attacking the army.

As a bizarre aside to the upheaval, Pancho Villa provoked an intervention by the United States in 1916. Having failed to mediate an end to the fighting, President Wilson recognized Carranza's very successful forces as the de facto government. Whether this abandonment by his former supporter drove Villa beyond reason is unclear. Whatever the cause, Villa's men stopped a train in Chihuahua and shot 15 Americans. Then Villa sent troops across the border into Columbus, New Mexico, to acquire arms. Instead they terrorized the village, shouting "Death to the gringos!", burning the town, and killing 18 residents.

Some in the U.S. Senate called for the occupation of all of Mexico. Instead, Wilson sent a punitive expedition under General Pershing to execute Villa. Violating Mexican sovereignty, Pershing searched for many months but left without ever setting eyes on Villa. The expedition cost the United States $130 million and a good deal of Mexican ill will.

Although Villa was somewhat contained in Chihuahua, the Carranza government had other uprisings to control. The most important was Zapata's. Carranza sent an army of 30,000 against Zapata's 20,000 and attempted to return confiscated estates to wealthy *hacendados*. The army managed to fight Zapata back into the confines of the state of Morelos, but later Zapata drove out the federal forces and organized an independent government with its own land commission.

The Constitution of 1917

The First Chief controlled much of Mexico, yet the situation was far from peaceful. Carranza also needed a constitutional convention in order to bring about a new legal framework to legitimize his government and his own election as president. Others supported the convention, but from it they intended to incorporate the goals and aspirations of the many peoples who had fought in the Revolution.

Hoping to revive the Constitution of 1857 with a few minor changes, Carranza convened 200 national delegates in Querétaro on December 1, 1916. They were far from representative. Delegate qualifications were so restrictive that relatives of Madero could not attend. All Zapatistas and Villistas were barred, and 80 percent of the delegates were from the middle class and only a third represented the military. Half were well educated and many were young. Even with a stacked convention, Carranza suffered a devastating defeat: under the leadership of Obregón, his minister of war, radical amendments were made to the constitution.

With their nation still suffering from civil war, the delegates struggled for two months to hammer out a constitution that would permit, and even mandate, fundamental social change. The most astounding amendment, Article 27, concerned land reform. Twenty-five hundred words in length, it comprised half the constitution and was an exposition on the relationship between private and public property, on individual rights versus the public good. In a section that alarmed all foreign corporations, it eliminated all monopolies on water and mineral resources and, reverting to the Spanish law that Díaz had repealed, it gave the nation rights to such natural resources. It made the communal Indian *ejidos* inalienable and limited the size of estates. It provided for land redistribution to be paid for by government bonds. And it restricted foreign ownership to those who agreed to be treated like Mexicans: no foreign interventions were to be allowed on their behalf.

Article 123 protected workers and destroyed debt peonage. A minimum wage was mandated, adequate to provide for education, "lawful pleasures," and the subsistence needs of workers. Work hours and a day of rest were also mandated, as was government insurance in times of unemployment, retirement, sickness, and death. In addition, the rights to organize, bargain collectively, and strike were granted by this amendment. It was an amendment that protected Mexican workers to the same degree as in industrial nations.

Many of the amendments included clauses that limited the role of the church. Huerta's considerable support from the church had revived anticlerical sentiments among the revolutionaries. All church properties were proclaimed government property, without compensation. Monastic orders were outlawed. Priests were not permitted to vote. Important mandates for universal and free primary education stipulated that only secular schools would be constitutional. Freedom of religion was granted; the Catholic church would no longer be the sole religion permitted in Mexico.

For the first time the social concerns of most Mexicans and most revolutionaries were formulated. Institutions that had crippled the state in the past were weakened: the church, foreign interests, and haciendas. The Constitution of 1917 provided a legal framework for the government that, though amended, continues to this day. It would take two decades to implement.

The Carranza Presidency, 1917–20

Even Carranza never openly challenged the constitution—perhaps because the First Chief didn't wish to acknowledge his humiliating political defeat at a hand-picked convention. The constitution also legitimized his election to a four-year term as president in March 1917. The constitutional president simply ignored the rest of the provisions.

Carranza's election did not usher in the end of the military phase of the Revolution; rather his policies continued the social violence and fighting. He did nothing to implement change, and he was properly criticized for his failure to conform to the constitution. Instead of setting up the commissions that would have implemented a minimum wage, he fought the unions. Strikes, organized by the anarchist Casa del Obrero Mundial, plagued industry. Because organized labor had supported Carranza, he had subsidized the various unions and permitted them to be armed. But with the economy disrupted and foreign powers complain-

The Trench, *mural (c. 1930) by José Clemente Orozco in the National Preparatory School, Mexico City*

ing, he banished the Casa del Obrero and disbanded their armies. When the rail workers declared a strike, he conscripted the workers into the army. Despite his efforts to weaken the unions, however, in 1918 the first national organization, the Regional Confederation of Mexican Workers (CROM), was formed.

In regard to land reform his performance was equally regressive. He actually gave back communal *ejido* lands to the Porfiristas. Further, he was relentless in his pursuit of Zapata. The army killed thousands of innocent civilians in its search for the rebel leader and burned crops and killed cattle to starve even more. The Zapatistas responded in kind, blowing up a civilian passenger train. Zapata wrote a letter to Carranza:

> It never occurred to you that the Revolution was fought for the benefit of the great masses . . . you have given or rented our haciendas to your favorites . . . and the people are mocked in their hopes.
> ■
> —*Emiliano Zapata, 1919 (translated by Meyer & Sherman:548)*

Carranza responded with an elaborate plot to assassinate the revolutionary hero. On April 10, 1919, his plot succeeded: Zapata was shot point blank in an ambush. His body was displayed to convince the Zapatistas and the peasants for whom he had struggled so long that their leader was, in fact, dead.

The End of Military Revolution: 1920

When Carranza's presidential term ended, the Revolution had ravaged Mexico without accomplishing its primary social objectives. Carranza had also undermined its liberal political objectives by instituting martial law and rigging elections. He didn't dare openly challenge the no reelection clause of the constitution; he did try, however, to subvert it by nominating one of his puppets to run against Alvaro Obregón, the minister of war.

Patience ran out with Carranza. Generals from around the country declared against him; regions declared independence. It was Obregón who finally chased him out of office. Carranza's presidency ended with the corruption and violence typical of the period: he fled with all the public treasury he could carry, allegedly 20 train-cars' worth; he was captured en route to Veracruz and shot.

The Devastation of War

Thinkers . . . prepare the Revolution; bandits carry
it out. At the moment no one can say with any assurance:
'So-and-so is a revolutionary and What's-his name is a bandit.'
Tomorrow perhaps it will be clearer.
■
—The Flies, *Mariano Azuela, 1918*

A decade of civil war devastated the people, countryside, and economy. As armies of tens of thousands moved back and forth across the land, they took with them whatever crops were in the fields and drove the cattle along as provisions. Revolutionaries burned haciendas and destroyed mills. Any crops they missed could not be harvested because the able-bodied were carried off with the armies. In the cities, fires raged, too; in Mexico City alone more than 50 elementary schools were burned down.

Payment, when it couldn't be avoided, was in chits or recently printed paper called "money." Each army printed currency as needed. Not only were different currencies used in the various regions, but they changed with the arrival of each new army, being exchangeable one day, but not the next—except for Zapata's coins, that is, which were minted from the silver of confiscated mines. There was an unending supply of money for the armies and inflationary prices for everyone else. Guadalajara reported that the price of corn and beans tripled in 1918.

Mexicans were hungry during the Porfiriato, but they were hungrier during the Revolution. Even when the government attempted to fix food prices, its efforts were inadequate. Transport systems, especially the railroads, had been expropriated by the armies or destroyed in the fighting; slow grain distribution was one result. With the United States and Europe engaged in World War I, not enough foodstuffs could be imported to alleviate the problem. The amount of maize available per capita was the lowest since colonial times. In 1917 the government officially recognized a corn famine. Malnutrition was common. Food riots broke out in some towns. Others reported 100 deaths a day due to starvation. Even in 1918 when there weren't marching armies sweeping the land, food production was low.

The War Economy

With the prolonged fighting, Mexico's economy should have stopped short. Instead, World War I gave it a boost. Yucatecan *henequén* was in high demand for cordage; profits from its trade stabilized the revolutionary government's finances into the early 1920s. Oil and metals, too, were in higher demand than ever because of the war. During the Revolution, foreign oil companies bribed the armies to protect their equipment and industry. Oil production boomed and Mexico became the fourth largest supplier in the world. Production, often wasteful and exploitative—gasoline cost more in Mexico than abroad—increased from almost 4 million barrels in 1910 to almost 200 million in 1921. Although the mines, mostly foreign owned, had suffered during the Huerta period, silver, zinc, and copper production under Carranza increased and even surpassed that of the Porfiriato—and prices had never been higher.

The Mexican government was kept afloat during World War I by its trade and by the taxes on extracted materials. But when its debts were reckoned, the nation couldn't have been in worse shape. Foreign debt was high even for Mexico: in 1923, it amounted to $750 million, three times higher than after the first round of fighting when Madero took office. Then, there was an additional $1 billion of foreign claims against Mexico for damage done to their companies during the Revolution. The domestic debt was no less impressive. All those army chits and paper monies and forced loans on businesses and the church became claims against the government. And the military was a continuing financial burden, with many soldiers and officers owed back pay. There were years in which the cost of the military was 70 percent of expenditures. Not even a war boom could finance so much debt.

COMMODITY PRODUCTION 1910–20					
Year	Corn	Sisal	Copper	Oil	Silver
1910	@3,219,624	94,790	48,160	3,634,080	2,416,669
1912	2,062,971	139,902	57,245	16,558,215	2,526,715
1914	1,961,073	169,286	26,621	26,235,403	810,647
1916	**	201,990	28,411	40,545,712	925,993
1918	1,899,625	140,001	70,200	63,828,326	1,944,542
1920	**	160,759	49,192	157,068,678	2,068,938

In metric tons except oil in barrels; from John Womack in Bethell 1991:133
** not available

The Revolutionary Reconstruction, 1920–40

> We too could produce a Kant or Hugo. We too
> could wrest iron from the bowels of the earth and fashion it . . .
> We could raise prodigious cities and create nations, and
> explore the universe. Was it not from a mixture of the
> races that the Titans sprang?
> ■
> —José Clemente Orozco (translated by Ramón Eduardo Ruiz)

Mexico finally was about to embark on a period of political stability. Its leadership would be assumed by social revolutionaries such as Alvaro Obregón, Plutarco Calles, and Lázaro Cárdenas. Each president would lead Mexico toward social and economic changes as envisioned by the Constitution of 1917. Only Cárdenas wasn't from the north, however, and only he would understand the indigenous communities that dominated central and southern Mexico. With increasing political stability, Mexico created a national identity as well, one that esteemed its blending of races into a new culture and a mestizo people. As a new Mexico took shape, a few violent episodes occurred, but they did not succeed in ripping the nation apart. Mexico was well on the way to solving its conflicts without the military.

President Alvaro Obregón, 1920–24

Obregón (1880–1928) brought political ingenuity, not just military might, to the Mexican presidency. As one of the great military strategists of the Revolution, Obregón had won many battles, including the decisive ones against Villa, with his Yaqui Indian soldiers and union supporters. He was a listener, a general who could sit and discuss strategy with his troops. He was a keen observer and chose his sides carefully and successfully. Although committed to social change and the implementation of the constitution, he was practical and knew how to compromise.

Knowing peace was imperative, Obregón granted an amnesty to all factions. He appointed Villistas and Zapatistas to his government. In exchange for remaining outside of politics, Pancho Villa was given a ranch and substantial pension. A Zapatista was put in charge of the Morelos troops that had once been the enemy. Other "generals" were bought off by well-paid positions in the army, but in an attempt to separate the government from the military, Obregón reserved most cabinet posts for civilians.

Obregón was the first revolutionary president committed to social reform. He was well aware of the simmering discontent of the peasants and organized labor who had received nothing after a decade of war. He had fought alongside them and heard their complaints. As a first step toward implementing the land reforms mandated in the constitution, he granted the Indians title to their lands that had been stolen. He also permitted peasants to keep the land they had occupied during the Revolution. Worried that agricultural production would be adversely affected if he moved too quickly on the haciendas before smaller enterprises got under way, Obregón's land redistribution was significant but tentative: on the whole, about 3 million acres returned to over 600 villages. Not even the vast estates of the Terrazas clan were diminished in the process.

Obregón supported labor, as long as it did not attempt to disrupt the structure of the capitalist system. In collaboration with Luis Morones, the head of CROM, the government encouraged the growth of that union, even if it was not always so generous with more radical ones, especially when they had foreign leaders. During Obregón's term, CROM grew from 50,000 members to well over 1 million.

The Mexican Vision: Vasconcelos

For the first time in Mexican history, the government attempted to educate people of all classes. Obregón chose not to strictly enforce the anticlerical laws; it would have closed 20 percent of the schools, not to mention create political unrest. Instead he put a remarkable man in charge of education, José Vasconcelos (1882–1959). A man of letters, a lawyer by training and a self-taught philosopher, Vasconcelos desired a cultural identity for Mexico and inspired intellectuals and artists to collaborate with him in its creation. He conceived of a populist nationalism, a blending of all ethnic groups into a new 20th-century Mexican "cosmic race." This mixing of peoples would turn Mexico into a perfect mestizo nation.

The new Mexico needed education to incorporate all the peoples into the nation, from the rural Mayas in the south to the mestizo miners in the north. The education budget increased from 15 million pesos in 1921 to 35 million in 1923. Under Carranza, education accounted for less than 1 percent of the federal budget; under Obregón it went up to 15 percent. The Vasconcelos budget more than tripled the amount spent by the Porfiriato.

Vasconcelos sent Peace Corps–style volunteers to live with village families and help them build schools. Then, the teachers would move in, as well as artisans and technicians to provide skills training and agricultural assistance. Determined to provide more than technical education to the poor, Vasconcelos published Spanish translations of the classics— Plato, Homer, and Dante—to stock the school houses.

Vasconcelos's vision of Mexico captured the Mexican spirit. Volunteers joined a campaign to go to the remotest areas to teach children and adults how to read. (The enormity of the undertaking can best be judged by the statistics: under Díaz, illiteracy was at least 80 percent; in 1934 it had been reduced only to 62 percent.) Artists joined in the educational campaign, too. Vasconcelos insisted that a Mexican identity required cultural nationalism and funded the Department of Fine Arts to sponsor painting, music, folk art, and songs. The walls of public buildings were given to artists such as Diego Rivera (see page 3) to paint with subjects relating to Mexican history and culture. From this was born Mexico's great muralist movement (see Mexican Art and Society, page 183).

Relations with the United States

Despite his popularity within Mexico, Obregón did not initially receive recognition from the United States under President Harding. There were matters to be resolved, such as the outstanding debt overdue since the Porfiriato and payment for damages to U.S. property during the Revolution. Furthermore, American corporations were alarmed about the constitutional restrictions on subsoil rights. Recognition would not be easily forthcoming.

The biggest oil companies had lobbied Harding and supported his election, so much so that their influence eventually was exposed as the Teapot Dome scandal. But in the interim, their business concerns became U.S. concerns. Looked at carefully, the Constitution of 1917 gave the Mexican government control over the very oil, silver, copper, and other natural resources that foreigners thought they owned. The United States wanted an exemption from the newly wrought Mexican constitution.

The de la Huerta Rebellion

Obregón could not meet U.S. conditions. But in 1923, he was forced to seek U.S. support. The two strongmen of his administration were Plutarco Elías Calles, minister of the interior, and Adolfo de la Huerta, minister of finance. As Obregón's term approached its end, he declared support for Calles as his successor. Although Calles had been a general in the Revolution in support of Obregón, most of his backing came from labor and Zapatista agrarians. Conservatives thought Calles was too radical. The military was unhappy with Obregón's reduction of the army, and there were other disgruntled groups who joined in encouraging de la Huerta to declare himself against Obregón. It was around the time of this tense juncture that Pancho Villa, having threatened to come out of political retirement, was assassinated.

Such powerful opposition in the past would have disrupted Mexico for untold years. This time it was quashed in a matter of a few months, but at a price. In return for U.S. recognition and support against the insurgents, Obregón conceded that the constitutional provisions in regard to natural resources would not be applied retroactively to properties exploited before 1917. At a critical moment, the United States blockaded the Gulf and sent munitions to Obregón. Obregón put down the uprising quickly and brutally. Seven thousand rebels were killed; their leaders, 54 of them Obregón's former supporters and friends, were rounded-up and shot. The age of the *caudillos* was ending.

President Calles: *Jefe Máximo*

When Obregón finally transferred his power to Calles, it was the first peaceful transition in almost half a century. Despite the brief violent outburst in 1923, Mexico was achieving a semblance of political stability. The economy was prospering after the post-World War I recession, and the treasury was in good shape. Although Obregón retired having gained considerable respect for his accomplishments, there were concerns that more progress had not been made toward implementing the constitutional reforms. Some, such as Vasconcelos, resigned from government. Others thought any progress was a worthy accomplishment.

Calles (1877–1945), the poor school teacher who had risen through the Revolution to general, governor of Sonora, and Obregón's cabinet, believed the primary role of his government was to get the Mexican economy working. With classic capitalist policies, he streamlined the government (the education budget dropped from 15 percent to 7 percent of the total), increased taxes on oil, and created a government surplus. The money went to creating financial and banking institutions that enabled Calles to begin much needed highway and rail construction, and agricultural improvements, such as irrigation. National industries were encouraged through protective legislation.

Luis Morones, the head of the most powerful union, CROM, was minister of industry, commerce and labor (1924–28). He was charged to set constitutional standards for labor—improved working conditions, minimum wages, pensions—but to do so while constantly mediating these matters with both business and workers. His efforts saved the Mexican textile industry and often were appreciated by other businesses that were protected from wildcat strikes. Unions that did not cooperate, rivals of Morones's CROM, ceased to be protected by the state.

Oil Problems

An ardent nationalist, Calles repudiated Obregón's compromise with U.S. oil companies and insisted that the constitution be implemented in regard to natural resources. There already were signs that the oil wells had been wastefully exploited rather than managed for market demand and longevity. As Mexico threatened nationalization, the oil companies retaliated by decreasing production (by 42 percent in 1926–27) and investing in other countries like Venezuela. The pressure on Calles was unmistakable; oil duties fell from one-third of government revenues to one-eighth in 1927. As a further blow, the companies pulled their money out of the banks, causing a devaluation of the peso.

Because Mexico's economy had become so dependent on oil, which represented 70 percent to 76 percent of exports, it was easily disrupted and, worse, disrupted by foreign interests. Only 3 percent of the investments in the oil industry were Mexican. Mexican relations with U.S. banking and manufacturing concerns were good (for example, Ford, Colgate, British-American tobacco), but they could not replace oil revenues. The result was an empty treasury, unemployment, strikes, and nonpayment of interest on foreign debt. All this foreign retaliation, and the oil fields hadn't even been nationalized yet. The economic situation worsened with the Cristero Rebellion and sunk fully into the quicksand with the depression of 1929.

The Cristero Rebellion

As if Mexico weren't confronting enough crises, Bishop José Mora y del Río granted a newspaper interview in which he adamantly attacked the anticlerical provisions of the constitution. This political attack in and of itself was in violation of the constitution, and Calles countered swiftly. Many of the anticlerical laws had not been implemented; now they were: foreign priests were deported, religious processions banned, monasteries closed. The church responded on July 31, 1926 by refusing to provide any religious services. For the first time since the conquest, not a single mass was performed in Mexico. There was no baptism, no Christian burial.

The stalemate continued between church and state for almost three years. Because the state owned the churches, they remained opened and most Mexicans, being devoutly Catholic, found solace in them. The clergy had hoped that their parishioners would instead rise in rebellion. Only a few did. Called Cristeros for their battle cry of "Viva Cristo Rey" ("Long Live Christ the King"), they burned schools and killed teachers; they also attacked peasants who supported the government because they had received redistributed lands. In sum, it was another ugly episode in Mexican history. It was ugliest in the states of Michoacán and Jalisco where, in 1927, the Cristeros dynamited a passenger train and then set it on fire so the survivors could not escape.

The U.S. ambassador Dwight Morrow negotiated a facesaving compromise between the church and Mexico. But before it could be implemented, a Cristero assassinated Obregón. Obregón, under an amendment to the constitution that permitted reelection after a term out of office and that extended the term to six years, had just been reelected. The outrage at the Cristeros ended the armed uprising.

The Maximato, 1928–34

It is believed that Calles and Obregón planned to alternate as president under the new amendment. But Obregón's campaign had brought out deeply held Mexican fears about reelection. After Obregón's assassination, Calles had no intention of giving up power—it was unclear who could have successfully replaced him at that time—but he thought it wiser to control the country from behind a puppet president. For this he was known as the *Jefe Máximo* (the Big Boss), and his extended term was the *Maximato*. The problems with the succession in 1929 also brought him to concentrate power in the hands of a single party, the PNR, or the Partido Nacional Revolucionario; the party would enable the state to transcend personality politics. Eventually it would become the PRI, the Institutional Revolutionary Party that controls the government today.

Calles was remarkable for the enemies he fought, because he believed they weakened the nation. He never backed down from the task of national integration and progress even when seriously challenged by foreign oil interests and the Catholic church. But he didn't resolve the problems involved with them, either, and they festered. Under the Jefe Máximo, elections once again were a political charade for a string of presidential puppets, but the government remained stable and power was concentrated in the PNR, a party open to many social forces, such as agrarian leagues and labor unions.

Lázaro Cárdenas: The People's Hero 1934–40

As his control over Mexican politics continued, Calles became increasingly cynical and corrupt. Like many before him, his personal wealth and that of his cronies became a major preoccupation, and his politics became more conservative after the depression put an end to so many of his programs. It seemed the initial energy imbuing the Revolution and the idealism engaging the Mexican intelligentsia were spent. Repeatedly in Mexican history, individuals born to humble circumstances were catapulted into power and succumbed to greed. Lázaro Cárdenas (1895–1970) should have been another *político* distorted by power. Instead he was incorruptible. At the moment history might have written the end of the Revolution, Lázaro Cárdenas became president.

Calles personally approved of the PNR's selection of Cárdenas as the presidential candidate. As a young man, Cárdenas fought under Calles in the Revolution, became a general himself at the age of 25 then, in 1928, became governor of the state of Michoacán where he was born. He was the first president of the Revolution who was not from the north, but rather from a traditional indigenous state: he understood the importance of *ejido* lands to the peasants. Cárdenas also was a leader of the younger radical wing of the PNR, yet Calles thought he would be easy to control, given his reputation for loyalty and honesty. Instead, it would take Cárdenas only a year to defeat Calles's control of the presidency and one more year to force him into exile.

Although the results of his election were foreordained, Cárdenas campaigned diligently, traveling to small towns and factories and covering 1,800 miles, some of them on horseback. He campaigned on a platform formulated by the younger wing of the party, the "Six-Year Plan" that emphasized greater land distribution and agrarian assistance, more support of organized labor, the elimination of illiteracy, and less foreign dependence. The campaign educated him about the populace, and the platform gained him support, especially among peasants and workers. His election went smoothly and no *caudillo* or assassin disrupted his assumption of the presidency in 1934. In contrast to Calles's lavish lifestyle, Cárdenas cut his salary by half and gave up Chapultepec Palace, formerly belonging to Maximilian and Carlota, as the presidential residence and made it into a museum. Throughout his presidency he received delegations of the people and patiently heard their concerns; he mandated one hour a day of free telegraph service for citizens wishing to communicate with him.

Cárdenas inherited a nation of pent-up frustrations. The economic impact of the 1929 depression had finally ended in 1934, but workers had suffered wage cutbacks and were engaged in escalating strikes and more radical politics. The agrarian movement had been abandoned by an increasingly conservative Calles; many peasants remained without land, and production of maize and beans had been falling since the already devastatingly low levels of the Porfiriato. Meanwhile, Calles never stopped his attacks on the church, and the country festered with the conflict.

Agrarian Reforms

In 1936 Mexico's agrarian policy appeared to be failing. Investments had encouraged mostly export crops, not the subsistence crops of the peasants. The depression, however, revealed the flaws in this export policy. Yucatán with its *henequén* plantations, for example, was destitute. The peasantry was starving. Since the end of the Revolution, less than 15 percent of cultivated land had been redistributed, and only 10 percent of the villages had been given *ejidos*. But Cárdenas, unlike his predecessors, made agrarian reform a hallmark of his presidency. In the quarter of a century before he took office, about 10 million hectares changed hands. Cárdenas alone redistributed 18 million hectares—about 49 million acres. The landless population fell from 2.5 million to less than 2 million. Forty-seven percent of the cultivated land belonged to *ejidos*.

Cárdenas not only gave traditional Indian villages land. He expropriated export crop haciendas and gave them to the peons working them: cotton in the north became the product of former peons, as did *henequén* in Yucatán. Cárdenas also took advantage of a healthy economy to pour resources into the *ejidos*, creating a special bank to extend credit to the communal lands to provide the infrastructure for success: irrigation, electrification, fertilizers, and seed. The *ejidos* were also encouraged to mobilize into organizations representing their interests, and the National Peasants Confederation (CNC) was formed.

LAND DISTRIBUTION BY ADMINISTRATION, 1915–40	
President	Percentage
Carranza	1
Obregón	5
Calles & the Maximato	28
Cárdenas	66
Based on Meyer and Sherman 1983:599	

Unfortunately, these experiments in collective commercial farming failed to be adequately productive (partially because they received no further support after Cárdenas's six-year term) and, with an explosion in the rural population, the amount of *ejido* land itself sometimes proved inadequate. But as a social reform, the success was unquestioned: the institution of the hacienda, a feudal legacy from the conquest, was finally destroyed. Anita Brenner described the changes in 1943:

> Before and after pictures of most Mexican villages would not show any great change. But once upon a time a stranger who happened to ride in would find deserted streets, closed doors, rustlings in the houses; famished dogs . . . if he dismounted, some elder with suspicion on his face, fear in his eyes, would inquire about his business. Today no one, not even the women and children, hides. Doors stay open . . . small boys tag along asking to act as guides. The women, if they get a chance, like to show the community prides . . . the public corn-grinder, run by an old car motor at the rate of a few pennies for the day's supply of dough; the pump, the school . . .

Real Wages

Cárdenas also supported the labor unions. CROM was in disarray and politically discredited due to corruption. Cárdenas asked labor organizer Vicente Lombardo Toledano to organize another national union that could work with the government. Three thousand unions formed the Confederación de Trabajadores de México (CTM), which soon had over a million members. Under Lombardo Toledano, CTM struggled to increase real wages. Although the average daily minimum wage was 1.6 pesos, it cost a head of household 4 pesos to support a family of four each day. Business resisted an increase in the minimum wage, but finally a compromise of 3.5 pesos was reached. Real wages in Mexico had finally increased.

Nationalization of Oil

> In how many of the villages bordering on oil fields is there
> a hospital, or school, . . . or even an electric plant fed by the
> millions of cubic meters of natural gas allowed to go to waste? . . .
> Who is not aware of the irritating discrimination governing construction
> of the company camps? Comfort for the foreign personnel; misery,
> drabness, and insalubrity for the Mexicans . . . Another inevitable
> consequence of the presence of oil companies . . . even more harmful
> than all those already mentioned has been their persistent and
> improper intervention in national affairs . . .
>
> ■
>
> —*Lázaro Cárdenas, March 18, 1938*

Cárdenas implemented a policy by which companies that failed to comply with the constitution, especially when they could not resolve workers' strikes in accordance with it, would be confiscated. A number were. The most famous of these were the foreign oil companies, which had a long history of taking fortunes out of the country but giving little in return. Constantly interfering in Mexico's internal politics and seeking special favors, they were an obvious target of the country's new-found nationalism. Company policies towards Mexican workers had always been a problem: they were not given the better positions nor trained for management or technical jobs. Also, the companies did not respond seriously to union strikes and demands.

In 1938, the companies refused to settle a labor conflict in accordance with binding arbitration. They instead appealed the decision to the Mexican Supreme Court. Even after the court upheld the arbitration board, the companies failed to comply with the order. Cárdenas, claiming they had defied Mexico's law and sovereignty, nationalized the holdings of 17 U.S. and British oil companies—with compensation. For Mexicans it was an order for national respect. All classes rejoiced, even the archbishop encouraged support for the president, and the poor walked barefoot into the city to contribute coins and chickens—whatever would help pay for the expropriation.

The U.S. oil companies waged a newspaper campaign at home, claiming that Cárdenas's action was no less than theft and that Mexico's oil industry would collapse without foreign know-how. The world

OIL AND XENOPHOBIA

The nationalization of oil is no less an icon of Mexican consciousness than the Virgin of Guadalupe. Oil symbolized foreign dominance and discrimination against Mexican workers. In 1914, both U.S. and French investors owned more of Mexico than Mexicans; the total foreign holdings were triple that of Mexican holdings. Reacting to centuries of foreign intervention, the Revolution called for a Mexico for Mexicans. The expropriation of the petroleum industry finally satisfied the xenophobic Mexicans that their day had come. It was celebrated as Economic Independence Day with the commemoration of a monument in the capital.

economy, they said, would suffer because Mexico was not technically competent to manage its own oil reserves. The sides angrily disagreed as to how much compensation was just: Mexico offered $10 million; the companies demanded $200 million. Fortunately for Cárdenas, Franklin D. Roosevelt had just become president on a platform of nonintervention in Latin America. The amount was settled peacefully between the two nations by a commission that agreed on $24 million dollars as fair. Initially there was a drop in oil production, partly because of untrained workers and aging equipment. It didn't take Mexico long, however, before it was outproducing the foreign companies.

Church and Education

The younger generation of the PNR had emphasized education and the elimination of illiteracy as a six-year goal. Their kind of education had no room for the catechism—in fact, the government thought the uneducated could not progress because they were superstitious rather than scientific in their approach to the world and its problems. This they blamed on the Catholic church. Cárdenas didn't want his educational program to stir up the fanaticism of the Cristero Rebellion, however, and worked out a compromise with the church. The church would be forbidden under the constitution to run schools; but the curriculum of the schools would not attack either religion or the church.

Cárdenas increased the education budget to the highest it had ever been. The money for rural schools, half the budget, emphasized a practical curriculum—the reading teacher was accompanied by agricultural experts, midwives, home economics instructors, and artisans. The efforts did increase literacy, but because the population was increasing so rapidly, the funds were inadequate to be completely successful. In 1930 the population of Mexico was 16.5 million; in 1940 it had leaped to 20 million. Although the absolute number of illiterate individuals increased, the literacy rate nonetheless grew to 42 percent.

Not all of the government's efforts were welcomed. In the thinly populated region of Quintana Roo, some Maya had managed to live independently of government interference except for a few years at the end of the Caste Wars in 1901. But in the 1930s, the value of the resin in the native sapodilla trees, used to make chewing gum, increased on the international market. The government reasserted itself in the region, regulating schools and issuing licenses for bleeding the trees. The Maya, wishing to manage their own schools and work the land and its resources according to their traditions, challenged the government's right to interfere.

Mexican Art and Society

> Even the smallest manifestations of the material or
> spiritual vitality of our race spring from our native midst.
>
> —*1923 Manifesto of the Technical Workers, Painters
> and Sculptors Union (quoted by Dore Ashton:555)*

The Revolution ushered in dramatic social changes. Contrasting the simplicity of Cárdenas's lifestyle with that of Díaz properly emphasizes some of the change. Instead of women in their embroidered Parisian dresses, one thinks of the artist Frida Kahlo dressed in indigenous clothing (see page 184). Instead of champagne parties, one is reminded of university students volunteering as teachers in Zapotec and Maya villages.

Revolutionary Mexico extolled its own traditions, its native peoples, and pre-Columbian past. Indians no longer were considered inferior as they had been since the Spanish conquest, rather, the destruction of their culture and their exploitation became major themes in the arts (see pages 3 and 49). The glories of their ancient history were revived and studied. An archaeology institute was established in 1925 to preserve and excavate pre-Columbian ruins. The ruins at Chichén Itzá in Yucatán, for example, were excavated in conjunction with the Carnegie Institute from the United States and restored in a manner to attract tourists to a Mexico now proud of its distinctive heritage. Sophisticates in the capital collected pre-Columbian artifacts and decorated their homes with rugs from

Oaxaca, tiles from Puebla, and handpainted gourds from Michoacán. The Teatro de Belles Artes, begun by Díaz in the Belle Epoque style, was furnished with art deco native designs.

A national culture was in the making and comprehended both urban dwellers and rural farmers. Mexicanness, or *mexicanidad*, encompassed folk art traditions as well as the paintings of the Mexican mural masters: Diego Rivera (1885–1957; see pages 3 and 49), José Clemente Orozco (1883–1949; see pages 107 and 168), and David Alfaro Siqueiros (1896–1974; see page 145). Encouraged by the public walls given them by education minister Vasconcelos, they created paintings that enabled all Mexicans, even those who couldn't read, to understand the grander themes of their history and culture. They depicted people who looked

FRIDA KAHLO

Frida Kahlo (1907–54) represents the progress some women made in the early 20th century. She was educated at the capital's highly respected National Preparatory School during Mexico's most brilliant artistic period. Unlike the famous muralists, she painted smaller canvases that nonetheless captured the epoch's spirit of *mexicanidad*. Her work was greatly admired by the French surrealists, but only in the last decade has it been fully appreciated in the United States.

Thinking About Death, *(1943) a self-portrait by Frida Kahlo*   (Courtesy of the Mexican Ministry of Tourism)

like most Mexicans, brown-skinned peasants and bureaucrats, rather than idealized Greek figures. They painted narratives about conquistadors and foreign capitalists, about Mexican heroes called Hidalgo and Zapata. These painters created works that constituted one of the greatest artistic periods in the Americas. The period boasted more than the paintings of the famous trio: many others contributed lasting works, such as Rufino Tamayo (1899–1991), whose reputation belongs a bit later in art history, Fernando Leal (1900–64), Jean Charlot (1898–1979), and Juan O'Gorman (1905–82). And then there were other fine painters who primarily confined themselves to canvas-size works such as Frida Kahlo (1907–54), Miguel Covarrubias (1904–57), and Francisco Goitia (1882–1960). All these artists found inspiration in Mexico's rich history and artistic traditions, especially those from pre-Columbian times.

The Revolution also inspired great works of music and literature. Carlos Chávez (1899–1978) was among Mexico's most distinguished musicians; he not only conducted the symphony, but composed works such as *Sinfonía India* (1935) to be played with pre-Columbian instruments or their modern substitutes. And to reach out to the people he wrote more popular works such as *Llamadas* (1934). The famous revolutionary war novel, *Los de Abajo* (The Underdogs), was written in 1916 by Mariano Azuela who had traveled as a doctor with Villa's army. Martín Luis Guzmán (1887–1976) fictionalized his experiences as a university student who joined the Villistas in his 1928 *El águila y la serpiente* (The Eagle and the Serpent). These and other novels revealed the dehumanization of the long struggle and the personal corruption that too frequently accompanied success: as Azuela said, the underdogs merely replaced the "top dogs" in their violence and demagoguery. In his second novel, *La sombra del caudillo* (The Shadow of the Political Boss; 1929), Guzmán expressed disappointment in the strong-arm policies of Calles. Another novelist, Gregorio López y Fuentes viewed a vaguely incomprehensible Mexico through Indian eyes in his 1935 *El indio*.

Apart from the artistic outpouring, life in Mexico was made easier by stability and modernization. In education, the rate of illiteracy fell from the 80 percent of the Porfiriato to 38 percent. Greater opportunities were offered to women, too; in the cities increasing, if small, numbers graduated from the universities (500 in 1930) and a league was formed for achieving the right to vote.

Running water and electricity, radio stations, paved roads for cars, trucks, and buses became commonplace, uniting city and village. Mexico remained predominantly rural, however, with 65 percent of its popula-

INFANT MORTALITY		AVERAGE LIFE EXPECTANCY	
		Male	Female
1910	450 per 1000	30 years	
1930	222 per 1000	36.1 years	37.5 years
1940	125 per 1000	40.4 years	42.5 years

Based on Charles C. Cumberland and Fieldstaff Reports

tion living outside urban areas in 1940. Life in the countryside changed for the better. Village buildings were whitewashed and bandstands built along with schools. With more clinics and health volunteers, life expectancy improved remarkably. Social reforms permitted former peons to travel freely and work in new locations. Migration to the cities increased markedly: Mexico City's population jumped from 1910 by over a million to 1,726,858 in 1940. Problems remained, including poverty, but the improvements were unmistakable.

The End of the Revolution

Cárdenas's term ended without a single assassination attempt or rebellion. He resigned from the presidency in accordance with the no reelection clause of the constitution, just as every president after him would. He and his predecessors finally had achieved a nation that could settle its disputes within a legal and political framework. Cárdenas also reorganized the PNR into the Party of the Mexican Revolution (PRM), enabling it to officially embrace more diverse interests, including the new peasant and labor confederations, CNC and CTC. This trend towards consolidating the political forces under one powerful governmental organization, begun under Calles and continuing today as the PRI (Institutional Revolutionary Party), has been called "one party democracy"—as well as, more recently, "one party dictatorship."

The church and state had defined their roles and Mexico, remaining primarily a devout Catholic society, also left its government to control matters of civic and public concern. The society had been demilitarized as well. The military absorbed less than 20 percent of expenditures by 1940 and had been professionalized: most of the disruptive *caudillos* had been killed in the many squirmishes or absorbed into the new party structure. Foreign businesses had learned to obey Mexican law. Peasants and workers had been organized and given a voice in politics.

The progressive restructuring of society had certainly not solved all the problems of Mexico. Poverty remained a painful reality, and centuries of racism could not be eliminated easily, even in the new *mestizo* nation. Yet the period of restructuring was ending. The impetus of the Revolution was about to give way to more moderate politicians who would consolidate the gains already made.

MODERN MEXICO

1940–1988

Mexico . . . is changing at a rate
approaching the vertiginous.
■
—*Lesley Byrd Simpson (1962:xvii)*

uilding on the foundations of the Revolution, Mexico entered a
period of exceptional political stability and extraordinary economic
growth and industrialization. The nation approached self-sufficiency in
many important commodities and crops. New oil discoveries in the
1980s gave Mexico reserves comparable to the entire Persian Gulf;
"petrodollars" brought greater economic and political independence
as well as world stature: Mexico became a leader of the developing
nations.

Mexico was transformed. The military and its budget were so reduced
that more money was available for education and health care. Illiteracy
was lowered significantly. Improved health services and the increased
production of subsistence crops contributed to a growth in population
that almost doubled every two decades. The middle class also doubled
in size and, for a while at least, real wages grew. Industry attracted so
many to the cities that by 1960 more people lived in urban areas than in
the countryside for the first time in the nation's history.

Yet for all the changes in the modern period, Mexico was left with
severe problems to overcome, including ones that were unknown in 1910
such as environmental pollution and overpopulation, as well as old ones,
such as rural poverty and political corruption. The gap between the
wealthy and poor widened even during periods of growth in the gross
national product. The one-party state ruled by the Institutional Revolutionary Party (PRI) since the time of Calles increasingly failed to respond
adequately to demands for greater democratization. Despite the phe-

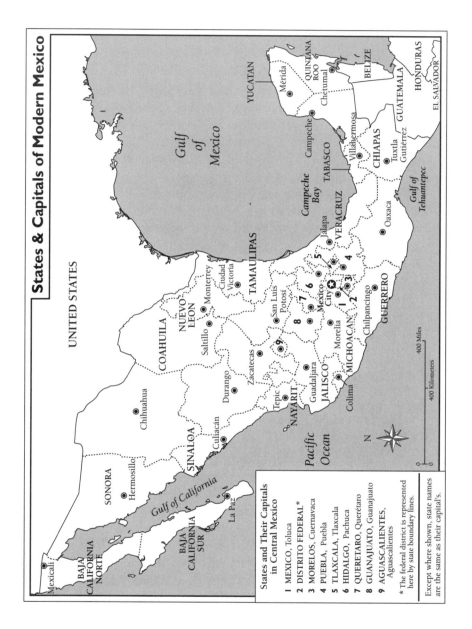

States & Capitals of Modern Mexico

States and Their Capitals
in Central Mexico

1 MEXICO, Toluca
2 DISTRITO FEDERAL *
3 MORELOS, Cuernavaca
4 PUEBLA, Puebla
5 TLAXCALA, Tlaxcala
6 HIDALGO, Pachuca
7 QUERÉTARO, Querétaro
8 GUANAJUATO, Guanajuato
9 AGUASCALIENTES,
   Aguascalientes

* The federal district is represented
here by state boundary lines.

Except where shown, state names
are the same as their capital's.

nomenal gains in Mexico, the old problems lingered and have contributed to an intellectual debate over whether the ideals of the Revolution were furthered or undermined during the "institutionalized" Revolution.

A Conservative Shift: 1940–58

Following the reforms of Lázaro Cárdenas, the government shifted course. Cárdenas himself must have thought a period of consolidation was needed, because he supported the conservative General Manuel Avila Camacho as his successor. President Avila Camacho (1940–46) believed the Revolution had been accomplished: all that was needed was evolution towards a more industrialized economy.

Avila Camacho, a fighter in the Revolution but not one of its heroes, was nicknamed "the unknown soldier." Mexico had achieved enough stability so that war heroes were not the only presidential candidates. Camacho, in fact, would be the last military president in Mexico. His successors were all civilians with experience in government, not war. Unlike many Latin American countries, Mexico controlled its militarism and decreased its military spending to the lowest in the hemisphere. Military spending dropped from 20 percent of the federal budget in 1934 to less than 10 percent in 1958.

World War II: Relations with the United States

Because of Mexico's immediate revolutionary past,
it is something like a school for . . . many other Latin American
republics; its moral leadership is beyond its size. Therefore it has
had an enormous effect on the conduct of the war, for without its
diplomatic work, the line-up of twenty-one American republics
against the Axis could not have been achieved."

■

—*Anita Brenner (1943:105)*

Although Mexican nationalism had been fueled by a distrust of the United States and an antipathy toward Spain and other European meddlers, Mexico did not hesitate to support the democratic powers against fascism. As early as Cárdenas's presidency, refugees from the Spanish Civil War and Jews fleeing Nazi persecution were welcomed into the country. Under Camacho, Mexico organized Latin American countries in condemning warmongering among the Axis powers. When German submarines attacked two Mexican tankers in the Caribbean, Mexico formally declared war.

Mexico and the United States entered into a mutually supportive relationship during the war, encouraged by President Franklin Roosevelt's Good Neighbor policy. In 1943, Roosevelt became the first U.S. president to visit the interior of Mexico. The result was Roosevelt and Camacho's *bracero* (hired hand) program to provide Mexican contract labor to make up the labor shortages affecting American farms and factories. Mexico exported to the United States the zinc, copper, and other materials necessary for the war effort—without inflating the prices. And Mexicans fought in the war with the United States: an air squadron saw active combat in the Philippines, and Mexicans residing in the United States joined its army. This period of cooperation set a new tone for the nations' policies toward each other. When President Harry Truman visited Mexico City in 1952, he made a conciliatory gesture to Mexicans by laying a wreath at the monument to the Niños Héroes, Mexico's military cadets who had been killed by U.S. troops a century earlier.

Mexicanization of Industry

World War II certainly gave Mexico's industrialization effort an early boost. The war provided a steady demand for Mexican products, and Mexico was forced to produce substitutes for items that formerly had been imported but no longer were available. But it was really the government's policies that created the nation's economic miracle.

Camacho's goal was to make Mexico self-sufficient in all the most important manufactured goods and, once the domestic goals were achieved, to export finished products. Mexican capital, Mexican industry, and Mexican raw materials would be used in this important endeavor. If foreigners wanted to invest, they were restricted to manufacturing industries rather than extractive ones. Even in manufacturing, foreign investments could not control a majority interest in any company: the so-called 51 percent rule. After World War II, the yields from Mexican investments were so satisfactory that U.S. and European investors were not deterred by such restrictions: Coca-Cola and Pepsi, General Motors and Ford, Dow Chemical, John Deere, Sears, and many others established themselves in Mexico.

Camacho's emphasis on industrial development and technological solutions would become the template for succeeding administrations. Not purely capitalist or socialist, the economic program was a uniquely Mexican mix, just as it had been under Cárdenas and others. The economy was too important to be left to private ownership, the lawmakers believed; government leadership was essential. Oil prices were controlled to fuel the national economy. If new equipment was needed, then government loans and tax breaks were made available. Fledgling businesses that were integral to attaining the goal of national self-sufficiency received tariff protections. When private enterprise failed to materialize, the government didn't avoid taking ownership of critical industries, not only oil and electricity, but also insecticide and fertilizer factories.

Mexico's industrialization efforts were successful into the 1980s. In Camacho's six-year term, the textile, food-processing and chemical industries, and breweries and cement factories developed rapidly. Electrical capacity jumped by 20 percent and tripled by 1952. Steel production increased from less than 100,000 metric tons in 1930 to more than 142,000 in 1946 alone. During President Miguel Alemán's term (1946–52), oil production doubled. By 1958 the gross national product had doubled. And Mexico did finally achieve self-sufficiency in iron, oil, and steel in 1964.

Throughout the initial phase of industrialization, Mexico's infrastructure was improved. Dams were built not just for electricity, but for land reclamation and irrigation as well. Oil pipelines and refineries were constructed. Alemán invested in massive public works that resulted in 7,500 miles of new highways. The Pan American Highway linking the United States with Guatemala was completed along with a road linking the Pacific and Gulf along the Isthmus of Tehuantepec. These roads encouraged not only commerce but tourism from the United States to the improved resort facilities at Acapulco and Puerto Vallarta. The

AGRICULTURAL AND INDUSTRIAL PRODUCTION					
	Maize*	Cotton*	Steel**	Zinc*	Oil***
1930	1,377,000	38,000	102,859	124,084	39,529,901
1940	1,640,000	65,000	149,655	114,955	44,448,191
1950	3,122,000	260,000	332,631	223,510	73,881,472
1960	5,386,000	470,000	1,491,778	262,425	108,771,583
1970	8,997,000	398,000	3,881,201	266,400	177,599,055
1980	11,081,000	340,000	7,300,000	236,050	708,942,000

Based on Robert Ryal Miller:372–74
*metric tons ** tons; *** barrels

irrigation and land reclamation works coincided with the Department of Agriculture's successful development of new, more fruitful plant varieties that created a "green revolution." During Alemán's term, corn yields increased from 300 kilos per hectare to 1,300. The infrastructure laid the foundation for the later, more phenomenal periods of growth.

Labor Policies

Economic growth led to a burgeoning middle class, and by 1958 there were 1.5 million industrial workers. The national income almost tripled: from 1940 to 1946 the per capita income rose from 325 to 838 pesos. These heartening figures, however, did not mean the gains were spread equitably throughout the population. They especially did not always work to the advantage of the lower classes.

Avila Camacho's first act in regard to labor was to remove the progressive Lombardo Toledano as the head of CTM and replace him with the conservative Fidel Velázquez. A firmer hand on labor was considered necessary to accomplish the economic growth desired. Throughout the period, Fidel Velázquez did the bidding of the presidency more often than that of his constituents: he signed numerous blatantly anti-labor documents that declared most strikes illegal. Without government support, most workers were afraid to strike. In 1958, the situation changed, however: the railway workers did strike. Initially, the government tried to co-opt the strike by granting some concessions. When the workers persevered, the government displayed its ability to bring them under control. The army was ordered to run the trains, the union leader was arrested (and replaced by the government), and thousands of strikers were jailed. The union leader was convicted of sabotage and imprisoned for 16 years.

Labor peace was achieved not only through coercion, but through persuasion as well. The government had become unsympathetic to labor, yet the ruling party, PRI, recognized the need to provide for workers' basic well-being—the devastation of the Revolution remained a vivid memory. Although labor did not share proportionately in the growing economy, the minimum wage maintained most of its purchasing power well into the 1970s. Unemployment was a serious problem, however: Population growth was so stupendous that the government found it impossible to create enough jobs to absorb the new workers. Alemán attempted to address the issue by using the healthy government treasury in massive public works projects.

Another significant labor effort began in 1943. Avila Camacho created the Instituto Mexicano de Seguro Social (IMSS), a social security system to provide unemployment insurance and pensions, disability and death assistance, as well as health care benefits to workers and their families. The program began slowly, with less than 250,000 enrolled. Under President Adolfo Ruiz Cortines (1952–58), all workers were insured. The number of clinics increased from 42 to 226 and the number of hospitals from less than 20 to over 100.

Agrarian Policy

It is fair to say that during the first years of industrialization the agrarian revolution was abandoned. The emphasis on technology and industrialization seemed to exclude more human concerns. The more conservative presidents were concerned that land be efficiently used rather than justly distributed. Loans to buy tractors, government construction of dams for irrigation, and factories to produce fertilizer were the priorities. Whereas Cárdenas had distributed almost 50 million acres, Avila Camacho distributed less than 12 million, and every acre went to small, privately owned farms, not the *ejidos*.

In the battle for productivity, policymakers showed a preference for the larger, private commercial farms that could supply the rapidly growing cities as well as contribute to the export capital of the nation. These policies favored the north, where the plains were most amenable to tractors and technology, and the nearby United States border made exporting more efficient.

In Mexico's central and southern regions, *ejido* farming became more productive by 1960. The government, however, remained dissatisfied: the *ejidos* constituted 43 percent of all crop land but produced only 40 percent of the crop value. The private farms were more productive per acre on a per capita basis.

Some economists have criticized the government assessment of the *ejido* program, and various administrations during the modern period have agreed. They contend that the lower harvest rates for *ejidos* resulted from government policies: only one-fifth of all tractors made their way to *ejido* land and, with the growing population, the figures per capita distorted the output. In addition, the most fertile land remained in private hands even after Cárdenas's redistribution because *hacendados* were permitted to select the plots they wished to retain. Apart from the issues of productivity, *ejido* farming guarantees the poor a subsistence: the basic

CORRUPTION

ne of the most striking buildings of the new campus built for the
National University of Mexico in 1953, the library was covered with
a mosaic mural by artist Juan O'Gorman. But inside there were only
empty shelves: graft, unbridled during the Alemán presidency, had "di-
verted" the money for books.

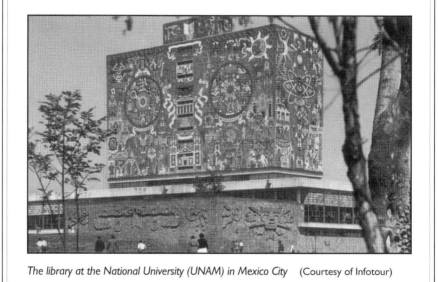

The library at the National University (UNAM) in Mexico City   (Courtesy of Infotour)

crops are produced and consumed by peasants regardless of international
market forces. Indeed, in 1960 more corn, wheat, and beans were
produced on the *ejidos* than on all crop lands in the non-*ejido* system of
the 1910 Porfiriato.

Education Under the Conservatives

Education remained important, but the more socialist, anticlerical cur-
riculums of the revolutionary period were abandoned. Education minister Jaime Torres Bodet, a poet and scholar, did build more schools,
libraries, and museums. More indicative of the times, however, was the
volunteer program against illiteracy. Rather than paying more teachers,
Camacho proclaimed the "Each One Teach One" program and set the

proper example himself by setting aside one hour a day for tutoring. During the 1940s illiteracy was reduced from 58 percent to less than 43 percent, but the "voluntary" program lost its momentum when disgruntled government employees complained of being coerced into participating.

President Alemán constructed the impressive three-square-mile campus of the National University of Mexico (UNAM). Planned by the mural artist Juan O'Gorman, its facades were covered with works by the great muralists Rivera and Siqueiros. A symbol of national progress and *mexicanidad,* the campus lacked basic library facilities and other educational necessities. It was much like the many new elementary schools in 1958 without teachers because salaries were too low. Less than 1 percent of rural children finished sixth grade.

The Need for Change

As President Ruiz Cortines confessed at the end of his conservative tenure in 1958, masses of Mexicans had not sufficiently benefited from the economic miracle. They did receive, however, plenty of revolutionary

WOMEN WIN THE VOTE

In 1954 Mexican women finally were granted the right to vote. The United Front for Women's Rights was founded in 1935, demanding not only the right to vote, but organizing women's hospitals and child care centers. As the Front's membership swelled to 50,000, it was asked by Cárdenas to join the official party that became the PRI. The Front's absorption failed to result in the right to vote, even during the war years when growing numbers of women joined the work force to fill the jobs vacated by men in the *bracero* program. After almost two decades, the PRI honored its commitment to universal suffrage, and in 1954 women were finally granted the right to vote. In 1974 it once again embraced women's issues by passing an Equal Rights Amendment to the constitution. In 1990 women represented 63 percent of the registered voters and held 10 percent of the seats in the Chamber of Deputies, and 12 percent in the Senate. More than one-third of women work, and some have assumed nontraditional roles, such as police work and movie direction as well as a few governorships. Yet 52 percent of women workers still earn less than the minimum wage.

rhetoric—including the change in the party name to Institutional Revolutionary Party (PRI) in 1946. Yet too much poverty, illiteracy, and social pain remained. One reason for this was the PRI's change in dynamics: the peasant and labor organizations had been supplanted in influence by business. Intellectuals, too, lost their influence. The party, less open to reconciling diverse interests, failed to implement policies that might have better distributed the increasing wealth, and it failed to even address the frightening population growth that also undermined any progress.

Public funds, estimated at well in excess of half a billion dollars under President Alemán, that could have been spent on social programs and education instead ended up in the foreign bank accounts of high-ranking members of government. Corruption became so notorious that the PRI had to bring in as president the colorless, but honest Ruiz Cortines to enhance its credibility.

A Liberal Correction: President López Mateos

In 1958 Adolfo López Mateos was elected over the National Action Party (PAN) opposition candidate by 90 percent of the vote! If any proof was necessary that the PRI had preempted democracy and that its nomination of a candidate was equivalent to election, it was such recurring statistics. Yet the PRI remained in control because it had the good sense to change course when necessary in order to accommodate a broad base of interests. In the case of President López Mateos (1958–64), the party had selected a candidate who would be one of the most popular in the post-revolutionary era. An energetic 47 year old, the new president appealed to both intellectual youths and the masses with his promise to revive the ideals of the Revolution.

Declaring himself "on the extreme left within the constitution," the new president used his term to prove it. Taking advantage of a strong economy and healthy treasury, he invested in people, not just infrastructure. He distributed 30 million acres of land (only Cárdenas had distributed more) to both *ejidos* and private farmers and cleared new lands in the south to alleviate population pressures. He expanded the social security system, IMSS, and conducted successful public health campaigns against polio, tuberculosis, and malaria. He implemented a clause of the constitution requiring profit sharing with labor and thereby increased many workers' earnings by 5 to 10 percent.

Education again became a priority. New schools were constructed quickly and in a cost-effective manner: the schools were prefabricated,

URBANIZATION: PERCENTAGE OF POPULATION IN CITIES					
1910	1920	1930	1940	1950	1960
29.3	25	33.5	35	43	50.7

Based on *Mexico: Facts, Figures and Trends*, Mexico, 1968

the communities provided the land and the labor to assemble them. In order to attract more teachers to rural areas, their living quarters were included as part of the school construction. Free federal textbooks enabled more poor children to remain in school. The rate of illiteracy was further reduced from 80 percent in 1910 to 38 percent in 1960, but still the swelling population increased the absolute numbers of those who could not read or write: from 11,658,000 in 1910 up to 13,200,000 in 1960.

Like his predecessors, the president failed to implement any program to curb population growth. But he did attempt to rectify some of its worst impact on the cities. As rural farmers flooded urban areas, the cities could no longer provide adequate support services such as housing, running water, and sewerage. Shanty towns appeared on the outskirts of every city. López Mateos initiated a program of low-cost public housing. A slum in Mexico City was replaced with new units for 100,000 individuals.

LAND EROSION IN THE MIXTEC SIERRA AND MIGRATION

The Mixteca Sierra of Oaxaca has been eroded into red "badlands" by too many years of overgrazing by goats and sheep. Land that produced agricultural surpluses in the 16th century now barely yields enough for subsistence. For decades many have been forced to find work elsewhere in the dry season in order to survive. As the population increased and the land could not yield more food, migration became wider ranging with Mexico City the primary destination. There Mixtecs squatted in new slums or joined family members. The country was brought with them: roosters perched on the roofs, and cornstalks grew on every available inch of land.

On the international economic front, López Mateos encouraged French and British investments for the development of the new petrochemical industry, Petróleos Mexicanos (PEMEX). Yet he also purchased foreign interests in essential electric companies and bought out U.S. control of the burgeoning motion-picture industry, so that Mexico became the major distributor of Spanish-language films in the world. In a gesture typical of his presidency, López Mateos also guaranteed that movie tickets would remain affordable to the poor. Agricultural and industrial production continued to grow strongly and the foreign tourism industry, supported by luxury hotels in Acapulco and Puerto Vallarta, brought in almost twice as many travelers as under President Alemán.

Renewed Conservatism: The Tlatelolco Massacre

President Gustavo Díaz Ordaz (1964–70) was probably the worst choice the PRI could have made for the 1960s. At a time when student activism led to demonstrations and police confrontations around the world, the PRI selected one of its most conservative presidents. When the nation demanded greater openness in the PRI, the new president not only annulled the victories of opposition parties, but also the liberalizing reforms of his predecessor, López Mateos. Just when Mexico was receiving world attention in its preparation for the 1968 Olympics, it presented a government that would not easily tolerate public criticism and ruled more by coercion than persuasion.

In bidding for the 1968 Summer Olympic Games, the Mexican government hoped to find a global forum to show off the nation's miraculous economic progress. Side by side with the games, a cultural Olympics showcasing Mexican art and artisanship would add to the nation's prestige. The cost of constructing the stadiums and infrastructure for the games was excessive for a nation with so much poverty, or so the critics said. The total was estimated at between $150 million and $200 million, but the government argued that it was not money thrown away. A modern subway system, new housing, and sports facilities would remain, as would the money spent by visitors. The government implemented its plans, and everything was built on time. The games, too, were successful. The most troublesome events, however, happened before the Olympics began.

Against the background of the Olympic preparations, a public dispute between two schools in the capital erupted. The mayor responded by calling in a despised paramilitary police force, the *granaderos*. They

One of the modernization projects for the 1968 Olympic Games, the Mexico City metro system incorporated an Aztec temple uncovered during construction.

dispelled the students with the excessive brutality for which they were known and in so doing politicized most students in Mexico City. When the *granaderos* were again called in during a student parade celebrating the anniversary of the Cuban Revolution, they provoked a riot, using bazookas and barricades.

The situation continued to escalate. Students demanded that the mayor be removed and the *granaderos* disbanded. Failed negotiations led to the largest protest demonstration in Mexico's history on August 27: half a million people marched from Chapultepec Palace to the main square of the government palace. The government, fearful that the students would attempt to disrupt the upcoming Olympics in October, greeted them with tanks. Undeterred, the students threatened further action. Díaz Ordaz ordered 10,000 troops to take over the campus of the National University; 500 students were imprisoned. On October 2, just days before the games began, students planned a rally at the Plaza of Three Cultures in Tlatelolco. It was a peaceful rally, with about 5,000 participants, including children accompanying their parents. Army tanks arrived. The *granaderos* stormed in with tear gas. Someone fired shots: terrorists, according to the government; the police, others said. Whoever started it, the police finished it with their machine guns.

Díaz Ordaz said there were only 43 deaths; the *New York Times* said several hundreds. Two thousand were imprisoned. Mexico was shamed and Mexicans were stunned.

Crisis with the PRI

The advances made during Díaz Ordaz's term in economic growth and education have been completely overshadowed by his repressive handling of the student demonstrations. The PRI still has not recovered from the tragedy at Tlatelolco. Mexicans were convinced that the party, out of touch with the nation's needs, only served the ambitions of its own politicians. Luminaries such as the poet Octavio Paz and the writer Carlos Fuentes condemned the government. Intellectuals abandoned the PRI, and dissident youth looked for more progressive parties to support. Others went underground: in 1969, on the anniversary of Tlatelolco, a terrorist group bombed government and newspaper buildings.

The call for open elections and a broader-based government became a major issue in Mexican politics. Making the Mexican government more democratic was difficult. The government was, in fact, the PRI. Its control of the state apparatus was not technically illegal under the constitution, which permitted exceptionally centralized power in the office of the presidency. The autocratic party could not easily be removed either: the election apparatus was under its control, as was the television news. The newspapers could be influenced, because the government subsidized the cost of newsprint and hence financially controlled their ability to survive. There were alternative newspapers, and brutally critical ones at that, but their circulation was mostly among intellectuals. And there were opposition parties that gave the appearance of democracy to the electoral process; they just never were permitted to win. Congress did not serve as a check on the PRI or on the president, because the principle of no reelection applied to legislative office as well as to the presidency: the

PARTY ELECTION RESULTS IN 1970*				
Party	PRI	PAN	PPS	PARM
Percentage	80.0	13.6	1.4	0.8

Based on figures from the Federal Election Commission, Mexico City, and *Mexico: A Country Guide*, Tom Barry:33

legislators never served long enough to develop an independent power base. The PRI president held absolute power for six years. The struggle for reforms would preoccupy Mexico for the rest of the century.

The Miracle Slows

When Luis Echeverría became president (1970–76), he exacerbated the alienation many already felt from the PRI. As the minister of the interior under Díaz Ordaz, he was believed to be yet another party conservative and, worse, responsible for the Tlatelolco tragedy. A master of PRI politics, Echeverría campaigned hard among the working classes and spent considerable time talking to people in rural areas about their needs. Although he did nothing to reform the PRI structurally, his own style made the party appear more broad based.

Echeverría had the misfortune to manage the economic miracle during a period of crisis. Economic growth slowed to under 4 percent, creating a recession from 1971 to 1972. U.S. policies under President Richard Nixon also adversely affected Mexico; they included a 10 percent surcharge on all imports and the elimination of the gold standard for the dollar. Because the peso had always been pegged to the dollar, the peso became unstable. Inflation did more damage. By 1973 the economy was in severe straits.

Echeverría's response surprised the private sector. He delineated a new economic policy of "shared development" that included a government coalition with workers and peasants, not just with the private business sector, thus proving himself to be one of Mexico's most progressive presidents in this century. He raised prices on electricity and gas, but protected workers by increasing their wages. Price controls were ordered on tortillas, beans, and other basic commodities to make them affordable to the poor.

Businesses complained, threatening to put their capital in U.S. banks. Echeverría lost his temper and launched into a speech against "the little rich ones" who were unwilling to strengthen Mexico for the next generation. Throughout his term, the president favored greater government intervention in the economy—and alienated the private sector. Echeverría even traveled throughout the Third World championing the need for developing nations to steer a course between capitalism and socialism and the importance of narrowing the gap between the rich and poor.

To revive the economy Echeverría lavished public monies on social programs. He doubled the production of oil, electricity, and steel—with

MAIZE AND POPULATION INCREASES		
	Maize (in metric tons)	Population (in millions)
1960	5,386,000	34.9
1970	8,997,000	48.2
1980	11,081,000	67.4
Source: Statistical Abstract of Latin America		

borrowed money. He further regulated multinational corporations and attempted to lessen Mexico's reliance on the United States for exports and investment. He actively implemented the 51 percent Mexican control law and insisted that management, too, be mostly Mexican. He nationalized the tobacco and telephone industries and bought up smaller national companies to keep a strong Mexican corporate presence. (State-owned businesses increased from 86 to 740.) He invested in public works. The recession was left behind when the economy grew by over 5.5 percent annually. The problem was that inflation and the federal deficit grew even faster.

Maize Shortage

In 1970 maize production had increased 60 percent over that of 1960. Despite such phenomenal growth, the population had increased by 72 percent, so Mexico had to import 760,000 tons of corn to feed its people. Echeverría was disturbed that Mexico had failed to be self-sufficient in such a basic and, for Mexico, symbolic commodity. Unfortunately, it was only the most remarkable of the many foodstuffs that Mexico was forced to import. Echeverría made agriculture his priority, reinforcing it with 20 percent of the budget. Unlike his predecessors, he invested this money in the development of traditional farming communities and *ejidos*. Echeverría charged the agency CONASUPO with implementing an integrated program of credit, storage facilities, marketing advice, and price support for rural development and self-sufficiency in maize. The program, competing with older bureaucracies, was blocked from proper implementation which meant that it could never really succeed.

Population

> Here is the dilemma: either the developed Mexico
> will absorb and integrate the other, or the
> underdeveloped Mexico, by the sheer dead weight of
> demographic increase will end up strangling the
> developed Mexico.
>
> ■
>
> —*Octavio Paz (1972:45)*

Control of population growth was also necessary to any program of self-sufficiency. Like his predecessors, the Catholic president initially

CIUDAD NEZAHUALCÓYOTL

◆n the outskirts of the capital, one squatters' settlement grew up along the edge of what had formerly been Lake Texcoco, a dreadfully dusty area in the dry season and a muddy one during the rains. By the 1980s the camp had a population of over 2 million. Many of its residents had come from the Mixteca Sierra of Oaxaca; so many that weekly communication with the home villages was made possible, not by the postal service, but rather by the comings and goings of the Nezahuacóyotl community. The sheer size of the slum forced the government to recognize it. Streets and schools were built, electricity and water and sewerage were provided. A municipal government was instituted, and the town was named for the pre-Columbian ruler and poet, probably his most unusual honor. Some claim that Ciudad Neza, as it is more often called, is Mexico's unrecognized third largest city.

CITIES OVER 500,000 IN 1980	
Mexico City	12,000,000
Guadalajara	2,178,000
Monterrey	1,702,000
Puebla	771,000
Ciudad Juárez	680,000
León	596,000
Tijuana	542,000

Based on Meyer & Sherman: 691

resisted advocating any form of family planning. Instead he addressed the growing problems by spending public funds on housing and schools. By the middle of his term, however, he became the first president to support birth-control programs. His successor would follow suit, initiating public campaigns against large families. Posters in buses and television soap operas emphasized the importance of small families. Birth control was distributed at IMSS clinics.

Despite these efforts, which did eventually slow the birth rate, the population simply outstripped all efforts to keep up with it—in job creation, schools, and other necessities. A million young adults entered the labor force each year, yet the growth of the economy could not absorb them. In their search for work the unemployed migrated to the cities where they squatted on any available land. Mexico City became a megalopolis by 1980 with a population of 12 million: at least 5 million lived in poverty.

Undocumented Workers

Population pressure increased migration across the U.S. border. Because the official *bracero* program instituted during World War II had terminated in 1964, Mexicans crossed the border as illegal aliens. Even before its termination, Mexican workers in the United States had been the target of resentment and racism. The increase in their numbers during the 1970s and 1980s—and later in the 1990s—caused some alarmists to claim there was a "silent invasion" of eight to 12 million Mexicans into the United States. Studies in the mid-1980s, however, indicated only 1.5 to 3.5 million were in the United States at any one time. Those that were in the United States worked, many paid taxes, and few utilized available social services. Yet the hyperbole and tensions would only get worse, creating political problems between Mexico and the United States.

Echeverría Ends Term

Echeverría never stopped trying to woo new groups. For the youth he lowered the voting age to 18, but they would never forgive him Tlateloco no matter how revolutionary his policies: he still was pelted with rocks at the campus of the National University. He also negotiated the Equal Protection Amendment through the legislature and, with just days left in his term, distributed 250,000 acres to landless peasants in the state of Sonora. And in an unusual effort to let Mexicans comment on his successor—usually the PRI squabbled in private—he floated seven names to the public before making the final announcement that José López Portillo would be the next president of Mexico (1976–82).

OIL PRODUCTION, 1976–80		
	1976	1980
Barrels per day	800,000	2.3 million
Earnings	$500 million	$6 billion
Based on Meyer & Sherman:679		

Petrodollars

López Portillo came to office much like predecessors: he had worked in local politics, become active in the PRI, and taken a cabinet post that led to the presidency. He inherited a troubled economy with a large federal deficit, high inflation (up to 60 percent), and a trade deficit that, with imports outstripping exports by almost $3.5 billion, no longer could be balanced by foreign investment. At the end of his term, Echeverría had been forced to slow imports and make Mexican products more competitive on the world market by devaluing the peso—twice. First, it was devalued by almost 40 percent; then, only a month later, it was devalued again. The peso, equivalent to $.08 for twenty years, suddenly was worth less than $.04. The shock sent capital to the security of foreign banks and shattered the view that the Mexican economy was safe for investment.

Yet López Portillo knew he had an historic opportunity to resolve Mexico's economic problems. In 1974 new oil reserves had been discovered in the southern states of Chiapas and Tabasco. At the same time the Arab oil embargo was causing oil prices to skyrocket. In 1980 the reserves were estimated to be at least 60 billion barrels and probably as many as 200 billion. Finding oil was equivalent to finding the proverbial pot of gold. Mexico was jubilant. It suddenly was a wealthy nation, a member of the haves rather than the have-nots. By 1980, its production had tripled and with rising oil prices, its earnings increased twelvefold.

There was immense foreign pressure on López Portillo to increase oil production. He resisted, arguing that the Mexican economy could withstand only a gradual increase and that its reserves should be used wisely, like a savings account for Mexico's future.

Nonetheless Mexico was the world's fourth largest producer by 1981. In 1982 petroleum comprised 78 percent of all its exports. The growing industry also alleviated unemployment: it absorbed 150,000 new workers each year and the expanding economy created almost 1 million jobs in 1979 alone. Although this growth contributed to rampant inflation, the economy still grew from 8 percent to 9 percent annually—more than in the miracle years of the 1960s.

Independent Foreign Policy

Since World War II, Mexico had carefully nourished its friendship with the United States. Beginning with the López Mateos administration, however, it increasingly took more independent stands in the international arena. Its foreign policy was formulated on a principle that sprang from Mexico's centuries of struggle against foreign domination: the principle of noninterference in matters of national sovereignty. Based on this principle, López Mateos did not follow the U.S. lead in breaking off diplomatic relations with Fidel Castro's Cuba. But it did support the United States in areas where its security was threatened, as in the case of the Cuban missile crisis. Echeverría more flamboyantly separated himself from many U.S. policies, organizing Third World countries to make demands on the industrial nations and supporting the Chilean president, Salvador Allende against American interference. López Portillo, operating with the confidence of a major oil producer, felt free to disagree, too. As President Ronald Reagan increasingly involved the United States in Central American countries, such as El Salvador and Honduras, he found that López Portillo's support was not forthcoming. In fact, Mexico became a facilitator of the peace processes that finally occurred.

Financial Troubles

Although Mexico had intended to avoid dependency on oil, its other exports, especially in agriculture, diminished—partly because prices for items such as sugar and coffee fell. And foodstuffs increasingly needed to be imported along with the machinery and goods required for industrial expansion. Despite the petrodollars, Mexico's trade deficit remained troubling, offset only by the willingness of foreign governments and banks to grant loans to the oil rich nation.

Once again Mexico attempted to become self-sufficient in food production. López Portillo, with the help of a World Bank loan and oil monies, invested billions of dollars in a new rural development effort. Initially good weather yielded encouraging results, like 30 percent higher grain crops, but the following years were plagued by drought.

Debt Crisis

By the end of López Portillo's administration, the balance-of-payments deficit (resulting from more goods being imported than exported) approached a monstrous $12 billion. Government activism in agricultural and social development programs resulted in a budget deficit that grew phenomenally, from 7 percent of GDP in the 1970s to 18 percent in 1982. Mexico borrowed money from foreign banks to finance its deficits. The total national debt climbed to $80 billion, and the inflation rate to 100 percent! Despite its good intentions, Mexico had succumbed to petroleum fever.

As an oil glut inundated the international market, prices fell, and Mexico's overreliance on petrodollars became a disaster. A world recession exacerbated matters. A devaluation was imperative to slowing imports and preventing capital flight to foreign banks. As under Echeverría, the peso had to be devalued twice and its value sunk from $.04 to little more than a penny. Suddenly Mexico could not meet its dollar debt repayments.

The U.S. Federal Reserve, fearing a default, put together an emergency plan. López Portillo, attempting to curb capital flight, nationalized Mexican banks—exempting only those that were foreign-owned. He also imposed exchange controls on the peso to prevent any further devaluation. This was the final rupture in the economic alliance with the private and foreign sectors that had sustained Mexican growth for four decades. And it was the end of Mexico's dream of an easy future.

A Severe Reversal

Mexico did not face its crisis alone. Foreign banks, the International Monetary Fund (IMF), and the World Bank all owned a piece of the Mexican debt problem. The new president, Miguel de la Madrid Hurtado (1982–88), would not be as free as his predecessors to manage the economy.

De la Madrid quickly demonstrated a more conservative bent than his predecessors. The Harvard-educated former minister of budget and planning represented the growing class of technocrats in the PRI elite. His training made him sympathetic to the demands of the IMF, and he quickly acceded to its conditions for a bailout on the debt. Many of these conditions eliminated the efforts, as inadequate as they were, to protect the poor. De la Madrid devalued the peso again, and it fell from 80 to 150 pesos to the dollar. He lifted the price controls on thousands of commodities (tortillas increased 40 percent in price, bread 100 percent), and depleted the resources of his predecessor's rural development program by targeting federal funds on increasing export production rather than domestic foodstuffs—again, at the instigation of the IMF. In all, de la Madrid cut public spending by one-third.

These actions encouraged the foreign banks and investment community, and they reinstituted their alliance with the private sector in Mexico. In this regard the changes were successful. Inflation slowed and non-petroleum exports expanded until they comprised 70 percent of total exports by the end of the decade. Yet throughout the 1980s the economy contracted by 6 percent annually. Mexico renegotiated its debt, but to do so it committed 53 percent of the federal budget to repayments. Encumbered by such repayments, Mexico could not expect any economic growth for decades to come.

The political and social fallout was enormous. After the elation brought on by petroleum, Mexico was reduced to taking orders from foreigners about how to manage its affairs—an issue that brought back the most demoralizing moments in Mexican history. The left cried for a default on payments rather than accepting such an insult to the nation's sovereignty. Many Mexicans suffered, not just the poor, as food prices increased and the peso's value fell. Labor threatened massive strikes and demanded a government program of both price and wage freezes, but Fidel Velázquez (still in control of CTM) again managed to keep the workers in line.

The Earthquake of 1985

As if matters were not bad enough, they were worsened by two catastrophes. One was a collapse of the oil market beginning in December 1985, with prices falling from almost $24 a barrel to less than $9. The drop was temporary, but the cost in revenues was over $8 billion. The other event started on the morning of September 19, 1985, when the capital was devastated by a tremendous earthquake that measured 8.1 on the Richter scale. The next day another hit, registering 7.3. Buildings collapsed, including many newer apartment buildings and Mexico's most advanced medical center. The death toll was estimated at between 7,000 and 20,000 people. Over 100,000 were left homeless or injured. Mexicans who could not find their loved ones gathered at the great pilgrimage plaza of the Virgin of Guadalupe seeking solace and information. Here, at the spiritual center of Mexico, emergency centers were established.

The earthquake disaster unified the Mexican people. While the government bureaucracy stumbled to respond, citizens' groups were saving lives. The government suffered a great blow in prestige while a grassroots movement was born, and it would multiply. The Mexicans found solidarity, but their economy was succumbing to the continuing shock waves—the earthquake cost $4 billion in damages. More loans were necessary to enable Mexico to pay its debts, which rose to $96 billion.

A New Course: Free Trade

Realizing that the nation's economic ills required radical surgery, de la Madrid set a new course in economic policy. He hoped a more open economy would enable Mexico to recover from its debt and rapidly privatized many government holdings, some of which were used as a collateral exchange for debt payments. Although the government retained control of oil, electricity, railroads, and telecommunication, their operations were made more efficient.

De la Madrid also withdrew the government from the private sector by lifting protective tariffs from many products and joining the international free trade GATT (General Agreement on Tariffs and Trade) in 1986. Instituting purer forms of capitalism into the Mexican government, de la Madrid hoped to jump-start the Mexican economy. This complete reversal of Mexican postwar economic strategies would become the hallmark of the 1990s.

Moral Renovation

Hoping to ingratiate himself with the populace, de la Madrid initiated a policy of cleaning up corruption, or "moral renovation." Mexicans in the capital were subjected daily to demands for *mordidas* (or bribes; literally "bites") from traffic police—the chief of police built himself a house so large it was called "the Parthenon" by the press. The electorate's natural resentment had turned to disgust with the entire political system when President López Portillo and his cronies had too flagrantly enriched themselves while in office.

But Mexicans hoped that the president also meant to eliminate corruption in the electoral process itself, permitting opposition candidates to gain office. Their wishes were partly fulfilled when de la Madrid permitted the PAN, the conservative opposition party, to win important municipal elections in the north. Unfortunately, the record was made murky, and violent, when the PRI ousted a progressive candidate in Juchitán, Oaxaca, and insisted on total victory in the 1985 and 1986

gubernatorial elections. Citizens demonstrated against the corrupt practices of the PRI and received international attention when they blocked
a bridge across the U.S. border.

Mexico ended decades of expansion and optimism with deep concern
about its future. The PRI party dictatorship no longer would go uncon-
tested. The protectionist economy seemed out of step with the international climate of free trade. The first steps made by President de la Madrid
towards opening Mexico politically and economically became the foundation of radical changes in policies witnessed in the 1990s.

Modern Art and Culture

Mexico's expansion of education encompassed more than campaigns
against illiteracy. Many secondary schools, art schools, and state universities also were founded or expanded in the modern period and the highly
esteemed scholarly institute, El Colegio de México, was begun. The result
has been a modern period rich in literary journals, histories (Daniel Cosío
Villegras's multivolume history of modern Mexico, published in the
1940s, remains a valued resource to scholars today), political essays, and
a great diversity of intellectual life. In literature, Mexico can boast of two
exceptional writers: the Nobel prize-winning poet Octavio Paz (b. 1914),
whose *Labyrinth of Solitude* (1950), an essay on the Mexican character,
is his most famous work, and Carlos Fuentes (b. 1928), an essayist and
novelist who wrote, among other works, *Where the Air is Clear*, 1958,
and *The Death of Artemio Cruz*, 1964, both about the corruption of
revolutionary values, and *The Old Gringo*, 1984, again about the Revolution. These olympians do not stand alone in literature; a younger generation is making its contributions, including two women: Angeles
Mastretta (b. 1949) whose novel *Mexican Bolero*, 1986, continues the
tradition of Mexican historic fiction; and Laura Esquivel (b. 1950) whose
novel *Like Water for Chocolate*, 1989, is more in the Mexican tradition of
magical realism.

One scholarly field in particular has contributed to the national
identity: anthropology. The National Institute of History and Archaeology (INAH) funded the excavation of major pre-Columbian cities such
as Palenque in Chiapas, Monte Albán in Oaxaca, Uxmal in Yucatán, and
the Aztec Great Temple revealed in the 1980s from its cover of colonial
buildings (see page 57)—and literally hundreds more. The INAH trained
ethnologists who studied and recorded the customs of contemporary
Indians and discovered Mesoamerican traditions surviving in many

villages. The INAH has also opened superb museums to display the magnificent sculptures excavated at the many ancient cities; none is more fabulous than the National Museum of Anthropology in Mexico City, designed by architect Pedro Ramírez Vásquez and opened in 1964. All this work has contributed to the now enormous understanding of Mexico's past and has been a source of pride to all Mexicans.

The traditions of the great muralists and themes of *mexicanidad* continue in Mexico today. Although the first generation thrived well into the modern period and a second generation of painters continues to decorate the walls of town halls with regional history (see page 51), there has been a shift to a more international style. The renowned Rufino Tamayo (1899–1991) is the foremost example of this change. His work often was monumental and inspired by Mexican themes, but the subject matter was not historical and the style not didactic. Rather, it is often in the genre called magical realism, a fusion of the fantastic and the real that also is apparent in the work of Frida Kahlo. When the revolutionary spirit insisted on a purely Mexican style, Tamayo rebelled by emphasizing the influences on his work from the entire world of art. Francisco Toledo (b. 1940) is the preeminent living Mexican artist; his work is most emphatically in the realm of magical realism. Other contemporary artists have worked both in realistic Mexican styles as well as abstract ones, such as Carlos Mérida (1891–1984), and many eschewed any hint of *mexicanidad* in their work, preferring international styles, such as the abstract sculptures of Pedro Coronel (b. 1931) and the avant-garde work of José Luis

Man Facing Infinity (1971), mural by Rufino Tamayo in the Hotel Camino Real, Mexico City

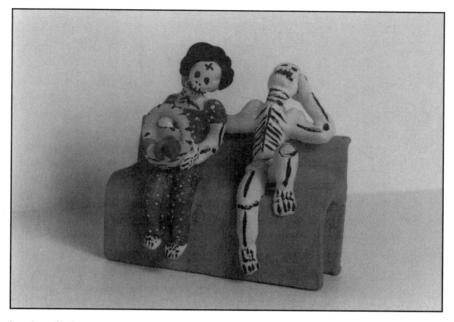

Laughing Skeletons *(1989), ceramic by Josefina Aguilar*   (Photo by Donnelly Marks)

Cuevas (b. 1934). The variety is enormous, from the haunting photographs of Gabriela Iturbide (b. 1942) to the narcissistic self-portraits of Nahum Zenil (b. 1947). They all have received international recognition by exhibits in world capitals. Mexico's artistic tradition has been rewarded by major exhibitions from Paris to San Francisco, but none was more outstanding than the world tour of "Mexico: Splendors of Thirty Centuries," exhibited in the most prominent museums during the quincentennial of Columbus's voyage.

Artisans have also evolved in style. Many today have brought ideas from art school to embellish the traditions of their villages. The copperware of Michoacán now can be seen fused with silver and made into lovely, but purely impractical shapes. Others have drawn on the broader artistic environment, such as the animal woodcarvers of Oaxaca who have been so inspired by magical realism and the majorlica ceramics of Guanajuato that incorporate Persian designs. Folk art has reached such heights that many of its finest practitioners sign their works, such as the woodcarver Manuel Jiménez, the ceramicist Capelo, and the figurine maker Josefina Aguilar. Their work often is sold in art galleries. Like the artists, they have international reputations, and many travel abroad to demonstrate their techniques.

Although much of popular culture has been overwhelmed by U.S. television programs and international rock and rap, Mexico is the creator and exporter of its own popular culture. With Latin music globally popular, both traditional Mexican music (such as the song "La Bamba") and pop artists (such as Gloria Trevi, "the Madonna of Mexico") are major export items.

The Mexican film industry, a thriving if not always an artistic medium, first received international notice when its stars showed up in Hollywood: Dolores del Río, Ricardo Montalban, and Anthony Quinn. But the films of Emilio Fernández (*Que Viva México*, 1931) and Fernando de Fuentes (*Allá en el Rancho Grande*, 1936) brought Mexican films to international attention, too. The industry grew rapidly in producing films for Spanish-speaking countries. Especially popular were films with the comedian Cantinflas and famous mariachi stars, such as Jorge Negrete and Pedro Infante. Most recently the industry has regained its international standing with the success of films such as *Like Water for Chocolate* (directed by Alfonso Arau; 1992), *El Danzón* (directed by María Novaro; 1992), and *Cronos* (winner of the 1994 Cannes Prize and directed by Alfonso Cuarón; 1992).

Decades of Accomplishment and Remaining Problems

By 1988 Mexico had progressed from a barely modernized nation to one with a complex economy of extractive and manufactured goods—processed foods, electrical machinery, petrochemicals, automobiles, textiles, and plastics have taken their place alongside livestock, coffee, and crude oil. Mexico's mining and agriculture remain important to the economy, just as they were in colonial times, but commerce and manufacturing are the two biggest contributors to the gross national product. The travel industry, initiated by Lázaro Cárdenas, attracted 4 million foreign tourists in 1980 who left behind $3 billion.

Socially the nation made exceptional progress as well. A middle class, numbering in the millions and constituting 25 percent of the population in 1991, had been created and took a prominent role in the nation's politics. Literacy had increased from 20 percent in 1910 to 82 percent in 1990. The average caloric intake had doubled since 1910, and life expectancy had jumped from 30 to almost 67 years. These accomplishments were remarkable, especially when compared with those of other developing nations.

Yet, as in the past, overpopulation compounded the problems still to be overcome. In the four decades of the modern period alone, the population grew from about 20 million to over 81 million in 1990, with 70 percent living in cities—in contrast to 20 percent in 1910. Millions remained illiterate, unemployment was high, and many peasants didn't have enough land to sustain themselves. By the late 1970s the economic miracle no longer sustained working-class wages: inflation (60 percent) finally outstripped wage increases (35 percent), and the minimum wage remained one of the lowest in the world (about $3.90 a day in 1991). In 1980 the gap between the rich and the poor had worsened: the poorest 20 percent owned only 3 percent of the national wealth; the richest 20 percent owned 54 percent. Much remained to be done.

Politically, Mexicans were increasingly alienated from their PRI-controlled government. In going from war heroes to technocrats as presidents, Mexico achieved a stupendous reduction in the role of the army in national affairs. The stability that enabled the economy to blossom must be attributed to the PRI's management of diverse interests while maintaining practically dictatorial control. Following a century of upheaval, this, too, was an impressive accomplishment, especially since it was achieved with little repression. In a world where the choice for new nations is too often either tyranny or constant upheaval, Mexico seemed to have successfully found a middle course. As the period ended, however, Mexicans clearly were ambivalent about their government. The time for liberalization seemed to have come. Some, such as the terrorists bands that robbed banks and kidnapped public figures in the 1970s, thought the time for another revolution was near. Even the PRI, under the leadership of its most recent presidents, agreed that profound changes were in order.

11

MEXICO AT THE CROSSROADS

The only thing that is not negotiable [in NAFTA] is
the virginity of the Virgin of Guadalupe. That stays.
Everything else is on the table.
■
—Official, Ministry of Finance (Barry:1992)

Anyone writing about Mexico only a few years ago would have predicted that the North American Free Trade Agreement (NAFTA) would be the most important event of the 1990s. Its passage in 1993 represented the Mexican government's total abandonment of its protectionist management of the economy that had been in effect since the Revolution. So fundamental a reversal did NAFTA represent that many questioned whether its wholesale opening of the economy to U.S. and Canadian investors wasn't a return to the old Profiriato gift of Mexico to foreign businesses. Others optimistically argued that it represented Mexico's chance to join the developed nations as a technologically advanced country.

The years following the ratification of NAFTA have not, however, been preoccupied with monitoring its impact on the nation. Instead, the worst recession since the Revolution knocked Mexico to its knees, threatening to affect financial institutions worldwide and undermining any expectations about Mexico's rosy future. Uprisings, political assassinations, and revelations of corruption on an unprecedented scale have shocked the country and absorbed its energies. Amid all the sensation, quieter and more encouraging moves have been made in the direction of democracy.

President Carlos Salinas de Gortari 1988–94

In 1988 Carlos Salinas faced the first serious political challenge of any PRI presidential candidate. The country was in recession; its fortunes were managed by the IMF in order to meet debt repayments. Calls for democracy and more open politics intensified in Mexico as the PRI's increasing favoritism for business alienated its traditional support from populist groups. The PRI was divided over its response to the mounting criticisms, and the rifts became public, most noticeably when one of its respected members, Cuauhtémoc Cárdenas, abandoned the party.

Cárdenas, the son of one of Mexico's most beloved presidents and named in honor of the last great Aztec emperor, gained immediate appeal when he announced his presidential candidacy and joined a coalition of progressive groups, the National Democratic Front (FDN), which later became the Democratic Revolutionary Party (PRD). Unlike Salinas, he had held electoral office as governor of Michoacán and could speak to the masses of Mexicans who had suffered the most during the repeated fiscal crises since 1982. He was cheered by large crowds as he campaigned throughout the country; many believed he could win the election—if it was conducted fairly. Another candidate, Manuel Clouthier of the conservative PAN, was well financed by northern industrialists and courted the active support of the Catholic church, which had been banned from politics since the Revolution. The PAN had gained popularity, not for its economic or social policies, but rather for its dramatic protests—hunger strikes and road blocks—against PRI-fixed elections.

Calls for Democracy

> This is a historic time. Everyone's clamoring
> for more democracy.
> ■
> —Carlos Salinas de Gortari, 1988 (Smith:393)

Both opposition candidates campaigned for greater democracy, and both made the conduct of the election a primary issue. The international press scrutinized the proceedings. Nonetheless, the PRI once again claimed victory for its candidate. Charges of a rigged election were difficult to confirm: the government computers storing the ballot data conveniently broke down. But the race had been too hotly contested for the PRI to claim its usual 80 to 90 percent victory. Carlos Salinas de Gotari became president with only a slim majority amid charges of fraud.

PRESIDENTIAL ELECTION RESULTS IN 1988			
Party	PRI	FDN/PRD	PAN
Percentage	51	31	18
Based on figures from the Federal Election Commission, Mexico City			

From such an inauspicious beginning, Salinas presided over one of the most admired presidencies in recent memory. To counter public disgust over his "election," he initiated reforms, giving greater access to the media and restricting party financing: no longer would the PRI be financed by the national treasury. Also, the opposition parties won 240 seats out of 500 in the chamber of deputies, forcing the PRI to negotiate with them over serious policy matters. The PAN won the governorship of Baja California in 1989, the first opposition gubernatorial victory in the PRI's 65-year history. Although Salinas's actions did much to assuage national and international opinions, they more deeply divided the PRI into two groups: the elite, foreign-educated "technocrats" involved in policy making and the elected politicos called "dinosaurs," who saw their patronage and power threatened by reforms and privatization.

Economic Recovery

A consumate technocrat, the 39-year-old Salinas had, like his predecessor de la Madrid, been the minister of planning and budget. He seemed to prove the value of his two master degrees from Harvard University, one in economics and the other in public administration, when he managed to end the onerous debt payments (although $98 billion in external debts remained, it was reduced from 79 percent of the GDP to 29 percent) and stabilize the economy (inflation dropped from triple digits to 8 percent in 1994). The economy was expanding by a miraculous 4 percent in 1991, faster than any of the Group of Seven industrial nations. Per capita income increased somewhat for the first time in a decade, despite population growth.

The miracle had partially been accomplished by continuing de la Madrid's sale of government businesses to pay off the foreign debt: 400 state-owned businesses were privatized or shut down; banks, a television channel, and even the telephone company were no longer under party control, but owned by joint foreign and domestic corporations. The miracle continued because Salinas's fluency in the language of world finance—reduced inflation, deficit reduction, export promotion— brought an onslaught of foreign investment, especially in stocks and high-interest bearing bonds.

NAFTA

Salinas convinced both the world and much of Mexico that the nation was on the fast track to modernity. Under the trade liberalization of GATT, foreign products poured into urban areas, and new technology such as cellular phones and bank ATMs became more readily available. Private investment fueled development. Superhighways spanned canyons and tunneled through the mountainous Sierra Madres. It was easy to believe that NAFTA would bring more of the same, speeding Mexico into the global market and "first world" status.

NAFTA and the Salinas modernization program required the jettisoning of the most fundamental principles of the Revolution. The free market, it was said, demanded the abandonment of protected *ejido* land—the safety net for the poorest Mexicans. Now permitted to sell their communal lands, the poor in need would do so—and many already have. Salinas also achieved a constitutional amendment eliminating the right of peasants to land for their subsistence. The land to grow maize and beans no longer would be available to them in desperate times.

Salinas also opened the economy further to foreign investors by lifting the 51 percent Mexican ownership rule and modifying the prohibition on foreign control of extractive commodities. Free trade and open markets stumbled over a few of the more charged symbols of Mexican identity, however—if only temporarily. In the case of maize, the Mesoamerican staff of life, even Salinas did not dare to make a change precipitously; he proposed phasing out tariffs protecting the grain over 15 years—the longest for any commodity. And the oil industry, that former symbol of foreign exploitation, was to remain closed to investment, yet even this might be fudged for the petrochemical industry in the near future. Free enterprise and free trade in the style of the United States had become the economic commitment for Mexico's future.

U.S. Borders

Despite Mexico's growing openness towards a stronger U.S. presence, the reaction in the United States was often tinged with financial fear. Many unions and environmental groups opposed NAFTA. As poverty and overpopulation increased illegal migration from Mexico, racism intensified in the United States. Some states passed laws making English the only official language. Border states like California agitated for protection from increasing numbers of illegal Mexican immigrants. While the two economies opened, ground sensors and night vision equipment were installed along the border and a $4-billion dollar, seven-kilometer metal fence was planned for the border where San Diego and Tijuana meet.

The Church Finds its Voice

Modernization seemed to sweep some Mexican fundamentals out the door. The long struggle during the Juárez reforms and the Revolution to delineate the boundaries between church and state ended with the Constitution of 1917. No one had been eager to reopen this debate, although many administrations permitted Catholic schools to operate quietly. In a highly criticized move, Salinas, like his PAN opponents, championed greater freedom for the church and achieved constitutional amendments on its behalf. Not only does the church now actively comment on political affairs, from elections to the content of textbooks, but the religious are permitted to wear their vestments in public.

Resurgence of Native Traditions

I feel I am more Maya than ever . . . I have no desire
to belong to another culture.
■
—*Pedro Meza (Foxx:209)*

VIRGIN OF GUADALUPE: SYMBOL OF MEXICAN FAITH

The church may sometimes find its newly permitted public profile a liability, at least in regard to the nation's patron saint. Monsigneur Guillermo Schulenber, abbot of the revered Basilica of the Virgin of Guadalupe, saw his preference for fancy cars exposed in a political magazine. With public interest aroused, his remarks about doubting that the Virgin actually appeared in 1531 before the Aztec boy, Juan Diego, also made the press. It caused such a stormy outburst from Mexicans that the abbot was forced to resign. Many are now demanding that the shrine's sizable assets be shared with Mexico's poorer parishes rather than lavished on cars.

The mestizo nation that was officially born with the Mexican Revolution embodied the ideals of two traditions and two races merging into one nation and one people. Racially, the desired mix was achieved in this country where the non-mestizo categories are most accurately described as "predominantly white" or "predominantly Indian." Culturally, national festivals, such as the Day of the Dead, have incorporated pre-Hispanic ancestor worship into the very Catholic All Saints' Day. Yet many Indians are culturally distinct from mestizos; at least 10 million speak the language of their pre-Columbian forebears. The "mestizo ideal" overlooked the fact that these Mexicans cherish their pre-Columbian heritage and have no desire to lose it through assimilation, especially into a society that provides few opportunities for them.

In the most isolated villages indigenous groups continue to live in the most traditional manner. Nahuas still calculate their corn planting according to ancient traditions of the cyclical New Year. A vestige of an old solar calendar is still used in the Chiapas village of Chamula. Pre-Hispanic myths pervade the contemporary religious beliefs of the Mixtecs; Yucatec Maya sages, based on old myths, foretell the day when their ancestors will rule once again. These Mexicans also are among the poorest: they live in homes without sewers (72 percent) or running water (48 percent), and their literacy rate (59 percent) is well below that for the nation as a whole (90 percent).

In 1992, the 500th anniversary of Columbus's voyage to the Americas, indigenous peoples organized within Mexico and throughout the Americas to present their concerns: they wanted the right to preserve their cultures while achieving greater economic parity. One result was an amendment to the Constitution of 1917: Mexico was designated as a multiethnic, not mestizo, nation. The hoped-for by-products are that schools will become more multilingual and native culture no longer will be treated as an anachronism in a mestizo world. It would take the 1994 Zapatista armed uprising, however, to make discrimination against Mexico's first peoples illegal.

The Problems Overlooked

Salinas's agenda, especially concerning NAFTA, was not greeted with equanimity by all Mexicans. Intellectuals believed national sovereignty and *mexicanidad* were threatened. Small businesses knew their survival was at stake. Economists predicted millions of jobs would be lost in the first five years. Many became concerned that their country was up for

Two Mexicos: above, Mexico City skyscrapers; below, a Mexico City street vendor making sopes, or flat corn-and-bean cakes (Photos courtesy of the Mexico Ministry of Tourism)

sale. When U.S. vice president Albert Gore defended NAFTA to U.S. citizens in a televised debate, his remark that NAFTA was an opportunity equivalent to the purchase of Alaska caused an uproar in Mexico.

Under Salinas, modernization ignored the basic needs of the citizenry and polarized Mexican society into the wealthy few and the increasingly poor masses. Hoping to impress global investors with the strength and stability of the peso, Salinas overinflated it while holding down wages. To further expand the export-driven economy, he thought low wages were essential. (Fifty-one percent of manufactured exports were produced by *maquiladoras*, foreign businesses operating with cheap Mexican labor in order to send competitively priced goods into the United States.) The economy grew, but

222

per capita income never increased enough to make up for the losses caused by the recessions during the 1980s. The purchasing power of the minimum wage declined 66 percent from 1982. The now grossly inadequate minimum wage, the lowest even among the more developed Latin American countries, became such a political issue in the United States—yet not for the PRI government—that NAFTA negotiations forced Salinas to increase it. The minimum wage varies regionally, but at the beginning of 1997 it was uniformly under $3.50 a day. A full-time job at minimum wage equals poverty.

More than wages were depressed. Salinas developed new social services under his highly publicized solidarity program, yet the monies—mostly from temporary reserves resulting from privatization—were used selectively to neutralize opposition from both Cárdenas supporters and the "dinosaur" wing of the PRI. They did little to compensate for the 10 percent cutbacks in social programs at a time when continued population growth meant the government could barely keep up with the basic educational needs of the nation. For the first time in its history, the National University (UNAM) considered ending its open door policy; primary schools required double shifts, but compensation was not always

OVERPOPULATION AND THE ENVIRONMENT

Family-planning efforts have reduced the birth rate from 3.5 percent in 1970 to 1.8 percent in 1995. Even at this rate, Mexico will double its population of 90 million in 40 years. Already it is the eleventh most populous nation in the world. The car and industrial pollution in urban areas cannot be missed by the naked eye; smog has become a major health hazard requiring no-car days in the capital and the relocation of factories. Demand has depleted the water table so much that Ciudad Juárez is expected to run dry before the millennium; in Mexico City the streets, built over the canals and lagoons of the Aztec city, have sunk 35 feet. In the countryside, overpopulation has forced families out of their communities in search of new farm land, and deforestation of 1.5 million acres each year has become a problem as potentially disasterous as it was to ancient Maya civilization. In response, an entirely new government agency, SEDUE, has been created to prevent further disintegration of the environment, and citizen activitist groups have sprung up to monitor its progress.

available for the teachers. The social security system, too, became over-taxed with state hospitals struggling to provide adequate care. At charity hospitals, people with broken bones could wait for weeks while the limited staff responded to more serious emergencies. Overpopulation had also resulted in land conflicts in some of the most indigenous, and poor, regions of Mexico. Little was done to resolve the disputes between peasants and ranchers.

Trouble: Zapatistas

Despite these undercurrents, Salinas remained genuinely popular among the middle class and, of course, the elite. The president's confidence in his policies and the respect he received worldwide gave hope to many Mexicans that an era of prosperity and development would be theirs.

Then, New Year's Day 1994, the first day NAFTA was to take effect, was greeted by an armed uprising of 2,000 Maya Indians in the poor southern state of Chiapas. Their leaders, faces covered with ski masks, appeared in the world media saying that NAFTA was a death sentence for Indians. Calling themselves the "Zapatista National Liberation Army," the Mayas demanded land to farm and the return of the constitutional provisions protecting their right to land. They demanded greater democracy. They demanded the end to discrimination against them. They wanted schools and medical care. Said Carlos Aguilar, a Zapatista, "The peasants have awakened and realized that they had to do something in order for them to listen to us. Now the whole world is listening" (Holden: 1994).

Suddenly Salinas's promise of a modern Mexico crashed against the reality of a Mexico that had been completely ignored by the policies of two successive conservative administrations. In Mexico's indigenous states, like Chiapas, some have estimated that 70 percent of the population lives below the poverty line. During the Salinas years extreme poverty increased by one-third.

The army was sent in to restore order, but Mexicans, ashamed of the abject poverty suffered by much of the peasant population, demanded negotiations, not war. Salinas adeptly avoided political catastrophe by unilaterally declaring a cease-fire. Negotiations began in earnest. They continue in 1997.

Assassination

This reality shock was followed by another in Salinas's final year in office. His hand-appointed successor as the PRI presidential candidate, Luis

Donaldo Colosio, satisfied many who had misgivings about Salinas's economic policies. Colosio had a political background that made him seem a progressive antidote to his two PRI predecessors: as minister of social development he was well known for his commitment to social programs; as an elected official, he was more attuned to the people than the technocrats. No one doubted that Colosio would be elected without the help of stuffed ballot boxes.

Despite democratic reforms and strengthened opposition parties, it looked as if Salinas had created so much support for the PRI and its new presidential candidate that the old political machine would once again be victorious. To further prove the PRI's commitment to an open election, Salinas invited international observers to monitor the election along with Mexican grassroots groups that had sprung up during the earthquake of 1985, such as Civil Alliance.

Colosio, however, was assassinated in March 1994 while campaigning in Tijuana. It was the first assassination of a presidential candidate or president in the PRI's history. Six months later, the PRI secretary general, José Ruiz Massieu, was gunned down. The combination of the Zapatista uprising and the political assassinations left Mexico profoundly shaken.

President Ernesto Zedillo and Democratic Reforms

Unlike Colosio, the new candidate, Ernesto Zedillo, had never run for office. A PRI technocrat with a doctorate in economics from Yale University, Zedillo was politically awkward. The PRI won anyway, bouyed on a wave of Colosio sympathy. Cuauhtémoc Cárdenas ran again, but the PRI had done much to undermine the PRD; the left was in disarray and Cárdenas's campaign, lackluster. The PAN candidate, Diego Fernández de Cevallos, more popular after Mexico's historic first televised presidential debate, seemed to stop campaigning at a critical juncture—some claimed in collusion with the PRI. The PRI victory came with a healthy margin, because many Mexicans feared the unknown that would result from a PRI defeat. For the first time, they did not believe their votes were mere protests and local elections proved them right: the PAN racked up enough victories that by 1996 it represented about one-third of the population in municipalities, state governments, and congressional delegations. These strides toward democracy culminated in 1996 when all parties agreed on a constitutional restructuring of the electoral process.

Although the PRI "dinosaurs" continue their efforts to weaken these reforms, the PRI can no longer simply dictate who rules Mexico.

La Crisis

While democracy made some advances under Zedillo, the fledgling president was immediately confronted with a fiscal crisis. Salinas, campaigning for the position of director of the World Trade Organization, had not seen fit to manage what would be a very unpopular devaluation of the peso. He left the dirty work to the new president, who had not yet earned the confidence of foreign financial markets. It was mishandled: the Mexico peso went into a downward spin, and the nation was catapulted into its fourth recession since 1982 and its worst since the Revolution. It took an emergency bailout loan from the United States, with Mexican oil as collateral, to prevent complete collapse of the peso.

By mid-1996 there were signs of a fragile recovery, but Mexico was suffering still. Two million jobs and thousands of small businesses had been lost. To avoid a complete collapse of the currency, interest rates had been quadrupled, and the price of gasoline and utilities had been increased, as had the value-added tax. The cost of food, increasingly imported under Salinas's restructuring of the economy, also rose as a result of the weakened peso. Half the Mexican population was estimated to be living in poverty. The devastated middle class was angry: it was government lies and ineptitude that had done this to them. Salinas's popularity plummeted with the peso, as did world confidence in Mexican markets. Only crime soared.

Corruption

At the time of Colosio's assassination, rumors were rampant about the PRI's possible involvement. With Ruiz Massieu's assassination, they became even more convoluted. The "dinosaurs" did it, some thought, in an attempt to end the liberalizing policies of Salinas. Salinas did it, others thought, because he wanted to run for a second term: his popularity was so great that some thought he could successfully amend the constitution, especially during a time of such crisis. Drug kingpins did it, others speculated, because they were being pursued by PRI prosecutors. As extraordinary as all these accusations may seem to those outside Mexican society, they continue to be held by the Mexican populace and press, and they are fanned into greater credibility by the television soap operas in which Salinas look-alikes play assassins.

A Mixtec Success Story

Eroded land and population pressures sent Isác López to Mexico City from the Mixteca Sierra as a young boy. Living with relatives in Ciudad Nezahuacóyotl, he attended school and, to contribute to the family's needs, sold chiclets on the public buses in the afternoon. While the rest of his family continued to struggle to make ends meet, they contributed what they could so that Isác could become a certified public accountant. For 15 years, Isác worked for major corporations in Mexico, such as Salinas y Rochas and Sheraton. In the 1990s, when interest rates had fallen under Salinas, he qualified for a mortgage on a new, two-story house in the resort of Huatulco, where he worked. With the crisis of 1995, the interest on his mortgage went from 24 to 100 percent. But Isác was one of the lucky ones during *la crisis*: he managed to hold on to his job and his house. The interest payments, however, affected the well-being not only of his immediate family, but also of his extended family who relied on him in times of trouble. In 1996, interest rates finally fell below 30 percent.

More seriously, however, these speculations remain credible because the government has failed to resolve the murders. In the process of untangling them, astonishing levels of corruption have been revealed. Initially Ruiz Massieu's brother was appointed by Salinas to investigate the deaths, but he resigned in protest, saying political pressures from high within the PRI prevented an honest investigation. Once Zedillo took office he encouraged confidence in his administration by appointing an attorney general from outside the PRI. Soon thereafter Zedillo daringly permitted the arrest and imprisonment of Salinas's brother, Raúl, for collusion in the murder of Ruiz Massieu, his own brother-in-law.

The arrest of Raúl Salinas has led to a series of revelations that even the most cynical Mexican would have thought impossible. After Salinas's arrest, the former attorney general Ruiz Massieu—hired to find his brother's murderer—fled the country and was arrested at a U.S. airport carrying a suitcase that contained large amounts of undeclared cash. Then, he was discovered to have millions of dollars in U.S. banks. Corruption is now known to have touched everything, from the way tortillas are made to the sale of state-owned agencies, from protection of drug kingpins to murder. Corruption was always known to exist, but it is the violence, even in regard to one's own family, and the scale of personal enrichment that now have made a farce of PRI. The once popular Carlos Salinas has been forced to join Hernán Cortés and Porfirio Díaz as among the most reviled figures in Mexican history. He sensibly sneaked out of Mexico; in 1997, he was living comfortably in Ireland, a country that does not have an extradition treaty with Mexico.

Drugs and Politics

The amount of money that is now known to have been squirreled out of the country is so great that outraged Mexicans believe corruption has bankrupted their nation. Not surprisingly, they feel personally robbed. Raúl Salinas alone had an estimated $300 million in European banks. He is charged with the additional crime of illicit enrichment, his government salary having been $190,000. It is increasingly clear that kickbacks and favoritism were involved in the sale of government businesses. Many of the government plums went to members of Salinas's campaign finance committee; the number of Mexican billionaires soared from two to 24. Even given the privatization scandals, the stupendous prices offered, say for a television channel, were well above market value. The amount of capital involved has led some of the more serious Mexican political scientists to conclude that drug money was welcomed by the Salinas administration. This, too, has shocked Mexico.

Mexico at the Millennium

For all that Mexico accomplished into the 1980s, it is now reeling from changes as profound as those resulting from the Revolution. It seems certain that economic, social, and political problems will continue to disrupt its progress toward becoming a unified and modernized nation for some time to come. Sporadic guerrilla outbreaks in 1996 by a group calling itself the People's Revolutionary Army (EPR) have added to the uncertainty of the times. Many believe this group is not a significant threat. Yet the existence of the EPR adds to the general bewilderment: no one is certain whether these violent outbursts are staged by PRI dinosaurs, impoverished peasants, or drug dealers. In response, the army has become increasingly visible throughout the country, raising concern about the role of the military in Mexican politics.

The traumatic events of the 1990s do have a brighter side. The disgrace of Salinas and his party has resulted in a reformed electoral system that enabled the opposition parties to upset the balance of power in the July 1997 elections, when they gained a slim but historic majority in the lower house of Congress. The exposure of scandals indicates a much freer press, one willing to take on the traditional authorities. Grassroots movements, from peasant organizations and environmental groups to urban ones like Civic Alliance, have given voice to citizens' demands and forced the government to resolve more issues in a public forum. Civic Alliance has even created a "corruption watch" in which citizens adopt a politician to monitor. Splinter unions have hope of influencing government policies with the death of Fidel Velázquez, PRI's labor leader for the past 50 years. Politics have become more complex and open; the citizenry more engaged.

Cut free of the stability provided by the one-party system and adrift in the new economy created by NAFTA, Mexicans naturally are skittish about what the future will bring. During the 1994 election, pundits predicted either civil war or repression. Neither happened. During the current fiscal crisis, they predicted a social explosion and, once again, they were proven wrong. It appears that the majority of Mexicans, well educated in the destructiveness of the Revolution of 1910, have little desire to seek violent solutions. The question remains as to whether unscrupulous politicians, phantom armies (or real ones), and drug kingpins will permit the nation to progress peacefully toward a more democratic government, a more stable and balanced economy, and a society less polarized between the rich and poor.

APPENDIX 1

BASIC FACTS ABOUT MEXICO

OFFICIAL NAME

Estados Unidos de México

GOVERNMENT

Under the Constitution of 1917, Mexico is a federal republic with a centralized government dominated by the office of the presidency. The presidential term is six years with no reelection. There is a bicameral federal congress comprised of a senate and chamber of deputies. The judiciary forms a third branch of government.

There are many parties, but the PRI (Institutional Revolutionary Party) has governed Mexico during the modern epoch. Recent electoral reforms have strengthened opposition parties such as the conservative PAN (National Action Party) and the progressive PRD (Democratic Revolutionary Party).

POLITICAL DIVISIONS

States

Thirty-one plus the federal district which includes the capital.

Capital

Mexico City

GEOGRAPHY

Area

Covering 761,604 square miles, Mexico is four times the size of Spain. Mexico is the thirteenth largest country in land area in the world and the fifth largest in the Western Hemisphere, after Canada, the United States, Brazil, and Argentina.

Boundaries

To the north, the United States and the Gulf of Mexico. To the east and south, the Caribbean Sea, Belize, and Guatemala. To the west and south, the Pacific Ocean.

Topography

Mountains (Sierra Madre Occidental) run from the northwest to the southeast near the Pacific coast. Another chain (Sierra Madre Oriental) runs near the Gulf coast. South of Mexico City the mountains become the Sierra Madre Sur.

Arid plateaus lie between the mountain chains with altitudes ranging from 6500 to 8000 feet. Coastal regions are tropical. One peninsula marks the west (Baja California) and another in the east (Yucatán).

There are few navigable rivers. The most important riverine systems are in the southeast with the Grijalva, Usumacinta, and Coatzacoalcos rivers draining into the Gulf. The Balsas River, draining into the Pacific, is the most important in the central plateau. The Río Bravo ("Rio Grande") defines the border with the United States.

Forty-five percent of the land is arid.

Highest Elevation

Citlaltépetl (Pico de Orizaba), at 18,696 feet, is the third highest mountain in North America.

DEMOGRAPHICS

Population (1995 Census)

With 91.1 million people, Mexico is the eleventh most populous country in the world.

Largest City

Mexico City; the metropolitan area has a population of 21 million.

Language

Official language: Spanish, spoken by 95 percent of the population.
Indigenous languages: Fifty distinct languages and hundreds of dialects are spoken by 10 percent of the population over five years old. Nahuatl (in central Mexico), Yucatec Maya, Zapotec (in Oaxaca), Mixtec (in Oaxaca), and Purépecha (in Michoacán) are among the most prevalent.

Religion
Roman Catholic, 93 percent
Protestant, 3 percent
Other, 4 percent

ECONOMY

GDP (1990)
$238 billion; the fifteenth largest in the world and the second largest in Latin America.

Economic Sectors
Financial services, 28 percent
Commerce, 25.5 percent
Manufacturing, 23 percent
Agriculture, 7 percent
Transportation and communication, 7 percent
Mining, 3.5 percent
Construction, 5 percent
Electricity, 1 percent

Most Important Sources of Foreign Revenues
Petroleum exports
Maquiladora exports
Automobile exports
Tourism
Mining exports
Agroexports

Appendix 2

Chronology

Pre-Columbian Mexico

pre-10,000 B.C.	Peopling of the Americas from Asia.
c. 5000	Extinction of mammoths.
c. 3000	Farming.
c. 2000	Sedentary villagers.
c. 1200	Rise of Olmec civilization and other early preclassic cultures.
c. 400	Protoclassic cultures: the first cities. The rise of Teotihuacán, Monte Albán, and Maya cities, such as El Mirador.
A.D. 250–900	Classic period flourishing of Teotihuacán, Monte Albán, and southern lowland Maya.
900–1200	Terminal classic and early postclassic horizon. Trade routes and population centers shift to cities such as Chichén Itzá, El Tajín, and Tula.
1200–1521	Aztecs gradually dominate much of Mesoamerica. A few other regional cultures flourish, such as the Mixtec.

Spain in North America

April 22, 1519	Hernán Cortés anchors his ships off the Veracruz coast.
June 30, 1520	The *Noche Triste*.
1521	Spanish conquistadors defeat Aztecs at Tenochtitlán.
	Mexico becomes the colony of New Spain and governed by Spain until 1821.

1523	Arrival of the first Franciscan missionaries. Alvarado conquers Guatemala and El Salvador.
1527–37	Spaniards struggle to conquer the Mayas of Yucatán while most of Central America is pacified.
1528	Spaniards explore Florida, and Cabeza de Vaca returns overland through Texas into Mexico.
1533	Founding in Mexico City of the first university in the Americas.
1535	Antonio de Mendoza, the first viceroy of New Spain, arrives.
1538	De Soto explores from Florida to beyond the Mississippi River.
1540–42	Coronado explores Arizona and New Mexico.
1542	New Laws promulgated by Spain: Indian slavery prohibited. Cabrillo explores California coast.
1565	Legazpi colonizes the Philippines: China trade initiated.
1571	Inquisition instituted in New Spain.
1610	Oñate founds a colony in Santa Fe.
1681	Padre Kino and the Jesuits attempt to establish missions in Baja California.
1697	The last Maya stronghold of Canek capitulates to Spain.
1700	Charles II dies, last of the Spanish Hapsburgs. Bourbons rule the colonies.

Struggle for Independence

September 16, 1810	Miguel Hidalgo's cry for independence.
1811	Hidalgo executed. José María Morelos continues the struggle.
1815	Morelos executed.
1821	Enlightened constitution in Spain; Mexican conservatives join in call for independence. Spain signs treaty granting independence.

Independent Mexico: Years of Chaos

1822	Agustín de Iturbide crowned emperor of Mexico. The monarchy lasts seven months.
1823	Central American countries secede from Mexico.
1824	Mexico becomes a federal republic under its first constitution.
1833–55	The age of Santa Anna in Mexican politics.
1835	Texas declares its independence from Mexico. Santa Anna leads the Mexican attack on the Alamo.
1845	The United States annexes Texas.
1846–48	The Mexican-American War. The United States marches into Mexico City and defeats Santa Anna. Under Treaty of Guadalupe Mexico loses half its territory to the United States.
1847–49	Maya Caste Wars in Yucatán.
1853	Santa Anna sells southernmost Arizona and New Mexico to the United States in the Gasden Purchase.
1855	Liberals chase Santa Anna out of government.
1857	The Laws of Reform. New liberal constitution separates the church and state; limits church property and restricts privileges of military.
1858–61	Reform War: liberals vs. conservatives; reforms vs. non-reforms.
1860	Benito Juárez becomes Mexico's first Indian president.
1862	French, Spanish, and British forces blockade port of Veracruz demanding payment of loans.
May 5, 1862	Mexicans defeat French troops at Puebla.
1863–67	French install monarchy in Mexico under Maximilian at the invitation of Mexican conservatives. Juárez withdraws his government to the north. Struggle culminates in French defeat and execution of Maximilian.
1867	Constitutional republic restored.

1872	Benito Juárez dies.

The Porfiriato and the Mexican Revolution

1876–1910	Porfirio Díaz rules Mexico.
1910	Centennial of Mexican independence. Francisco Madero calls for free elections. Mexican Revolution begins.
1911	Díaz forced into exile in France. Madero elected president of Mexico.
1913	Madero assassinated by Victoriano Huerta. Venustiano Carranza, Pancho Villa, and Emiliano Zapata fight Huerta.
1914	Wilson sends U.S. troops to blockade Veracruz against Huerta. Huerta defeated; flees. Factionalism among revolutionaries.
1917	Constitution of 1917 promulgated, instituting land reform and labor rights. Carranza elected first constitutional president.
1920	Alvaro Obregón becomes president, demilitarizes politics and initiates social reforms. José Vasconcelos, minister of education, begins muralist movement.
1924–34	Plutarco Elías Calles elected president. Becomes strongman of Mexico.
1926–29	Cristero Rebellion.
1929	Calles founds National Revolutionary Party, forerunner of today's PRI and political system of party dictatorship.
1934–40	Presidency of Lázaro Cárdenas and period of land and social reform.
1938	Cárdenas expropriates foreign oil companies.
1940	Cárdenas leaves office peacefully, the first president to be neither exiled nor assassinated since the Revolution.

Modern Mexico

1940–46	Presidency of Avila Camacho.
1942	Mexico declares war on the Axis powers. United States and Mexico agree on the Bracero Program for Mexican contract labor in the United States.
1946–50	Miguel Alemán's presidency. Ruling party renamed Institutional Revolutionary Party (PRI). New campus built for National Autonomous University of Mexico (UNAM).
1952–58	Presidency of Adolfo Ruiz Cortines.
1954	Women granted the right to vote.
1958–64	Presidency of Adolfo López Mateos.
1964–70	Presidency of Gustavo Díaz Ordaz.
1968	Tlatelolco student massacre. Olympic games held in Mexico City.
1970–76	Presidency of Luis Echeverría. First policy on population control. Nationalization of many businesses, including state takeover of banks.
1974	Passage of Equal Rights Amendment for women.
1976–82	The oil boom and presidency of José Lopéz Portillo.
1977	First electoral reforms to increase representation by opposition in congress.
1982	Mexico's foreign debt crisis.
1982–88	Presidency of Miguel de la Madrid marked by foreign banks' interference in economy due to debt crisis. Promises for "moral renovation" and political reforms prove disappointing.
1985	Earthquake devastates Mexico City.
1986	Mexico liberalizes trade policies by joining GATT; privatization of industries begin.

1988	Presidential election hotly contested by opposition parties. PRI's claim of victory results in massive demonstrations.
1988–94	Presidency of Carlos Salinas de Gortari. Austerity programs continue, coupled with free market and free trade policies.
1989	First opposition governor elected in over 50 years. Constitutional amendments permit greater electoral reform. Mexico's foreign debt reduced.
1992	Constitutional amendment recognizing that Mexico is a multiethnic society.
1993	NAFTA signed by Mexico, the United States and Canada.
1994	The Zapatista uprising in Chiapas. Assassinations of the PRI presidential candidate, Luis Donaldo Colosio, and the head of the PRI, José Ruiz Massieu.
1994	PRI candidate Ernesto Zedillo becomes president in internationally monitored election. Peso devaluation devastates economy and morale of nation.
1995–96	Investigations into assassinations lead to arrest of Raúl Salinas, former president's brother. Opposition parties make great gains in mid-term elections under new reforms.
1996	Sporadic rebellions intensify role of military Economy begins a fragile recovery. More electoral reforms approved.
1997	Opposition parties in lower house of Congress win slim but historic majority in July elections.

Appendix 3

Bibliography

Alamán, Lucas. *Historia de México, 1808–1849.* 5 vols. second edition. México, 1942.

Aridjis, Homero in "Mexicans Fear for Corn, Imperiled by Free Trade." *New York Times.* July 12, 1993.

Ashton, Dore. "Mexican Art of the Twentieth Century." In *Mexico: Splendors of Thirty Centuries.* New York: Metropolitan Museum of Art, 1990.

Azuela, Mariano. *The Flies.* In *Two Novels of Mexico.* Translated by Lesley Byrd Simpson. Berkeley: University of California Press, 1956.

———. *The Underdogs.* Translated by E. Munguía. New York: New American Library, 1963.

Barry, Tom, ed. *Mexico: A Country Guide.* Albuquerque: The Inter-Hemispheric Education Resource Center, 1992.

Benavides, Alonso de. *The Revised Memorial of 1634.* Translated and edited by Frederick W. Hodge, et al. Albuquerque: University of New Mexico Press, 1945.

Borah, Woodrow and Shelburne F. Cook. *The Aboriginal Population of Central Mexico on the Eve of the Spanish Conquest.* Berkeley: University of California Press, 1963.

Brenner, Anita. *The Wind that Swept Mexico.* Austin: University of Texas Press, 1971.

Burkhart, Louise M. "The Cult of the Virgin of Guadalupe in Mexico." In *South and Meso-American Native Spirituality.* Edited by G. H. Gossen. London: SCM Press, 1993.

Calderón de la Barca, Fanny. *Life in Mexico: The Letters of Fanny Calderón de la Barca.* Edited by Howard T. Fisher and Marion H. Fisher. Garden City: Doubleday, 1966.

Cárdenas, Lázaro. Quoted in *Mexico's Oil: A Compilation of Official Documents.* México: Gobierno de México, 1940.

Chance, John K. "Colonial Ethnohistory of Oaxaca." In *Supplement to Handbook of Middle American Indians, vol. 4 Ethnohistory.* Edited by

Victoria Reifler Bricker and Ronald Spores. Austin: University of Texas, 1986.

Charlot, Jean. *Mexican Art and the Academy of San Carlos, 1783–1915.* Austin: University of Texas Press, 1962.

Cook, Sherburne F., and Woodrow Borah. *Essays in Population Study.* 2 vol. Berkeley: University of California Press, 1971, 1973.

Cortés, Hernán. *Letters from Mexico.* Translated and edited by Anthony Pagden. New Haven: Yale University Press, 1986.

Crónica mexicana. México: Editorial Leyenda, 1944.

Cumberland, Charles C. *Mexico: The Struggle for Modernity.* London: Oxford University Press, 1968.

Daniken, Erick von. *Chariots of the Gods.* London: Souvenir Press, 1969.

Davis, Nigel. *The Aztecs.* London: Macmillan, 1973.

Denevan, William M., ed. *The Native Populations of the Americas in 1492.* Madison: University of Wisconsin Press, 1976.

Díaz del Castillo, Bernal. *The Discovery and Conquest of Mexico 1517–1521.* Edited and translated by A. P. Maudslay. New York: Farrar, Straus and Giroux, 1956.

Durán, Diego. *Books of the Gods and Rites and the Ancient Calendar.* (c. 1575). Norman: University of Oklahoma Press, 1971.

Farriss, Nancy M. *Maya Society Under Colonial Rule: The Collective Enterprise of Survival.* Princeton: Princeton University Press, 1984.

Fieldstaff Reports, North America Series, vol. 2, no. 1 (July 1974).

Florescano, Enrique. *Memory, Myth, and Time: From the Aztecs to Independence.* Translated by Albert G. Bork. Austin: University of Texas Press, 1994.

Foxx, Jeffrey Jay and Walter F. Morris, Jr. *Living Maya.* New York: Henry N. Abrams, 1987.

Gage, Thomas. *Travels in the New World, 1648.* Reprint. Westport, Conn.: Greenwood Press, 1981.

Garibay, Angel M., ed. and trans. *La literatura de los Aztecas.* México: Editorial Joaquín Mortiz, 1953.

González Casanova, Pablo. *Democracy in Mexico.* New York: Oxford University Press, 1972.

Guzmán, Martín Luis. *Memoirs of Pancho Villa.* Translated by V. H. Taylor. Austin: University of Texas Press, 1965.

Hammond, George P. and Agapito Rey, eds. *Narratives of the Coronado Expedition.* (1940). Reprint. Albuquerque: University of New Mexico Press, 1970.

Herrejón, Carlos. *Morelos, antología documental.* México: SEP, 1985.

Heyerdahl, Thor. *Kon-Tiki*. Chicago: University of Chicago Press, 1951.

Holden, Tom. "In Remote Mexican Village Roots of Rebellion are Bared." *New York Times*, January 17, 1994.

Israel, Jonathan I. *Race, Class, and Politics in Colonial Mexico 1610–1670*. London: Oxford University Press, 1975.

Jones, Grant D., ed. *El Manuscrito de Canek*. México: Instituto Nacional de Antropología e Historia, 1991.

Jones, Willis Knapp, ed. *Spanish American Literature in Translation*. New York: Frederick Ungar, 1966.

Katz, Frederick. "The Liberal Republic and the Porfiriato 1887–1910." In *Mexico since Independence*. Edited by Leslie Berthell. Cambridge: Cambridge University Press, 1992.

Keeler, Peter, trans. *Chilam Balam of Chumayel*. Unpublished, 1993.

Landa, Diego de. *Relación de las cosas de Yucatán*. Edited and translated by Alfred M. Tozzer. Papers of the Peabody Museum of American Archaeology and Ethnology, vol. XVIII. Cambridge: Peabody Museum of Harvard University, 1941.

Las Casas, Bartolomé de. *In Defense of the Indian*. Edited and translated by Stanford Poole. DeKalb: Northern Illinois University Press, 1974.

———. *History of the Indies*. Abridged. Translated and edited by Andree M. Collard. New York: Harper Torchbooks, 1971.

León-Portilla, Miguel, ed. *The Broken Spears: The Aztec Account of the Conquest of Mexico*. Translated by Lysander Kemp. Boston: Beacon Press, 1962.

López de Gómara, Francisco. *The Life of the Conqueror by His Secretary*. Translated by Lesley Byrd Simpson. Berkeley: University of California Press, 1964.

McCarty, J. Hendrickson. *Two Thousand Miles Through the Heart of Mexico*. New York: Phillips & Hunt, 1888.

Meyer, Jean. "Revolution and Reconstruction the 1920s." In *Mexico since Independence*. Edited by Leslie Bethell. Cambridge: Cambridge University Press, 1991.

Miller, Robert Ryal. *Mexico: A History*. Norman: University of Oklahoma Press, 1985.

Monaghan, John. *The Covenants with Earth and Rain: Exchange, Sacrifice, and Revelation in Mixtec Society*. Norman: University of Oklahoma Press, 1995.

Motolinía. *History of the Indians*. Edited by Francis B. Steck. Washington: Academy of American Franciscan History, 1951.

Nuttall, Zelia, ed. *Codex Nuttall: A Picture Manuscript from Ancient Mexico*. New York: Dover Publication, 1975.

Oviedo as quoted in *Memory, Myth and Time in Mexico* by Enrique Florescano. Translated by Albert G. Bork. Austin: University of Texas Press, 1994.

Paz, Octavio. *The Labyrinth of Solitude: Life and Thought in Mexico*. Translated by Lysander Kemp. New York: Grove Press, 1961.

———. *The Other Mexico: Critique of the Pyramid*. Translated by Lysander Kemp. New York: Grove Press, 1972.

Peden, Margaret Sayers, trans. *A Woman of Genius: The Intellectual Autobiography of Sor Juana de la Cruz*. Salisbury, Conn.: Lime Rock Press, 1982.

Poinsett, Joel R. *Notes on Mexico Made in the Autumn of 1822, Accompanied by an Historical Sketch of the Revolution*. New York, Frederick A. Praeger, 1969.

Quirk, Robert E. *The Mexican Revolution, 1914–1915: The Convention of Aguascalientes*. New York: Citadel Press, 1963.

Read, John Lloyd. *The Mexican Historical Novel, 1826–1910*. New York: Instituto de las Españas, 1939.

Roys, Ralph, ed. and trans. *Chilam Balam of Chumayel*. (1933). Reprint. Norman: University of Oklahoma Press, 1967.

Ruiz, Ramón Eduardo. *Triumphs and Tragedy: A History of the Mexican People*. New York: W.W. Norton, 1992.

Sahagún, Bernardino de. *General History of the Things of New Spain: Florentine Codex*. (c. 1583). Translated by J. O. Anderson and Charles E. Dibble. 13 vol. Santa Fe: School of American Research and University of Utah Press, 1950–82.

Santa Anna, Antonio de López de. *The Eagle: The Autobiography of Santa Ana*. Edited by Ann Fears Crawford, translated by Sam Guyler and Jaime Platon. Austin: University of Texas Press, 1967.

Sierra, Justo. *The Political Evolution of the Mexican People*. (c. 1902–06). Translated by Charles Ramsdell. Austin: University of Texas Press, 1970.

Simpson, Lesley Byrd. *Many Mexicos*. Berkeley: University of California Press, 1962.

Smart, Charles Allen. *Viva Juárez*. London: Eyre and Spottiswoode, 1964.

Smith, Peter H. "Mexico Since 1946: Dynamics of an Authoritarian Regime." In *Mexico since Independence*. Edited by Leslie Bethell. Cambridge: Cambridge University Press, 1991.

Spores, Ronald. *The Mixtecs in Ancient and Colonial Times*. Norman: University of Oklahoma Press, 1984.

Stein, Stanley J. and Barbara H. Stein. *The Colonial Heritage of Latin America: Essays on Economic Dependence in Perspective*. Oxford: Oxford University Press, 1970.

Taube, Karl. *Aztec and Maya Myths*. Austin: University of Texas Press, 1993.

Tedlock, Dennis, trans. *Popol Vuh: The Mayan Book of the Dawn of Life*. New York: Simon & Schuster, 1985.

Thomas, Hugh. *The Conquest*. New York: Simon and Schuster, 1993.

Womack, John, Jr. "The Mexican Revolution, 1910–1920." In *Mexico since Independence*. Edited by Leslie Bethell. Cambridge: Cambridge University Press, 1991.

APPENDIX 4

SUGGESTED READING

Although this brief history is intended for non-scholars, more in-depth works are available on the many issues that could be discussed only cursorily. The following works in English include not only history and politics, but also literature and art, anthropology, and ethnohistory.

Books Spanning Major Periods

Bethell, Leslie, ed. *Mexico Since Independence.* Cambridge: Cambridge University Press, 1992.

Brenner, Anita. *Idols Behind Altars: The Story of the Mexican Spirit.* (1929) Reprint. Boston: Beacon Press, 1970.

Bricker, Victoria Reifker and Ronald Spores, ed. *Supplement to the Handbook of Middle American Indians: Volume 4 Ethnohistory.* Austin: University of Texas Press, 1986.

Brushwood, John S. *Mexico in its Novel: A Nation's Search for Identity.* Austin: University of Texas Press, 1966.

Cumberland, Charles C. *Mexico: The Struggle for Modernity.* London: Oxford University Press, 1968.

Florescano, Enrique. *Memory, Myth, and Time in Mexico: From the Aztecs to Independence.* Translated by Albert G. Bork. Austin: University of Texas Press, 1994.

Frost, Elsa Cecilia, et al., eds. *Labor and Laborers Throughout Mexican History.* Tucson: University of Arizona Press, 1979.

Jones, Willis Knapp, ed. *Spanish American Literature in Translation.* New York: Frederick Ungar, 1966.

Mexico: Spendors of Thirty Centuries. New York: Metropolitan Museum of Art. 1990.

Meyer, Michael C., and William L. Sherman. *The Course of Mexican History,* fifth edition. New York: Oxford University Press, 1995.

Ruiz, Ramón Eduardo. *Triumphs and Tragedy: A History of the Mexican People.* New York: W. W. Norton, 1992.

Sanderson, Susan W. *Land Reform in Mexico: 1910–1980*. Orlando, Fla., 1984.

Simonian, Lane. *Defending the Land of the Jaguar: A History of Conservation in Mexico*. Austin: University of Texas Press, 1995.

Simpson, Lesley Byrd. *Many Mexicos*. Berkeley: University of California Press, 1962.

Smith, Bradley. *Mexico: A History in Art*. New York: Harper & Row, 1968.

Stevenson, Robert. *Music in Mexico: A Historical Survey*. New York: Thomas Y. Crowell, 1971.

The First Peoples: Pre-Columbian Mexico

Adams, Richard E. W. *Prehistoric Mesoamerica*. Revised edition. Norman: University of Oklahoma Press, 1991.

Aveni, Anthony F. *Skywalkers of Ancient Mexico*. Austin: University of Texas, 1980.

————. *Conversing with the Planets*. New York: Times Books, 1992.

Benson, Elizabeth P., ed. *Mesoamerican Sites and World Views*. Washington D.C., Dunbarton Oaks, 1981.

Boone, Elizabeth H., ed. *Ritual Human Sacrifice in Mesoamerica*. Washington, D.C.: Dunbarton Oaks, 1984.

Coe, Michael D. *Breaking the Maya Code*. New York: Thames and Hudson, 1992.

Coe, Sophie D. *America's First Cuisines*. Austin, Texas. University of Texas Press, 1994.

Davies, Nigel. *Voyagers to the New World*. New York: William Morrow, 1979.

Fash, William L. *Scribes, Warriors and Kings*. London: Thames and Hudson, 1991.

Freidel, David A., Linda Schele, and Joy Parker. *Maya Cosmos: Three Thousand Years on the Shaman's Path*. New York: William Morrow, 1993.

Landa, Diego de. *Relación de las cosas de Yucatán*. Edited and translated by Alfred M. Tozzer. Papers of the Peabody Museum of American Archaeology and Ethnology. vol. XVIII. Cambridge: Peabody Museum of Harvard University, 1941.

Scarborough, Vernon, and David Wilcox, ed. *The Mesoamerican Ballgame*. Tucson: University of Arizona Press, 1991.

Schele, Linda, and David Freidel. *A Forest of Kings: The Untold Story of the Ancient Maya*. New York: William Morrow, 1990.

Taube, Karl. *Aztec and Maya Myths*. Austin: University of Texas Press, 1993.

Tedlock, Dennis, ed. and trans. *The Popol Vuh: The Mayan Book of the Dawn of Life*. Revised edition. New York. Simon & Schuster, 1996.

Wauchope, Robert. *Lost Tribes and Sunken Continents*. Chicago: University of Chicago Press, 1962.

Diversity of Mesoamerican Civilization

Berrin, Kathleen, and Esther Pasztory, eds. *Teotihuacan: Art from the City of the Gods*. Thames and Hudson, 1993.

Clendinnen, Inga. *Aztecs: An Interpretation*. Cambridge: Cambridge University Press, 1991.

Coe, Michael D. *Mexico: From the Olmecs to the Aztecs*. Revised edition. London: Thames and Hudson, 1994.

Coggins, Clemency C., and Orrin C. Shane III, eds. *Cenote of Sacrifice: Maya Treasures from the Sacred Well at Chichén Itzá*. Austin: University of Texas Press, 1984.

Culbert, T. Patrick, ed. *Classic Maya Political History: Hieroglyphic and Archaeological Evidence*. School of American Research Advanced Seminar Series. Cambridge: Cambridge University Press, 1991.

Diehl, Richard A., and Janet Catherine Berlo, eds. *Mesoamerica After the Decline of Teotihuacan*. Washington, D.C.: Dunbarton Oaks, 1989.

Flannery, Kent V., and Joyce Marcus, eds. *The Cloud People: Divergent Evolution of the Zapotec and Mixtec Civilizations*. New York: Academic Press, 1983.

Grove, David C., ed. *Regional Perspectives on the Olmec*. New York: Cambridge University Press, 1989.

Kubler, George. *The Art and Architecture of Ancient America*. Third edition. New Haven: Yale University Press, 1993.

León-Portilla, Miguel. *Aztec Thought and Culture*. Translated by Jack Emory Davis. Norman: University of Oklahoma Press, 1978.

Miller, Mary Ellen. *The Art of Mesoamerica from Olmec to Aztec*. Revised edition. London: Thames and Hudson, 1996.

Morley, Sylvanus G., George W. Brainerd, and Robert J. Sharer. *The Ancient Maya*. Fourth revised edition. Stanford: Stanford University Press, 1983.

The Olmec World: Ritual and Rulership. Princeton: The Art Museum, Princeton University, 1996.

Paddock, John, ed. *Ancient Oaxaca*. Stanford: Stanford University Press, 1966.

Pasztory, Esther. *Aztec Art*. New York: Henry N. Abrahms, 1983.

Pohl, Mary, ed. *Prehistoric Lowland Maya Environment and Subsistence Economy*. Papers of Peabody Museum of Archaeology and Ethnology 77. Cambridge: Harvard University Press, 1985.

Spores, Ronald. *The Mixtec Kings and their People*. Norman: University of Oklahoma Press, 1967.

Townsend, Richard. *The Aztecs*. London: Thames and Hudson, 1992.

Weaver, Muriel Porter. *The Aztecs, Maya, and their Predecessors*. New York: Academic Press, 1993.

The Age of Conquest

Carrasco, David, and Eduardo Matos Moctezuma, eds. *Moctezuma's Mexico: Visions of the Aztec World*. Denver: University of Colorado Press, 1992.

Cortés, Hernán. *Letters from Mexico*. Translated and edited by Anthony Pagden. New Haven: Yale University Press, 1986.

Díaz del Castillo, Bernal. *The True History of the Conquest of New Spain*. Translated by A. P. Maudslay. New York: Farrar, Strauss and Giroux, 1956.

Elliott, J. H. *The Old World and the New 1492–1650*. New York: Cambridge University Press, 1970.

––––––. *Imperial Spain 1469–1716*. New York: New American Library, 1963.

Hale, J. R. *Renaissance Exploration*. New York: W. W. Norton, 1968.

Hassig, Ross. *Aztec Warfare*. Norman: University of Oklahoma Press, 1988.

León-Portilla, Miguel, ed. and trans. *The Broken Spears: The Aztec Account of the Conquest of Mexico*. Expanded edition. Boston: Beacon Press, 1992.

López de Gómara, Francisco. *Cortés: The Life of the Conqueror by His Secretary*. Translated by Lesley Byrd Simpson. Berkeley: University of California Press, 1964.

Sales, Kirkpatrick. *The Conquest of Paradise: Christopher Columbus and the Columbian Legacy*. New York: Penguin, 1990.

Thomas, Hugh. *The Conquest*. New York: Simon and Schuster, 1993.

The Founding of an Empire: 16th-Century Mexico

Aiton, Arthur S. *Antonio de Mendoza: First Viceroy of New Spain*. (1927). Reprint. New York: Russell & Russell, 1967.

Alvarado, Pedro de. *An Account of the Conquest of Guatemala*. Edited by Sedley J. Mackie. London: Melford House, 1972.

Bolton, Herbert E. *Coronado on the Turquoise Trail: Knight of Pueblos and Plains.* Albuquerque: University of New Mexico Press, 1949.

Bricker, Victoria Reifler. *The Indian Christ, The Indian King: The Historical Substrate of Maya Myth and Ritual.* Austin: University of Texas Press, 1981.

Cabeza de Vaca, Alvar Núñez. *Adventures in the Unknown Interior of America.* Translated and edited by Cyclone Covey. Albuquerque: University of New Mexico Press, 1961.

Clendinnen, Inga. *Ambivalent Conquests: Maya and Spaniard in Yucatán, 1517–1570.* Cambridge: Cambridge University Press, 1987.

Friede, Juan, and Benjamin Keen, eds. *Bartolomé de Las Casas in History: Toward an Understandings of the Man and his Work.* DeKalb: Northern Illinois University Press, 1971.

Gibson, Charles. *The Aztecs Under Spanish Rule: A History of the Indians of the Valley of Mexico 1519–1810.* Stanford: Stanford University Press, 1964.

———. *Tlaxcala in the Sixteenth Century.* New Haven: Yale University Press, 1952.

Greenleaf, Richard E. *The Mexican Inquisition of the Sixteenth Century.* Albuquerque: University of New Mexico Press, 1969.

Gruzinski, Serge. *Painting the Conquest: The Mexican Indians and the European Renaissance.* Translated by Deke Dusinberre. Paris: Flammarion, 1992.

Hassig, Ross. *Trade, Tribute, and Transportation: The Sixteenth Political Economy of the Valley of Mexico.* Tucson: University of Oklahoma Press, 1985.

Kubler, George. *Mexican Architecture of the Sixteenth Century.* 2 vols. New Haven: Yale University Press, 1948.

Liss, Peggy K. *Mexico Under Spain, 1521–1556.* Chicago: University of Chicago Press, 1975.

Lockhart, James. *The Nahuas After the Conquest: A Social and Cultural History of the Indians of Central Mexico, Sixteenth through Eighteenth Centuries.* Stanford: Stanford University Press, 1992.

McAndrew, John. *The Open-Air Churches of Sixteenth-Century Mexico.* Cambridge: Harvard University Press, 1965.

Phelan, John L. *The Millennial Kingdom of the Franciscans in the New World: A Study of the Writings of Gerónimo de Mendieta.* Berkeley: University of California Press, 1956.

Ricard, Robert. *The Spiritual Conquest of Mexico.* Translated by Lesley Byrd Simpson. Berkeley: University of California Press, 1966.

Robertson, Donald. *Mexican Manuscript Painting of the Early Colonial Period: The Metropolitan School.* New Haven: Yale University Press, 1959.

Sauer, Carl Ortwin. *Sixteenth Century North America: The Land and the People as Seen by the Europeans.* Berkeley: University of California Press, 1971.

Schurz, William L. *The Manila Galleon.* New York: E. P. Dutton, 1939.

Simpson, Lesley Byrd. *The Encomienda in New Spain.* Berkeley: University of California Press, 1950.

Spores, Ronald. *The Mixtecs in Ancient and Colonial Times.* Tucson: University of Oklahoma Press, 1984.

Wagner, Henry R. *Spanish Voyages to the Northwest Coast of America in the Sixteenth Century.* San Francisco: California Historical Society, 1929.

The Colony of New Spain

Altman, Ida, and James Lockhart, eds. *Provinces of Early Mexico: Variants of Spanish-American Regional Evolution.* Los Angeles: UCLA Latin American Center Publications, vol. 36, 1976.

Baird, Joseph Armstrong, Jr. *The Churches of Mexico: 1530–1810.* Berkeley: University of California Press, 1962.

Bakewell, Peter J. *Silver Mining and Society in Colonial Mexico: Zacatecas 1546–1700.* Cambridge: Cambridge University Press, 1971.

Cervantes de Salazar, Francisco. *Life in the Imperial and Loyal City of Mexico . . .* Translated by Minnie Lee B. Shepard. Austin: University of Texas Press, 1953.

Chevalier, Francois. *Land and Society in Colonial Mexico: The Great Hacienda.* Translated by Alvin Eustis, edited by Lesley Byrd Simpson. Berkeley: University of California Press, 1963.

Crouch, Dora P., Daniel J. Garr, and Axel I. Mundigo. *Spanish City Planning in North America.* Cambridge: MIT Press, 1982.

Farriss, Nancy M. *Maya Society Under Colonial Rule: The Collective Enterprise of Survival.* Princeton: Princeton University Press, 1984.

———. *Crown and Clergy in Colonial Mexico, 1759–1821.* London: University of London Press, 1968.

Foster, Nelson, and Linda S. Cordell, ed. *Chiles to Chocolate.* Tucson: University of Arizona Press, 1992.

Gage, Thomas. *Travels in the New World (1648).* Reprint. Westport, Conn.: Greenwood Press, 1981.

Gerhard, Peter. *Pirates on the West Coast of New Spain, 1575–1742.* Glendale, Calif.: Arthur H. Clark Company, 1960.

Gibson, Charles. *Spain in America.* New York: Harper & Row, 1966.

Israel, Jonathan I. *Race, Class and Politics in Colonial Mexico, 1610–1670.* London: Oxford University Press, 1975.

Leonard, Irving. *Baroque Times in Old Mexico: Seventeenth-Century Persons, Places, and Practices.* Ann Arbor: University of Michigan Press, 1971.

Palmer, Colin A. *Slaves of the White God: Blacks in Mexico.* Cambridge: University of Cambridge Press, 1976.

Paz, Octavio. *Sor Juana or, the Traps of Faith.* Translated by Margaret Sayers Peden. Cambridge: Belknap Press, 1988.

Peden, Margaret Sayers, trans. *A Woman of Genius: The Intellectual Autobiography of Sor Juana de la Cruz.* Salisbury, Conn.: Lime Rock Press, 1982.

Stein, Stanley J., and Barbara H. Stein. *The Colonial Heritage of Latin America: Essays on Economic Dependence in Perspective.* Oxford: Oxford University Press, 1970.

Taylor, William B. *Drinking, Homicide and Rebellion in Colonial Mexican Villages.* Stanford: Stanford University Press, 1979.

Toussaint, Manuel. *Colonial Art in Mexico.* Translated and edited by Elizabeth W. Weismann. Austin: University of Texas Press, 1967.

Weismann, Elizabeth W. *Mexico in Sculpture 1521–1821.* Cambridge: Harvard University Press, 1950.

The Bourbon Reforms and Independence

Anna, Timothy E. *Spain and the Loss of the Americas.* Lincoln: University of Nebraska Press, 1983.

———. *The Fall of the Royal Government in Mexico City.* Lincoln: University of Nebraska Press, 1978.

Archer, Christon I. *The Army in Bourbon Mexico, 1760–1810.* Albuquerque: University of New Mexico Press, 1977.

Bannon, John F. *The Spanish Borderlands Frontier, 1513–1821.* New York: Holt, Rinehart and Winston, 1970.

Bobb, Bernard E. *The Viceregency of Antonio María Bucareli in New Spain, 1771–1779.* Austin: University of Texas Press, 1962.

Brading, David A. *Miners and Merchants in Bourbon Mexico, 1760–1810.* Cambridge: Cambridge University Press, 1971.

Charlot, Jean. *Mexican Art and the Academy of San Carlos, 1785–1915.* Austin: University of Texas Press, 1962.

DeVolder, Arthur L. *Guadalupe Victoria: His Role in Mexican Independence*. Albuquerque: University of New Mexico Press, 1978.

Farriss, Nancy M. *Maya Society Under Colonial Rule: The Collective Enterprise of Survival*. Princeton: Princeton University Press, 1984.

Fisher, Lillian Estelle. *The Background of the Revolution for Mexican Independence*. Gainesville: University of Florida Press, 1966.

Flores Caballero, Romeo. *Counterrevolution: The Role of the Spaniards in the Independence of Mexico, 1804–1838*. Translated by Jaime E. Rodriguez O. Lincoln: University of Nebraska, 1974.

Gálvez, Bernardo de. *Instructions for Governing the Interior Provinces of New Spain, 1786*. Edited by Donald E. Worcester. Berkeley: Quivira Society, 1951.

Hamnett, Brian R. *Politics and Trade in Southern Mexico, 1750–1821*. Cambridge: Cambridge University Press, 1971.

Harris, Charles H., III. *A Mexican Family Empire: The Latifundio of the Sanchez Navarro, 1765–1867*. Austin: University of Texas Press, 1975.

Humboldt, Alexander von. *Political Essay on the Kingdom of New Spain*. Edited by Mary Maples Dunn. New York: Alfred A. Knopf, 1972.

Kicza, John E. *Colonial Entrepreneurs: Families and Business in Bourbon Mexico City*. Albuquerque: University of New Mexico Press, 1983.

Ladd, Doris M. *The Mexican Nobility at Independence 1780–1826*. Austin: University of Texas Press, 1976.

Lafaye, Jacques. *Quetzalcoatl and Guadalupe: The Making of Mexican National Consciousness, 1531–1813*. Translated by Benjamin Keen. Chicago: University of Chicago Press, 1976.

Lieberman, Mark. *Hidalgo: Mexican Revolutionary*. New York: Frederick A. Praeger, 1970.

McAlister, Lyle N. *The "Fuero Militar" in New Spain, 1764–1800*. Gainesville: University of Florida, 1957.

Mörner, Magnus, ed. *The Expulsion of the Jesuits from Latin America*. New York: Alfred A. Knopf, 1965.

Motten, Clement. *Mexican Silver and the Enlightenment*. Philadelphia: University of Pennsylvania Press, 1950.

Poinsett, Joel R. *Notes on Mexico Made in the Autumn of 1822, Accompanied by an Historical Sketch of the Revolution*. New York: Frederick A. Prager, 1969.

Sprague, William F. *Vicente Guerrero, Mexican Liberator*. Chicago: University of Chicago Press, 1939.

Thomas, Alfred B., ed. and trans. *Teodoro de Croix and the Northern Frontier of New Spain, 1776–1783*. Norman: University of Oklahoma, 1941.

Timmons, Wilbert H. *Morelos*. (1963). Reprint. El Paso: Texas Western College Press, 1970.

Years of Chaos

Anderson, William Marshall. *An American in Maximilian's Mexico, 1865–1866: Diaries of William Marshall Anderson*. Edited by Ramon Eduardo Ruiz. San Marino, Calif.: Huntington Library, 1959.

Anna, Timothy E. *The Mexican Empire of Iturbide*. Lincoln: University of Nebraska Press, 1990.

Barker, Nancy Nichols. *The French Experience in Mexico, 1821–1861: A History of Constant Misunderstanding*. Chapel Hill: University of North Carolina Press, 1979.

Bazant, Jan. *Alienation of Church Wealth in Mexico: Social and Economic Aspects of the Liberal Revolution, 1856–1875*. Cambridge: Cambridge University Press, 1971.

Berry, Charles R. *The Reform in Oaxaca, 1856–76: A Micro-history of the Liberal Revolution*. Lincoln: University of Nebraska Press, 1981.

Brack, G. M. *Mexico Views Manifest Destiny 1821–1846, An Essay on the Origins of the Mexican War*. Albuquerque: University of New Mexico Press, 1975.

Brading, David A. *Haciendas and Ranchos in the Mexican Bajío*. Cambridge: Cambridge University Press, 1978.

Bricker, Victoria Reifler. *The Indian Christ, The Indian King: The Historical Substrate of Maya Myth and Ritual*. Austin: University of Texas Press, 1981.

Cadenhead, Inie E., Jr. *Benito Juárez*. New York: Twayne Publishers, 1973.

Calderón de la Barca, Fanny. *Life in Mexico: The Letters of Fanny Calderón de la Barca*. (1847). Reprint. Edited by Howard T. Fisher and Marion H. Fisher. Garden City: Doubleday, 1970.

Castañeda, Carlos E., ed. and trans. *The Mexican Side of the Texan Revolution*. Dallas: P. L. Turner Company, 1928.

Charlot, Jean. *Mexican Art and the Academy of San Carlos, 1785–1915*. Austin: University of Texas Press, 1962.

Costeloe, Michael P. *Church and State in Independent Mexico: A Study of the Patronage Debate*. London: Royal Historical Society, 1978.

Cotner, Thomas E., and Carlos E. Castañeda, eds. *Essays in Mexican History*. Austin: Institute of Latin American Studies, 1958.

Hale, Charles A. *Mexican Liberalism in the Age of Mora 1821–1853*. New Haven: Yale University Press, 1968.

Hanna, Alfred Jackson, and Kathryn Abbey Hanna. *Napoleon III and Mexico: American Triumph over Monarchy*. Chapel Hill: University of North Carolina Press, 1971.

Harris, Charles H. III. *The Sanchez Navarros: A Socio-economic Study of a Coahuilan Latifundio, 1846–1853*. Chicago: University of Chicago Press, 1964.

Haslip, Joan. *The Crown of Mexico, Maximilian and his Empress Carlota*. New York: Holt, Rinehart and Winston, 1971.

Jones, Oakah L., Jr. *Santa Anna*. New York: Twayne Publishers, 1968.

Monaghan, John. *The Covenants with Earth and Rain: Exchange, Sacrifice, and Revelation in Mixtec Society*. Norman: University of Oklahoma Press, 1995.

Ramírez, José Fernando. *Mexico During the War with the United States*. Edited by Walter V. Scholes and translated by E. B. Sherr. Columbia: University of Missouri Press, 1950.

Read, John Lloyd. *The Mexican Historical Novel, 1826–1910*. New York: Instituto de las Españas, 1939.

Reed, Nelson. *The Caste War of Yucatan*. Stanford: Stanford University Press, 1964.

Rives, George L. *The United States and Mexico, 1821–1848: A History of the Relations between the Two Countries from the Independence of Texas to the Close of the War with the United States*. 2 vols. New York: Charles Scribner's Sons, 1913.

Ruiz, Ramón Eduardo, ed. *The Mexican War: Was it Manifest Destiny?* New York: Holt, Rinehart and Winston, 1963.

Santa Anna, Antonio López de. *The Eagle: The Autobiography of Santa Anna*. Edited by Ann Fears Crawford and translated by Sam Guyler and Jaime Platon. Austin: State House Press, 1988.

Sinkin, Richard N. *The Mexican Reform, 1855–1876: A Study in Liberal Nation-Building*. Austin: University of Texas Press, 1979.

Smith, George W., and Charles Judah, eds. *Chronicles of the Gringos: The U.S. Army in the Mexican War, 1846–1848*. Albuquerque: University of New Mexico Press, 1968.

Stephens, John L. *Incidents of Travel in Central America, Chiapas & Yucatán (1841)*. 2 vols. New York: Dover Publications, 1969.

————. *Incidents of Travel in Yucatán (1843)*. 2 vols. New York: Dover Publications, 1963.

Ward, Henry G. *Mexico in 1827*. 2 vols. London: H. Colburn, 1828.

The Porfiriato Dictatorship

Anderson, Rodney. *Outcasts in Their Own Land: Mexican Industrial Workers, 1906–1911*. DeKalb: Northern Illinois University Press, 1976.

Bernstein, Marvin D. *The Mexican Mining Industry, 1890–1950*. Albany: State University of New York at Albany, 1965.

Charlot, Jean. *Mexican Art and the Academy of San Carlos, 1785–1915*. Austin: University of Texas Press, 1962.

Coatsworth, John. *Growth against Development: The Economic Impact of Railroads in Porfirian Mexico*. DeKalb: Northern Illinois University, 1980.

Cockcroft, James. *Intellectual Precursors of the Mexican Revolution*. Austin: University of Texas Press, 1968.

Cosío Villegas, Daniel. *United States versus Porfirio Díaz*. Lincoln: University of Nebraska Press, 1963.

Cumberland, Charles C. *Mexico: The Struggle for Modernity*. London: Oxford University Press, 1968.

Flandrau, Charles M. *Viva Mexico*. (1908). Reprint. Urbana: University of Illinois Press, 1964.

Friedrich, Paul. *Agrarian Revolt in a Mexican Village*. Englewood Cliffs, N.J.: Prentice Hall, 1970.

Hannay, David. *Díaz*. (1917). Reprint. Port Washington, N.Y.: Kennikate Press, 1970.

Joseph, G. M. *Revolution from Without: Yucatán, Mexico and the United States, 1880–1924*. New York: Cambridge University Press, 1982.

Kroeber, Clifton B. *Man, Land, and Water: Mexico's Farmlands Irrigation Policies 1885–1911*. Berkeley: University of California Press, 1984.

McCarty, J. Hendrickson. *Two Thousand Miles through the Heart of Mexico*. New York: Phillips & Hunt, 1888.

Sierra, Justo. *The Political Evolution of the Mexican People*. (c. 1902–06) Translated by Charles Ramsdell. Austin: University of Texas Press, 1969.

Thompson, Edward. *People of the Serpent: Life and Adventure Among the Mayas*. (1932) Reprint. New York: Capricorn Books, 1965.

Turner, John Kenneth. *Barbarous Mexico*. (1910). Reprint. Austin: University of Texas Press, 1969.

Tyler, Ron, ed. *Posada's Mexico*. Washington: Library of Congress, 1979.

Vanderwood, Paul J. *Disorder and Progress: Bandits, Police and Mexican Development.* Lincoln: University of Nebraska Press, 1981.

Weismann, Elizabeth Wilder. *Art and Time in Mexico: From the Conquest to the Revolution.* New York: Harper & Row, 1985.

Zea, Leopoldo. *Positivism in Mexico.* Translated by Josephine H. Schulte. Austin: University of Texas Press, 1974.

The Revolution of 1910 (1910–40)

Azuela, Mariano. *The Underdogs.* Translated by E. Munguia, Jr. New York: New American Library, 1962.

Bailey, David. *Viva Cristo Rey: The Cristero Rebellion and the Church-State Conflict in Mexico.* Austin: University of Texas Press, 1974.

Bernstein, Marvin D. *The Mexican Mining Industry 1890–1950: A Study of the Interaction of Politics, Economics, and Technology.* Albany: State University of New York, 1964.

Billeter, Erika, ed. *Images of Mexico.* Dallas: Dallas Museum of Art, 1987.

Brenner, Anita. *The Wind that Swept Mexico: The History of the Mexican Revolution.* (1943). Reprint. Austin: University of Texas Press, 1971.

Charlot, Jean. *The Mexican Mural Renaissance, 1920–1925.* New Haven: Yale University Press, 1967.

Clark, Marjorie. *Organized Labor in Mexico.* Chapel Hill: University of North Carolina Press, 1934.

Clendenen, Clarence C. *The United States and Pancho Villa: A Study in Unconventional Diplomacy.* Ithaca: Cornell University Press, 1981.

Cockcroft, J. D. *Mexico: Class Formation, Capital Accumulation, and the State.* New York: Monthly Review Press, 1983.

Cumberland, Charles C. *Mexican Revolution: Genesis under Madero.* Austin: University of Texas Press, 1952.

———. *Mexican Revolution: The Constitutionalist Years.* Austin: University of Texas Press, 1972.

Dulles, John W. *Yesterday in Mexico: A Chronicle of the Revolution, 1919–1936.* Austin: University of Texas Press, 1961.

Guzmán, Martín Luis, ed. *Memoirs of Pancho Villa.* Translated by V. H. Taylor. Austin: University of Texas Press, 1965.

———. *The Eagle and the Serpent.* Translated by Harriet de Onis. Garden City: Doubleday and Company, 1965.

Haddox, John H. *Vasconcelos of Mexico.* Austin: University of Texas Press, 1967.

Hall, Linda. *Alvaro Obregón: Power and Revolution in Mexico, 1911–1920.* College Station: Texas A and M University Press, 1981.

Hamilton, Nora. *The Limits of State Autonomy: Post Revolutionary Mexico.* Princeton: Princeton University Press, 1982.

Herrera, Hayden. *Frida Kahlo: A Biography.* New York: Harper & Row, 1983.

Katz, Frederich. *The Secret War in Mexico: Europe, the United States, and the Mexican Revolution.* Chicago: University of Chicago Press, 1981.

Lieuwen, Edwin. *Mexican Militarism: The Political Rise and Fall of the Revolutionary Army.* Albuquerque: University of New Mexico Press, 1968.

Link, Arthur S. *Wilson: Campaigns for Progressivism and Peace, 1916–1917.* Princeton: Princeton University Press, 1965.

López y Fuentes, Gregorio. *El Indio.* Translated by Anita Brenner. New York: Frederick Ungar, 1961.

MacKinley, Helm. *Mexican Painters: Rivera, Orozco, Siqueiros and Other Artists of the Realist School.* (1941). Reprint. New York: Dover Publications, 1989.

Niemeyer, Eberhardt V. Jr. *Revolution at Querétaro: The Mexican Constitutionalist Convention of 1916–1917.* Austin: University of Texas Press, 1974 and 1991.

Reed, John. *Insurgent Mexico.* (1914). Reprint. New York: Simon and Schuster, 1969.

Ross, Stanley. *Francisco I. Madero: Apostle of Mexican Democracy.* New York: Columbia University Press, 1955.

Ruiz, Ramón Eduardo. *Mexico: The Challenge of Poverty and Illiteracy.* San Marino, Calif.: Huntington Library, 1963.

Rutherford, John D. *Mexican Society during Revolution: A Literary Approach.* Oxford: Oxford University Press, 1971.

Salas, Elizabeth. *Soldaderas in the Mexican Military: Myth and History.* Austin: University of Texas Press, 1990.

Sommers, Joseph. *After the Storm: Landmarks of the Modern Mexican Novel.* Albuquerque: University of New Mexico Press, 1968.

Sullivan, Paul. *Unfinished Conversations: Mayas and Foreigners Between Two Wars.* Berkeley: University of California Press, 1991.

Wasserman, Mark. *Capitalists, Caciques, and Revolution: The Native Elite and Foreign Enterprise in Chihuahua, 1854–1911.* Chapel Hill: University of North Carolina Press, 1984.

Weyl, Nathaniel, and Sylvia Weyl. *The Reconquest of Mexico: The Years of Lázaro Cárdenas.* New York: Oxford University Press, 1939.

Whetten, Nathan L. *Rural Mexico.* Chicago: University of Chicago Press, 1948.

Wilkie, James W. *The Mexican Revolution: Federal Expenditure and Social Change since 1910*. Berkeley: University of California Press.

Wolfskill, George, and Douglas W. Richmond, eds. *Essays on the Mexican Revolution: Revisionist Views of the Leaders*. Austin: University of Texas Press, 1979.

Womack, John Jr. *Zapata and the Mexican Revolution*. New York: Alfred A. Knopf, 1968.

Modern Mexico

Barry, Tom, ed. *Mexico: A Country Guide*. Albuquerque: The Inter-Hemispheric Education Resource Center, 1992.

Beacham, Hans. *Mexico: Architecture of Yesterday and Today*. New York: Architectural Book Publishings, 1969.

Billeter, Erika, ed. *Images of Mexico*. Dallas: Dallas Museum of Art, 1987.

Camp, Roderick A., ed. *Mexico's Political Stability: The Next Five Years*. Boulder: Westview Press, 1986.

Cline, Howard. *Mexico: From Revolution to Evolution*. New York: Oxford University Press, 1962 and 1968.

Cline, William R., ed. *International Debt and the Stability of the World Economy*. Washington DC: Institute for International Economics and MIT Press, 1984.

Cole, William E., and Richard D. Sanders. *Growth and Change in Mexican Agriculture*. Knoxville, 1970.

Cornelius, Wayne A. *Politics and the Migrant Poor in Mexico City*. Stanford: Stanford University Press, 1975.

Fuentes, Carlos. *The Death of Artemio Cruz*. Translated by Sam Hileman. New York: Noonday Press, 1966.

Galarza, Ernesto. *Merchants of Labor: The Mexican Bracero Story*. San Jose, Calif.: Rosicrucian Press, 1964.

Gentleman, Judith, and Peter H. Smith, eds. *Mexico's Alternative Political Futures*. San Diego: Center for U.S.-Mexican Studies, 1986.

Goldman, Shifra M. *Contemporary Mexican Painting in a Time of Change*. (1981). Reprint. Albuquerque: University of New Mexico Press, 1995.

González Casanova, Pablo. *Democracy in Mexico*. 2nd edition. Translated by Danielle Salti. New York: Oxford University Press, 1970.

Grayson, George. *Oil and Mexican Foreign Policy*. Pittsburgh: University of Pittsburgh Press, 1988.

———. *The Mexican Labor Machine: Power, Politics, and Patronage*. Washington D.C.: Center for Strategic Studies, 1989.

Grindle, Merilee Serrill. *Bureaucrats, Politicians, and Peasants in Mexico: A Case Study in Public Policy.* Berkeley: University of California Press, 1977.

Hellman, Judith A. *Mexico in Crisis.* New York: Holmes and Meier, 1983.

Hodges, Donald C. and Daniel Ross Gandy. *Mexico 1910–1980: Reform or Revolution.* Revised edition. London: Zed, 1983.

Johnson, Kenneth F. *Mexican Democracy: A Critical View.* Revised edition. Boston: Allyn and Bacon, 1984.

King, Timothy. *Mexico: Industrialization and Trade Policies since 1940.* New York: Oxford University Press, 1970 and 1982.

Lamartine Yates, Paul. *Mexico's Agricultural Dilemma.* Tucson: University of Arizona Press, 1981.

Langford, Walter M. *The Mexican Novel Comes of Age.* Notre Dame: University of Notre Dame Press, 1971.

Levine, Daniel B., Kenneth Hill, and Robert Warren, eds. *Immigration Statistics: A Story of Neglect.* Washington, D.C.: National Academy Press, 1985.

Levy, Daniel C. *University and Government in Mexico: Autonomy in an Authoritarian System.* New York: Praeger, 1980.

Levy, Daniel C., and Gabriel Székely. *Mexico: Paradoxes of Stability and Change.* Revised edition. Boulder: Westview Press, 1987.

Lewis, Oscar. *The Children of Sánchez: Autobiography of a Mexican Family.* (1961). Reprint. New York: Random House, 1987.

Mexico: Splendors of Thirty Centuries. New York: Metropolitan Museum of Art, 1990.

Mora, Carl J. *Mexican Cinema: Reflections of a Society, 1896–1980.* Berkeley: University of California Press, 1982.

Morton, Ward. *Woman Suffrage in Mexico.* Gainesville: University of Florida Press, 1962.

Mosk, Sanford A. *Industrial Revolution in Mexico.* Berkeley: University of California Press, 1950.

Murphy, Arthur D., and Alex Stepick. *Social Inequality in Oaxaca: A History of Resistance and Change.* Philadelphia: Temple University Press, 1991.

Newell, Roberto G., and Luis Rubio F. *Mexico's Dilemma: The Political Origins of Economic Crisis.* Boulder: Westview Press, 1984.

Pastor, Robert A., and Jorge Castañeda. *Limits to Friendship: The United States and Mexico.* New York: Alfred A. Knopf, 1988.

Paz, Octavio. *The Labyrinth of Solitude: Life and Thought in Mexico.* Translated by Lysander Kemp. New York: Grove Press, 1961 and 1991.

———. *The Other Mexico: Critique of the Pyramid.* Translated by Lysander Kemp. New York: Grove Press, 1972.

Reynolds, Clark W. *The Mexican Economy: Twentieth-Century Structure and Growth.* New Haven: Yale University Press, 1970.

Riding, Alan. *Distant Neighbors: A Portrait of the Mexicans.* New York: Alfred A. Knopf, 1985.

Ronfeldt, David, ed. *The Modern Mexican Military: A Reassessment.* San Diego: Center for U.S.-Mexican Studies, 1984.

Ross, Stanley R., ed. *Is the Mexican Revolution Dead?* Revised edition. New York: Alfred A. Knopf, 1975.

Sanderson, Steve. *The Transformation of Mexican Agriculture.* Princeton: Princeton University Press, 1986.

Smith, Peter. *Labyrinths of Power: Political Recruitment in Twentieth Century Mexico.* Princeton: Princeton University Press, 1978.

Solís, Leopoldo. *Economic Policy Reform in Mexico: A Case Study for Developing Countries.* New York, 1981.

Vázquez, Josefina Zoraida, and Lorenzo Meyer. *The United States and Mexico.* Chicago: University of Chicago Press, 1986.

Vernon, Raymond. *The Dilemma of Mexico's Development: The Roles of the Private and Public Sectors.* Cambridge: Cambridge University Press, 1963.

Vogt, Evon Z. *The Zinacantecos of Mexico: A Modern Maya Way of Life.* New York: Holt, Rinehart and Winston, 1970.

Williams, Edward J. *The Rebirth of the Mexican Petroleum Industry.* Lexington, Mass.: D.C. Heath, 1979.

Mexico at the Crossroads

Barkin, David. *Distorted Development: Mexico in the World Economy.* Boulder: Westview Press, 1990.

Barry, Tom, ed. *Mexico: A Country Guide.* Albuquerque: The Inter-Hemispheric Resource Center, 1992.

Bustamante, Jorge, and Wayne Cornelius, eds. *Mexican Migration to the United States: Origins, Consequences, and Policy Options.* San Diego: Center for U.S.-Mexican Studies, 1989.

Casteñeda, Jorge G. *The Mexican Shock: Its Meaning for the United States.* New York: New Press, 1995.

Craig, Ann. *The Mexican Political System in Transition.* San Diego: Center for U.S.-Mexican Studies, 1991.

Cypher, James M. *State and Capital in Mexico: Development Policy Since 1940.* Boulder: Westview Press, 1990.

Dornbusch, Rudi, and Alejandro Werner. *Mexico: Stabilization, Reform and No Growth.* Cambridge: MIT Press, 1994.

Foweraker, Joe, and Ann Craig, eds. *Popular Movements and Political Change in Mexico.* Boulder: Lynne Rienner Publishers, 1990.

Foxx, Jeffrey Jay, and Walter F. Morris, Jr. *Living Maya.* New York: Harry N. Abrahms, 1987.

Haber, Stephen. *Industry and Underdevelopment: The Industrialization of Mexico.* Stanford: Stanford University Press, 1988.

Lowenthal, Abraham F. *Partners in Conflict: The United States and Latin America in the 1990s.* Baltimore: Johns Hopkins University Press, 1990.

McAnany, Emile G., and Kenton T. Wilkinson, eds. *Mass Media and Free Trade: NAFTA and the Cultural Industries.* Austin: University of Texas Press, 1997.

Menchaca, Martha. *The Mexican Outsiders: A Community of Marginalization and Discrimination in California.* Austin: University of Texas Press, 1995.

Monaghan, John. *The Covenants with Earth and Rain: Exchange, Sacrifice, and Revelation in Mixtec Society.* Norman: University of Oklahoma Press, 1995.

Mumme, Stephen P. *Preemptive Environmental Reform under Salinas.* Boulder: Colorado State University, 1991.

Oppenheimer, Andrés. *Bordering on Chaos: Guerrillas, Stockbrokers, Politicians, and Mexico's Road to Prosperity.* Boston: Little Brown, 1996.

Sandstrom, Alan. *Corn is our Blood: Culture and Ethnic Identity in a Contemporary Aztec Indian Village.* Norman: University of Oklahoma Press, 1991.

Stoddard, Ellwyn R. *Maquila Assembly Plants in Northern Mexico.* El Paso: Texas Western Press, 1987.

Sullivan, Paul. *Unfinished Conversations: Mayas and Foreigners Between Two Wars.* Berkeley: University of California Press, 1991.

Weintraub, Sidney. *Transforming the Mexican Economy: The Salinas Sexenio.* Washington D.C.: National Planning Association, 1990.

———. *A Marriage of Convenience: Relations between Mexico and the United States.* Oxford: Oxford University Press, 1990.

INDEX

Note: Entries are filed in letter-by-letter format. Page numbers in *italics* refer to illustrations; *m* = map; *t* = table.

M